Dreaming Gardens

Center Books on the International Scene
George F. Thompson, publishing director

Dreaming Gardens

Landscape Architecture
and the Making of Modern Israel

Kenneth Helphand, FASLA

Published by the Center for American Places
Santa Fe, New Mexico, and Harrisonburg, Virginia

in association with the University of Virginia Press, Charlottesville

PUBLISHER'S NOTES

Dreaming Gardens: Landscape Architecture and the Making of Modern Israel is published in an edition of 3,000 clothbound copies. It is the second volume in the series *Center Books on the International Scene*, created and directed by the Center for American Places. The inaugural volume in the series is *Anglo-Celtic Australia: Colonial Immigration and Cultural Regionalism* (2002) by Alyson L. Greiner and Terry G. Jordan-Bychkov (ISBN 1-930066-04-x). For more information about the Center for American Places and the publication of *Dreaming Gardens*, please see page 242.

Published 2002. First edition.
Printed in Canada on acid-free paper through HLN PRINTING, Inc.

All photographs are by the author, except as otherwise noted.

The Center for American Places, Inc.
P.O. Box 23225
Santa Fe, New Mexico 87502-4318, U.S.A.
www.americanplaces.org

Distributed by the University of Virginia Press
P.O. Box 400318
Charlottesville, Virginia 22904, U.S.A.
www.virginia.edu/~press/
Book orders: 800-831-3406
Information: 434-924-3468

9 8 7 6 5 4 3 2 1

Library of Congress Cataloging-in-Publication Data
Helphand, Kenneth I.
  Dreaming gardens: landscape architecture and the making of modern Israel /
Kenneth Helphand.
  p. cm. — (Center books on the international scene)
ISBN 1-930066-06-6 (alk. paper)
  1. Landscape architecture—Israel—History. 2. Landscape design—Israel—History. 3. Gardens—Israel—Designs—History. I. Title. II. Series.
SB470.55.175 H46 2002
712'.095694—dc21   2002073864

For Margot
who first brought me to Israel

Contents

Special Acknowledgments

 This book was initiated and supported by the Israeli Association of Landscape Architects, whose members share the dream and its realization.

 The Faculty of Architecture and Town Planning at Technion—Israel Institute of Technology provided key financial and institutional support to help the completion of this project.

THE RESEARCH AND PUBLICATION of this book would not have been possible without the generous financial support of others:

Ackerstein Industries. Giora Ackerstein dedicates his contribution to the loving memory of his dear parents, Haya and Zvi Ackerstein, who were true pioneers and among the first to offer unique landscape architecture products in the Israeli market.

Derech Eretz, Israel.

The Graham Foundation for Advanced Studies in the Fine Arts.

Elaine and Norman Winik, U.S.A.

W HAT DO I, AN AMERICAN LANDSCAPE ARCHITECT and educator, bring to this study of landscape architecture in Israel? I had briefly visited in 1972, I first taught at Technion—Israel Institute of Technology in 1980 for a year, and returned again on numerous occasions for shorter periods. In the course of living, working, and visiting in Israel I have traveled to all corners of the country, to places I discovered, and almost every place anyone recommended. I am indebted to my many students, colleagues, and friends for their numerous suggestions. I have traveled alone, with family, friends, and colleagues, on organized tours and informal trips. I have rarely passed up any opportunity or invitation to experience the life of the landscape. It is difficult to understand behavior without observing or participating in it. It is important to have spent days at the beach, on nature hikes, gone with my children to playgrounds, walked with them to school, spent *Shabbat* at picnics with friends, sat in people's gardens, looked out from balconies, gone on *tiulim*, celebrated holidays and festivals. I cannot have the innate deep feeling and visceral relationship of one who grew up imbibing and ingesting the landscape as part of his or her upbringing, but I have done my best to understand, to listen carefully and observe closely. I have spoken with and interviewed scores of persons, mostly landscape architects, but also architects, planners, writers, and artists as well as non-professionals. Everyone had more suggestions of places to see, people to visit, things to read. It is a never-ending chain reaction. The outsider's viewpoint has its dilemmas but also its opportunities. Fresh eyes may see what is ignored, ask questions that everyone takes for granted, or offer comparisons not previously imagined.

Throughout the text is found a selection of exemplary landscape architecture designs. I have striven to be discerning and equable, and I have also chosen to emphasize what I think is critical. The places discussed here reflect the recommendations of many individuals, and a desire to do justice to an extraordinarily rich and complex body of work. It is important to include work from various periods in the past century. I have included work representative of broad areas of

Preface and
Acknowledgments

practice, as well as designs widely recognized to have special, emblematic status. When I interviewed designers, a few sites, not surprisingly, emerged as universally acknowledged at the top of the list of canonical designs. It is essential that the scope of this investigation is broad, reflecting the range of practice, its historical contribution, and the breadth of its contribution. Thus work at all scales—from gardens to the nation, including all types of design work—and all areas of the country are represented. Despite the size of Israel, the diversity of its landscape architecture is remarkable. A single volume cannot begin to convey or acknowledge all those individuals responsible for its conception, design, and execution. More research and scholarship needs to be done, and my hope is that this volume acts as a catalyst and road map for future endeavors. In writing I have tried to balance the demands of uninitiated and expert alike.

For readers outside of Israel who only know the country from the nightly news it is my hope that the book will give them a more complete awareness of the country and its character. While the book is not about politics it is an unavoidable topic. Politics in all its manifestations from the local to the geo-political does influence landscape architecture design and construction. At the same time it transcends political concerns, for the landscape itself is a client and design serves places and their inhabitants irrespective of their political beliefs. At the time of this writing the on and off again peace process still has glimmers of hope. Even the map of the nation is subject to debate. Taking my cue from the landscape architects whose work is described here I have not included projects done on the Golan Heights, or in areas beyond the Green Line, the Israeli term for the 1967 border of the West Bank. The key exceptions are projects in and around Jerusalem whose significance transcends the concerns of both Israelis and Palestinians.

The images in the following pages are essential to communicating the story of landscape architecture in Israel. There are contemporary and historic photographs, plans, drawings, maps, paintings, and sketches. The diversity of imagery reflects the difficulty of communicating both landscape experience and the process of design. Most of my photographs were taken with the intention of communicating the life of these places, as well as their formal and spatial qualities. The color photography begins to suggest the sensory richness of these designs. Images are dated only when relevant, and sources and permissions are noted in parentheses.

There are numerous names, places, and terms that have been transliterated from Hebrew. I have tried to be consistent, but readers may be familiar with other spellings. Hebrew words are italicized, but certain terms which occur with great frequency or that are used in English, such as kibbutz, are only italicized at their first mention. A glossary is included to facilitate use.

I have many people to thank for assistance. They have shared their knowledge and love of the country, showed me their work and offices, given me essential advice, taken me on tours, consented to interviews, and offered hospitality. Israeli invitations are always sincere. While Israelis have a tremendous pride in their country, they are also its harshest critics. These people were my *madrichim* (guides) during this wonderful journey. It has been a privilege to work on this project and an honor to write about the work of such an extraordinary collection of design professionals. I have done my best to transmit their thoughts and feelings.

Many thanks are due to many individuals. My colleagues at Technion, Shaul Amir, Ruth Enis, and Gideon Sarig, from my first days shared their knowledge and insight, as did other on the faculty, including Arza Churchman, Nurit Lisovsky, Judy Green, Ayala Misgav, Sofia Rosner, Elissa Rosenberg, Zev Naveh, Gilbert Herbert, and Aharon Kashtan.

I worked with a committee from the Israeli Association of Landscape Architects whose members helped guide the project and read and critiqued the text: Prof. Gilbert Herbert, Alisa Braudo, Nurit Lissovsky, Gil Hargil, Shlomo Aronson, and Tal Alon-Mozes, who was particularly indispensable in acting as a liaison and as my proxy in Israel.

Many persons consented to interviews and took me to visit, or directed me to their work, and generously shared their office archives: Shlomo Aronson, Lippa Yahalom, Dan Zur, Gideon Sarig, Joseph Segal, Zvi Dekel, Uri Miller, Shlomi Zevi, Zvi Miller, Moshe Blum, Gil Har-Gil, Daphna Greenstein, Alisa Braudo, Dani Karavan, Tamar Darel-Fossfeld, Ruth Maoz, Yael Moriah, Ariel Barnet, Yigal Steinmetz, Hanna Yaffe, Racheli Merchav, Maya Shafir, Iris Bernstein, Ronald Lovinger, Revital Shoshany, Avinoam Avnon, Haim Kahanovitch, Paul Friedberg, Dorit Shahar, Esther Zandberg, David Reznik, Ariel Hirshfeld, Ilana Ofir, Jacob Fuchs, Jeremy Epstein, Judith Garmi, Arye Dvir, Bruce Levin, Tally Tuch, Tami Wiener Saragossi, Itzchak Blank, and Mira Engler. Also thanks to Alon Raab, Hanale Rosen, and Hal and Esti Applebaum for their fine helpful translations.

I have been the privileged recipient of the home hospitality of many, especially the Amirs in Haifa, Braudos in Savyon, Sarigs in Ramat HaSharon, and Isenbergs in Kibbutz Sarid, all of whom allowed me to share their family lives as well as their homes. In Jerusalem my home is that of Zvi and Sarah Novoplansky, my guides and most perceptive analysts. Through them I learned the fundamental meaning of Zionism and the life of true *halutzim* (pioneers) of the country.

I feel a special debt and kinship with landscape architects and architects who came to study at the University of Oregon and returned to practice in Israel: Alisa Braudo, Daphna Greenstein, Nava Novoplansky, Shmuel Burmil, Amit Segal, and Itamar Raayoni.

And there are many others: Hazel Amir, Yael Sarig, Ofer Greenstein, Cushy Braudo. Sharon Hefer, Arye Rachamimoff, Nir Burras, Ronit Sassoon, Arye Peled, Chava Barkan, Yoram Bar-Gal, Eran Schlesinger, Itzhak Biran, Ofra and Moti Peri, Mark Isenberg, Lee and Leah Harris, Shaul Cohen, Shelly Egoz, Anne Spirn, Peter Jacobs, Jolie Kaytes, Matt Myers, Cathleen Austin, Tricia Martin, and Melissa Barkin. There are also the scores of Technion students I was privileged to have in my classes. I apologize to any individuals I have omitted.

George F. Thompson, president of the Center for American Places, was an ardent advocate for this project. I am most grateful for his unwavering support and assistance. Nearing completion Denis Wood provided copyediting and insightful critique that helped refine the prose and tighten the discussion. And David Skolkin's superb design merged text and image to help communicate this story.

The project would not have come to fruition nor would it be presented in its current form replete with color images without the financial and institutional support of the Israeli Association of Landscape Architects, Akerstein Industries,

Derech Eretz, Elaine and Norman Winik, the Graham Foundation for Advanced Visual Studies in the Fine Arts, Technion and Deans Dani Shefer and Robert Oxman, as well as the support of my institution and colleagues at the University of Oregon.

My most personal debt is to my family who often accompanied me to Israel. I have seen the country through the eyes of my children, Sam and Ben, and their experiences, from kindergarten through high school, from parties to archeological digs. It was my wife Margot who first brought me to Israel, and transmitted to me her infectious and deep love of the people, language, and landscape. She has my never-ending thanks and everlasting love, and it is to her that this book is dedicated.

Dreaming Gardens

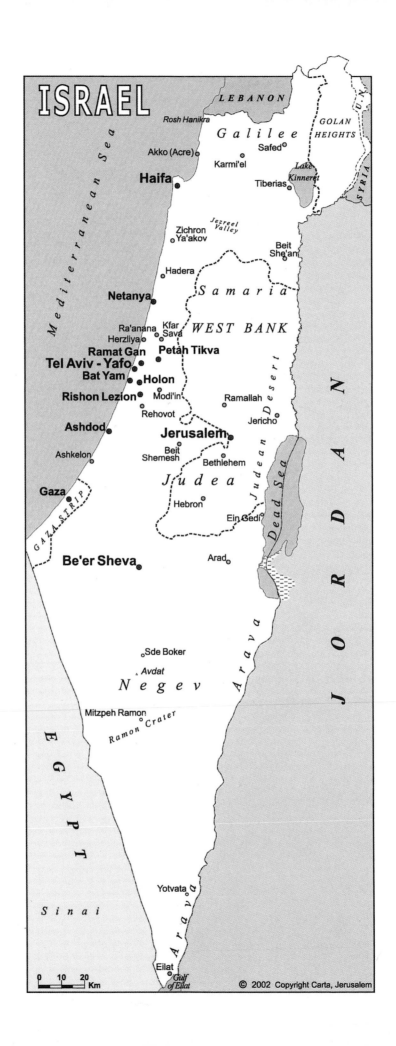

D URING THE PAST CENTURY landscape architects have been central to the development of Israel's physical, cultural, and social environment. They have made significant contributions in the design and planning of parks, gardens, and communities. They have literally helped construct and build the nation and their work has enriched the lives of citizens and visitors. At a personal and professional level they have been engaged ideologically and pragmatically with the fundamental issues and questions that have confronted Israel.

Landscape architects have designed places that have become symbolic icons of the nation. A brief list of outstanding places reveals the importance of their work: the Valley of the Destroyed Communities at Yad Vashem, Haas-Sherover Promenade in Jerusalem, Ben Gurion's Gravesite at Sde Boker, Yarkon Park of Tel Aviv, and Ramat Hanadiv in Zichron Yaakov. All of Israel's national parks, university campuses, most *kibbutzim* (communal agricultural settlements), and even whole cities have been designed and planned by Israel's landscape architects. Numbering only a few hundred, they have had a remarkable collective impact, but their contribution is little known. Fortunately, public recognition is on the rise. In 1998 Lippa Yahalom (b. 1913) and Dan Zur (b. 1926) were awarded the Israel Prize for their extraordinary lifetime contributions in design. Their personal honor was also recognition of the profession's significance.

Landscape architecture in Israel has reached an important crossroads. With roots in garden design, landscape architecture emerged as a profession in the United States and Europe during the nineteenth century. Within Israel its history paralleled that of the development of the state, as immigrants brought skills and ideas from the Diaspora. Many designers were self-taught or attended agricultural school. Others were educated abroad, and beginning in 1977 professional education has been offered at Technion—Israel Institute of Technology, in Haifa. The time is ripe to collect and share the works of Israel's landscape architects with a broad audience of both professional and lay persons, and to offer a critical appraisal of a significant body of work.

The goal for this volume is to provide a framework for understanding landscape architecture in Israel, its place in space and time, its cultural context, materials, design language, use, meaning, and evolution. This includes the examination of broad themes and the specifics of places; the shifting attitudes of a culture along with the ideas of individuals; the commonplace and the extraordinary; the iconic and the prosaic.

The book is divided into two parts. Part I, "The Vocabulary of Design," explores the development of an Israeli language of landscape architectural design. One cannot understand this landscape architecture without understanding its larger landscape and cultural context. These are the frameworks for design, and they are introduced and examined. "Land," "garden," and "landscape" each have distinct meanings in Israel, and the materials of design and construction are unique as well. Each is discussed in turn. Part II, "Speaking a Landscape Language," is about how this design language is spoken and its meaning. It focuses on four themes that are all fundamental to landscape architectural design. They are not unique to Israel, but each is given an Israeli definition: 1) the opposing forces of the relationship of inside to outside; 2) the designing of change in terms of the poles of tradition and innovation, and preservation and transformation; 3) the shaping of time in the landscape and the centrality of memory; and 4) the making of the frame, the creation of design structure in terms of community design and open space systems from the local to the national scale, all of which is focused in the *tayelet* (promenade). Part II concludes with some observations on the future of landscape architecture and the Israeli landscape.

The history of Israeli culture is the creation of modern "Israelis" in their many guises and varieties. Defining the modern Israeli identity and character has been a central personal and cultural concern. Characteristics of Jewish civilization in its shared fundamentals, historical experience, and cultural variety are part of the equation, as is language and shared experience. The Israeli-Arab community and its cultural contributions are also part of this mixture. The quest for this identity is reflected in literature, visual art, craft, and in the arts of environmental design, architecture, and landscape architecture.

The landscape speaks and we can choose to listen and hear its voice or not. Designers have sought to understand the Israeli *genius loci*, the spirit of the place, and explicitly to create designs that express this landscape at a particular moment in time. Gardens are designed dialogues between people and places. The gardens of Israel are grounded in its environments, the Mediterranean and the desert. The gardens speak of the environments, but also of the places from which modern Israelis have come. They speak simultaneously in the languages of the *Eretz Yisrael* (The Land of Israel) and the Diaspora. Thus the attentive listener can hear the voices of the landscapes of Germany and Russia, Poland and Morocco, Persia and England, and scores of other places. Landscape architectural design is about the meshing of nature and culture. While there are universal aspects to these concepts, they are also bound to specific times and places. The best designs in Israel respond to the universal aspects but are rooted in Israeli nature and Israeli culture.

Zionism, which is both a return to the historic homeland and a return to the land, forms a critical part of this mix. My emphasis here is in on the last century of history in Israel, which roughly parallels that of modern Zionism. The first Zionist Congress was in Basel, Switzerland, in 1897; the first *aliyah* (wave of immigration) was from 1881 to 1904. The legacy of landscape design in Palestine is a necessary background for understanding the modern era. Israel's design history also parallels the development of the modern practice of landscape architecture, and Israel's local history has significant connections to the development of modernism in Central Europe, Mediterranean culture, and design developments of the post–World War II era.

Israel's modern history has been fraught with distinctive, dramatic, and difficult issues. The conventional historical division of Israeli history subdivides it by *aliyah*; or it is organized by political history, from the Ottoman Empire to British mandate and the *Yishuv* (the Israeli community in Palestine prior to 1948), to the establishment of the state in 1948 and its successive governments. The most common division is one punctuated by the succession of wars and conflict, with its changing territories, borders, problems, and opportunities. All of these events have had an impact on landscape architecture, for they all influenced what was constructed or preserved, where things were built, and what resources were brought to bear. It is imperative to understand and evaluate work in the context of its time, and especially in terms of Israel's development, which has been fast-paced and under extreme pressure. The contexts for understanding design, culture, and society are in continual flux.

In a half century Israel has gone from a new, precarious, and developing nation to an established, modern, and prosperous state. It is a place of continuing and constant debate, but there is no question of Israel's accomplishments. There is the long list of problems and issues that Israel has had to confront: mass immigration, war, security, nation building, and a variety of internal conflicts, all of which are reflected in design. In addition to these extra burdens, Israel faces issues common to the contemporary world: the impact of the automobile and mass communications, and the pressures of modernity on traditional society and community life. Landscape architecture's response to a half-century of statehood and a century of development is part of this historical drama. Some of these phenomena are common experiences of the second half of the twentieth century, while others are unique to Israel's historical circumstances.

My emphasis is on the work of professional landscape architects, but they are among many agents of change. Other environmental designers, including architects, planners, and artists, have also contributed, and the country's professional gardeners and their association have played a unique and vital role.

Landscape architects have been integral to the actual building of the country. Often they collaborated in activities that showed remarkable foresight, in making gardens, parks, and open spaces, in community planning and design, and in the establishment of national forests, national parks, and nature reserves. Much of this groundwork was accomplished under remarkable pressure. The establishment of parks and reserves, places of pleasure, recreation, and conservation that took place in the early years of nation building and conflict was seen by some as luxuries, but others were more optimistic and forward thinking, and the history of the past two generations has proven the essential rightness of those actions. Establishing a haven and homeland is insufficient. It must be accompanied by the desire to create a landscape imbued with a humanistic order, social justice, amenity, and beauty.

Design opens a window onto cultural identity and desires. While design and planning take place in the present, they are always future oriented, always represent aspirations; and in Israel idealism and even utopian desire are close to the surface of common experience. Dreams and visions are preludes to action. Immigrants to Israel confronted a reality that rarely conformed to expectations, but there remained, and still remains, a persistent idealism regarding the land. Landscape design expresses the history of the country, even as it has also been an actor in that drama. Landscape design has helped people settle the land, learn the landscape, and build the country. Landscape design has created much of the basic framework for daily life, while also creating and preserving places of lasting significance and profound artistry for dwelling, recreation, work, gathering, commemoration, and celebration.

PART I
The Vocabulary of Design

A man is but a piece of land
A man is but a mold
of his native landscape.

SHAUL TCHERNICHOVSKY

The landscape language of Israel is spoken in the material elements of stone, water, and plants, the construction of space, and a distinctive culture of use. These are the vocabulary of the Israeli landscape. Speaking them, an undeniable Israeli garden is emerging. It speaks through the powerful and subtle use of stone, the sparing yet dramatic use of water, a rich palette of plants, a sensitivity to scale that addresses the proximate and distant, and is subject to intense use. This Israeli garden is part of the history of modern design and its European roots, but is also grounded in the geography and culture of the Mediterranean and Middle East. One can speak of this as an Israeli style, but this is but the visible face of the many forces that have shaped it. In the following chapters I address each of the components of this vocabulary—stone, water, plants, space, and use—trying to understand their meaning and use in design. As landscape architects have gained fluency and mastery of their materials they have become more articulate, able to speak a language of design with eloquence and poetry.

J EWS, THE PEOPLE OF THE BOOK, are not conventionally thought of as connected to design and the material, although this is a stereotyped and simplistic reading of history. For almost two millenia of diaspora, the Jews were disconnected from *Eretz Yisrael*, but the connection to the land was spiritual, mystical, and ideological, the landscape in its ancient and modern guises. *The* book, the *Torah*, begins with the story of creation and the site is *Gan Eden* (the Garden of Eden), the first home of humankind. The most profound garden idea is that of paradise. The Edenic garden is peaceful and innocent, the site of and a microcosm of creation. Genesis begins with a garden and of that garden God says that it has everything pleasant to look at and good to eat. In this implicit commentary on the garden, the aesthetic, the art of the garden, and appreciation of nature is noted first, and then coupled with its utility. The criteria of artistry and the pragmatic are linked in an essential pair of art and function, fundamental to any garden creation or critique.

The garden is a place experienced, but also an important symbol and archetype. Gardens employ the immutable elements, forms, and forces of nature, stone, water, plants, and climate, along with the changing meanings we ascribe to them. In Hebrew, *gan* has implications that go beyond our word "garden." The *gan* is the kindergarten of young children. It is a place out-of-doors that can be at any scale. Thus a house or apartment will have a *gan*, a neighborhood park will be a *gan*, and at the scale of the country there are *Gan Leumi*, the national parks, and national gardens. In Israel, the boundaries between garden and park are not sharp, and in terms of public spaces the terms are used interchangeably. Perhaps this is because the boundaries between the more personal and private domain and that of the public are blurred, as everyone shares a sense of ownership in the public gardens and everyone will surely offer a comment on the private domain. Garden joined with house forms the fundamental building block of a settled landscape. It is this intimate scale which defines the personal and daily relationship to the larger

Chapter 1

Garden and Landscape: Gan and Nof

The Lord God planted a garden in Eden, in the east, and placed there the man whom He had formed. And from the ground the Lord God caused to grow every tree that was pleasing to the sight and good for food...
—GENESIS 2:8

opposite:
Courtyard in Safed.

9

Illustration from Ruth Tsorfarti. A Chapter in the Life of my Father – The Garden. *1982.*

below: Children's garden. Kibbutz Sdot Yam. The signs all say lettuce.

landscape. It is here, between building and open space, where the domains of landscape architecture and architecture overlap.

The garden is the master metaphor of landscape architecture. Israeli gardens display the full range of garden functions, themes, and ideas. The garden has the ability to crystallize, in form and space, ideas about our relationship to the natural world and society. There are Israeli gardens that explore, reveal, and celebrate both natural and cultural history. There are those that commemorate and memorialize, that attempt to provide a space for the deepest of emotions. There are those which create a frame for and give form to ideas. There are gardens that are integral with architecture and the city, where the lines of inside and outside are blurred. There are gardens that are contemplative and revisited in ritual fashion, others that are centers of activity, while others are only glimpsed at high speeds. There are gardens that are communities, that people live in, that enrich the commonplace occurrences of everyday life.

What does *nof* (landscape) suggest in Israel? The interaction of people and place is embodied in the creation of land-scape. Landscape is not scenery, although it does include the scenic, nor is it nature without the human presence, nor is it landscaping, the greening of places. These are all important, but landscape embraces a broader idea. The landscape is a creation, the record and repository of the discourse between people and the physical environment. It is human artifact and art, the product of individual and collective activity, a cultural phenomenon whose meaning has evolved through the centuries. Jerusalem architect David

Picnic. Park HaYarkon. Tel Aviv.

Reznik expresses this succinctly, stating that "landscape is the culture of the environment," where "environment is the way of life of the people." Reznik adds that humans are always changing nature. To explain how, he gives a simple example, a picnic, a superb model of how even the most modest human action is a transformer of landscape space.

The word landscape has a dual origin and multiple meanings. The English word derives from *landskip* and *landschaft*. *Landskip* referred originally to paintings, depictions of the domesticated countryside as a scene. The Hebrew *nof* is synony-

Jezreel Valley. View to Nahalal. Moshav designed by Richard Kauffmann.

mous with a panorama, a broad view, and emphasizes this visual and spatial conception of landscape. *Landschaft*, on the other hand, was a collective term for the whole of village, gardens, fields, and woodlot. It was the world of the rural resident. Modern *usage* emphasizes the *landskip* root, the visual and scenic; but modern *times* demand a return to other origins, to landscape as a social concept, the bond of people and place. In many ways in Israel this is already the case for, since the establishment of the state, the making of the landscape has been conceived not only as a design activity, but also as the conscious embodiment of a set of values. The Israeli landscape is laden with values beyond the scenic that carry much weight in the public mind. Land is not landscape, but land (*eretz*) and landscape (*nof*) are closely related. *Nof* is not only scene, but also habitation and in Israel there is a wealth of types of habitation. Many are unique to the country and its specific landscape situation. In no other place is found the exact equivalent of kibbutzim, *moshavim* (collective agricultural settlements), *mitzpim* (hilltop settlements), field schools, tayelets, and development towns. This largely rural landscape is a modern middle-eastern *landschaft*.

top: Landscape near Beit Shearim.

bottom: Working the land.

This modern history is built upon an ancient foundation, one that is physical, psychological, and spiritual. Zionism postulates the continuity of the ancient and contemporary. The Zionist ideal is rooted in the act of imagining a homeland. Theodor Herzl's (1860-1904) novel *Altneuland (Old—New Land)* carries the essential meaning in its title. Rooted in religious and spiritual values the connection to the land is complex, and Zionist ideology had profound landscape implications. As Anita Shapira notes, "The transformation of that link from a spiritual-religious bond into a concrete nexus rooted in action was a feat virtually unparalleled in the history of modern movements." The tie to the land is sacred. It represents a return to historic roots, the literal answer to two millennia of prayers, and the modern desire for a nation state. For some it also represented an opportunity for a more *grounded* connection to the land. The pioneering Jews of Palestine valued the transformation of the land by their manual labor, which gave it an added value. For Aaron David Gordon (1856-1922), Jews who in the European urban existence were alienated from nature could now reconnect to the natural world. In the first generations the connections to the land were the manifestation of a conscious desire, pragmatic necessity, religious history, and a degree of romanticism. For subsequent generations the affinity was second nature. In a more poetic vein, literary scholar Ariel Hirschfeld says that gardens and landscape were always part of the Zionist subconscious imagination.

Geography is the key. The immutable basics of climate, vegetation, geology, and soil set the frame within which culture is created. It is our habitat, the result of a dynamic process, as people both create and are created by their environments. The result is a landscape designed by people over time. In this process, landscape architects are but one of the actors. Sometimes their voice and impact are large while at other times they are muted. Sometimes their artistry serves to crystallize the relationship of people and their place.

The Bunting map of 1580 is a simple diagram of three intersecting ellipses that meet at a central circle. The three shapes represent Europe, Asia, and Africa. America is off in the far corner, a harbinger of its later significance. At the center is Jerusalem, Israel's location. It is simultaneously at the periphery of continents, habitats, and civilizations and it stands at the center—a meeting place of cultures. In environmental terms it is an ecotone, but at a continental scale it is a junction of distinct habitats and species. A place of very modest size, Israel possesses a remarkable range, richness, and diversity of climate, geology, and vegetation. With gradations and modulation due to elevation and situation, it is a nuanced landscape whose small area belies its variety. Within short distances there are dramatic changes, and given the hilly topography they are often visible from one place to the other. The effect is a conceptual foreshortening, much like a telephoto image, which compresses and appears to squeeze together the visual frame.

Three great environmental zones intersect in Israel: the Mediterranean coastal belt; an extension of the west Asian steppe belt, the Irano-

top: Bunting map of 1580,
Itinerarium Sacrae Scripturae.

bottom: View in the Galilee,
from hills to Mediterrean.

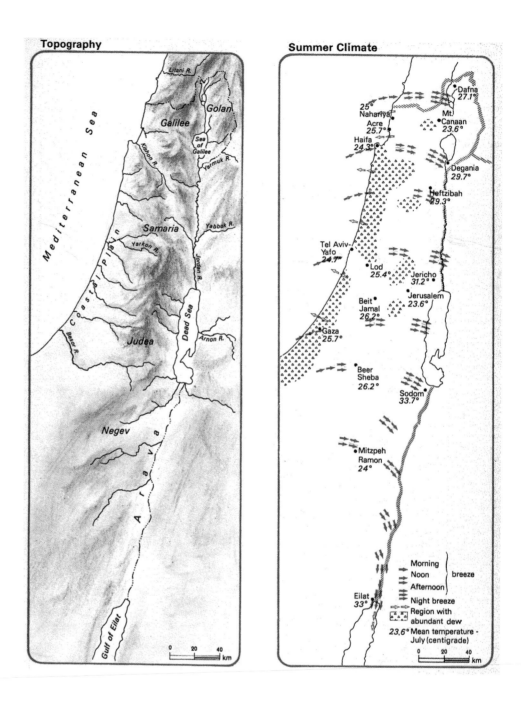

Maps of topography and climate. (CARTA)

Topography

Litani R.

Golan

Galilee

Sea of Galilee

Kishon R.

Yarmuk R.

Mediterranean Sea

Samaria

Yabbok R.

Yarkon R.

Jordan R.

Coastal Plain

Judea

Dead Sea

Arnon R.

Besor R.

Negev

A r a v a

Gulf of Eilat

0   20   40
km

Summer Climate

Dafna
27.1°

25°
Nahariya
Acre
25.7°

Mt.
Canaan
23.6°

Haifa
24.3°

Degania
29.7°

Heftzibah
29.3°

Tel Aviv-
Yafo
24.7°

Lod
25.4°

Jericho
31.2°

Jerusalem
23.6°

Beit
Jamal
26.2°

Gaza
25.7°

Beer
Sheba
26.2°

Sodom
33.7°

Mitzpeh
Ramon
24°

Morning
Noon   breeze
Afternoon
Night breeze
Region with
abundant dew
23.6° Mean temperature -
July (centigrade)

Eilat
33°

0   20   40
km

Turanian region; and in the Negev a fragment of the Saharo-Arabian desert, the great desert that cuts across Africa and into Arabia. The resulting landscape can be understood as a series of intersections and gradients. A journey from the Lebanese border in the north to Eilat in the south reveals the diverse character of the land and a transition from a Mediterranean to desert landscape. The gradient of rainfall is the key determinate as precipitation diminishes moving north to south and west to east. The upper Galilee averages almost 900mm of rain a year, which drops to about 500mm in Tel Aviv and Jerusalem, 162mm at Beersheva, and 2mm at Eilat. Most rain falls between November and April, the winter season, and summer throughout the country is hot and dry, but extremely so in the south and Jordan

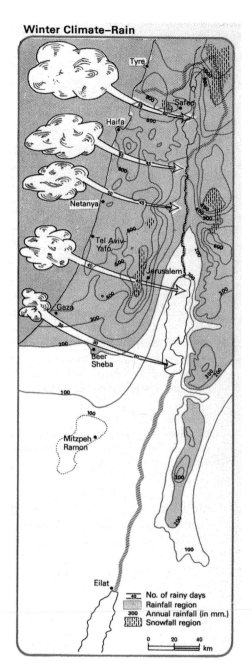

Winter Climate–Rain

No. of rainy days — 40
Rainfall region
Annual rainfall (in mm.) — 300
Snowfall region

0 20 40 km

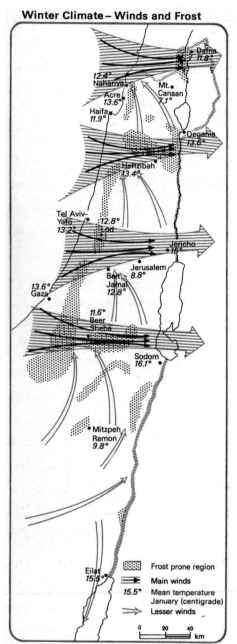

Winter Climate – Winds and Frost

Frost prone region
Main winds
Mean temperature January (centigrade) — 15.5°
Lesser winds

0 20 40 km

Valley. Haifa gets about 55 days of rain per year, Beersheva 30, while in the desert rain falls in sporadic bursts. The pattern of vegetation follows this moisture gradient. The hills of the Galilee and the uplands were historically wooded and many areas have been reforested. Traditionally slopes were terraced to create arable plots of land. A journey from west to east takes one from sea level, up and over the hills of the Galilee or Judea, into the Jordan Valley or down to the Dead Sea. The drop in elevation from Jerusalem to the Dead Sea is almost 1,200 meters.

Mediterranean landscapes characterize most of the densely habited portion of the country. The Mediterranean is the "middle sea." In the broadest sense it represents an overlap and meeting place of continents, environments, and cultures. Two

top left: Village. Galilee.

*top right: Galilee.
Mount Meron. Ruins.*

*bottom left: Courtyard
in Safed.*

*bottom right: Gan Ha Aliya
Hahshniyah. Givataim.
Meir Victor used traditional
terraces on the slopes of the
park.*

seasons, a cool wet "European" winter and a hot dry "African" summer, characterize the Mediterranean environment, reflecting its intermediary position. It is an
equable climate conducive to outdoor life. The natural vegetation represents a
meeting of northern forests and southern deserts. Mediterranean vegetation is distinguished by evergreen hardwoods, a schlerophyl forest of trees with hard, thick,
leathery leaves, gnarled low branching trees with thick bark, and large areas of
scrub and little ground vegetation. The colors are muted. It is an open forest of a
discontinuous canopy and a strained environment, where plants evolved to com-
pensate for summer's extreme water
deficit. Oaks and pines are part of the
forest mix, but the indicator species is
the olive. Once destroyed, many

16

species are non-regenerative, but the olive is able to survive after much abuse and live for centuries.

Like plants and animals, humans have similarly evolved methods for dealing with Mediterranean conditions. The key questions are how to stay cool and husband water for summer use and conserve heat and keep warm in winter. Environmental conditions set the limits, the ranges of possible options that can be pursued by a people. Throughout the Mediterranean basin there are certain landscape commonalties, and Israel is no exception. Much of the land bordering the sea is hilly and mountainous and historically terraced to create arable land and minimize erosion. Geographers refer to the Mediterranean triad of wheat, olives, and grapevines as characteristic and iconic crops. These are mainstays of diet, but they also refer more broadly to the fundamental components of a Mediterranean design vocabulary: terrace, orchard, field, and vineyard. In the Mediterranean landscape design has a certain tenuous quality. It thrives under human care, stewardship, and craft and easily degenerates without it.

The desert is not monolithic. Israel's deserts, the Negev and the Judean, are landscapes of great variety, from sand dunes to rocks, and a topography that encompasses broad plains, craters, cliffs, and canyons. The desert is an environment of extremes: hot and cold, drought and flash floods, sun and shade, desolation and intense, sporadic life. The desert accentuates the dichotomy of the functional and the aesthetic. The fundamental problem is how to make the desert habitable for

top left: Negev.

top right: Judean Desert in summer.

bottom: Dead Sea shoreline.

human use. Design needs to respond to its extreme conditions: heat, nighttime cold, glare, dryness, and the unpredictable.

Desert design has to confront the desert's scale and distinct qualities. The lack of vegetation dramatizes the material and the colors of the soil and rocks. The skeletal shape of the land is paramount as the lack of vegetation accentuates the topography. Natural processes create a landscape of great seasonal contrast and variety, as rain turns bare plains into colorful fields. Perhaps most fundamental is desert light. The basic division between land and sky is pronounced. There is the stark contrast of sun and the making of shade, which brings comfort and a landscape change felt viscerally through the skin.

While an extreme environment, the desert has immense appeal. Yet Israeli attitudes towards it have been ambivalent. A pioneering attitude of greening the desert co-exists with a desire to preserve its character. Its most ardent supporters and experts are those who dwell within its settled communities. For designers there is the double edged question of how to create places of human comfort in harsh and inhospitable conditions, but also how to get people, both visitors and those who dwell in the desert, to appreciate its qualities. The desert functions for Israelis much like the deserts do in the United States. It is the place that is wilder, where one can seek solitude, be away from civilization and connect back to nature. However, given the scale of Israel's deserts, one cannot actually go very far. Part of its attraction is its emptiness, but there is also a temptation to put things in it and fill it up. The allure is psychological as well as in the actual space, which is becoming even more essential and tenuous as almost the entire coastal plain is being transformed into a metropolis.

Conveyor belt for the Dead Sea Works. Shlomo Aronson. (Shlomo Aronson)

The desert captivates many Israelis, and for many landscape architects it has been a place they return to as a touchstone and for inspiration. They are well aware of how it casts design into relief, accentuating its formal qualities. The contrasts among elements can be exploited. Zvi Dekel speaks of the impact of just a few trees alone in the landscape. They act as landmarks, mark the change of seasons, shape space, and provide shade.

How to intervene is the question. Speaking largely about the siting of buildings, architectural historian Gilbert Herbert says that in the desert the scale of design does not have to be large, but it must have large scale. Design here benefits from simplicity, strength, and vigor, and structures must have a presence that situates them in space. Zvi Dekel says it is knowing when "to touch and do a lot and knowing when not to do something," but he also says sometimes one needs to make a mark just in contrast to it. The contrast of elements can be exploited. Oases do that, as does placing a road across the land, or the construction of an 18-kilometer long conveyor belt designed by Shlomo Aronson for the Dead Sea Works (1986).

In classic Mediterranean cultures there is a another cross section, the polarity of city and country, where the experience and meaning of each acquires dimension in reference to its opposite. This cross section takes on distinctive Israeli forms that are still evolving. There is a social cross section of development and density, going from wild austere desert and uninhabited landscapes, to pioneering settlements, to rural communities of kibbutzim and moshavim, to towns, cities, and metropolitan areas. In Israel the countryside is close to where most people live. Viewed from the opposite perspective, the city is always near. No place is very remote, all are easily accessible. Distances are small, dimensions are tight, divisions are powerful, and the diversity of experience is accentuated by these factors.

Landscapes are understood at a variety of spatial and temporal scales, which form a continuum. The experience of the landscape is evidence of great continental geological processes, minuscule sites, and ephemeral events. At one extreme it is possible to discern patterns that are universal or archetypal, those common to all cultures as they settle and transform the land. Next is the national, the development of national character and culture and its manifestations in the landscape. This aspect is essential to understanding Israel. But Israel itself is not monolithic. Despite its modest size the country's regions, and the design responses to these environments, are distinctive. There is the local, the minutia of places and their matrices of meaning. Finally, there is the personal landscape, and at the extreme the idiosyncratic, the wonderful peculiarities of individual personality.

Music Teacher's garden. Kibbutz Ayelet Hashachar. The gourds are musical instruments.

Page of Talmud.

T HE GRAPHIC LAYOUT of the *Talmud* (the codification and compilation of Jewish law) is striking. On each page a passage from the *Mishnah* (the oral law) and *Gemara* (commentaries on the *Mishnah*) occupies a central position surrounded by commentaries from the rabbis, additional notes, and cross-references. There are commentaries on commentaries and the implied interaction of the reader entering the discussion. Like books, landscapes can be read as texts; however, unlike most books, their authorship is collective. Landscape literacy—being able to speak "landscape"—necessitates an understanding of landscape vocabulary, grammar, syntax, and modes of expression. Landscapes speak in distinctive languages and dialects. Landscapes are much like pages of the *Talmud*. Over generations, there are commentaries—individual and collective designs—that address the core text and then begin to "speak" to each other. The form and content are subject to endless debate, annotation, and interpretation. It is in the context of that discussion, that is, in the experience of landscape, that its lessons and meaning lie. Landscape architecture offers one of the commentaries on the central text. Sometimes it even succeeds in reconfiguring a "page" by offering a bold new insight and interpretation, where the land and culture itself are seen anew. Occasionally, they even offer the moral and ethical equivalent of the guidance of the *Talmud*.

The basic question for Israel's designers is what is the language of design, the one that speaks of Israeli culture and landscape, its history, present and future. There has been a continuous and conscious search for such a language of landscape design, a quest for a design language of form, spaces, materials, and function. How to translate these raw elements, these seemingly inert elements, into places of substance and meaning has been a central task. A multitude of cultures has created the Israeli landscape; their values, beliefs, and aspirations are visible on the land, or lie hidden beneath the surface waiting to be revealed. As form embodies meaning the question is asked: what kind of landscape architecture is fitting in a nation which is the ancestral home of the Jewish people, a cradle of western civilization and its religious traditions, a historic crossroads, and the modern home to diverse peoples?

Chapter 2

Talmud and Ulpan

… And you shall learn Torah from the mouth of nature, the Torah of building and creating, and you shall learn to do as nature does in everything you build and in everything you create. And so in all your ways and in all your life you will learn to be a partner in creation.
—A.D. Gordon

Ein Gedi Field School (1950s). A dense oasis-like design along the shore of the Dead Sea. Yechiel and Joseph Segal.

The role of the physical environment is essential to the creation of Israeli identity, from a deep religious and ideological perspective, as well as being the site of a collective history and memory. But primarily it is the basis for daily life encompassing all levels of experience: the sensory environment of sound, smell, and sight; the natural and built worlds of material elements; the actual three-dimensional shape of the world and the activity of life. Just as the meaning and definition of Israel has evolved in a half century, so too has the design on the land.

We undoubtedly form an affinity, an emotional attachment, to places, what geographer Yi-Fu Tuan has called *topophilia*, a love of place. The most fundamental response is a reaction to what is inherent in a site itself. We may have instinctive, innate reactions to the qualities and characteristics of a site, be it the seashore, a mountain, or hidden valley. The ancient classical concept of seeking the *genius loci*, the spirit of the place, is a quest for essentials. A continuing process in design history has been to seek an understanding of these qualities in the landscape, to recognize that spirit once discovered, to evoke its messages, and to formulate an appropriate response, a design. The methods in this quest are varied and the responses may preserve, accentuate, contrast, or even deny the spirit. It is through this process that design transforms abstract space into meaningful place. In Israel this classical idea has a cultural variant in the concept of *Makom*. (A related Arabic term is *Makam*.) The word means place, but it also refers to a sacred place where God is manifest.

Israeli landscape architecture accentuates the modern world's critical task of rooting design in the essential qualities of a place and locale, the *genius loci* and *Makom*, while simultaneously being answerable to a broader set of contemporary concerns and forces. It is a matter of being responsible to concerns both cosmopolitan and local, universal and particular. This is a difficult and profound activity. Landscape architects have tried to understand what that spirit is in Israel. Given the land's rich and layered history and diversity of environmental conditions, this is a task of great complexity.

In Israel this quest has many forms and is sought in multiple ways. Understanding comes in looking closely at the landscape. The cultural landscape is layered over thousands of years of habitation. It is a place sacred to the Abrahamic faiths of Judaism, Christianity, and Islam. Each is profoundly connected to the actual land and the landscape as the embodiment of history. That spirit is evidenced in sacred texts, but it also resides in the rocks, the texture of stone, the quality of light, the pattern of plants, the shape of an arch. The spirit is layered with the resonance of tiers of history and association. Time is thick and deep, layered in the strata of the cultural landscape. This density has led to the creation of a modern landscape that accommodates diverse purposes and functions. It is one to which there are rival claims and to which various meanings are attributed. As Palestinian historian Rashid Khalidi notes, "the same rocks have different meaning."

Landscape architectural design must accommodate functions that vary from the mundane to the meaningful. There is the need for design to respond to diverse communities and to people as individuals and groups. The current users are the co-creators of design, breathing life into the body of form, and over time they render its spirit and invest it with meaning. There is a response to Israeli's behavior and habits, its outdoor culture, Mediterranean lifestyle, and the patterns and mores of religious and secular life. There is a response to issues and problems of the demands of security, army, and immigration, providing the essentials of housing and transportation, and the desire to preserve the land. Often there is a density of demands, which mitigates against simpler solutions. Design programs, the catalogue of functions, areas and requirements that need to be accommodated are typically complex and even full of contradictions.

Holy Place. Sign in Hebrew, Arabic, and English. Banias.

In a place of such complexity and mixed messages, often the problem for designers is to decide which spirits need to be served. While the aspirations of design are profound, most important is the creation of an environment at the prosaic level of daily life, places that facilitate and ennoble the ordinary: the walk to the store, the conversation on a bench, playing with friends, going for coffee. Design is both a functional and expressive language. It is prose and poetry. "Culture and site meet in design," says Uri Mueller (b. 1937) of the firm Tichnun Nof. Where this intersection is strongest it can crystallize and accentuate the character and quality of the place and bring something previously invisible or innate to a level of awareness.

What is the meaning of landscape and how do designers articulate that meaning? Meaning is embodied in design, the shaping of space, the creation of form, and the use of materials. However, it is more complicated. For any design, be it an artifact, building, or landscape, the pertinent question is, what does one want to say? Landscape design is not only about functional and programmatic concerns and about solving problems, but also at a profound level it is about expressing ideas through the medium of landscape. When this is accomplished with skill and artistry, one is invited to enter a created domain where the shape of space and the manipulation of materials creates places that are engaging and memorable, where we respond with our senses *and* our intellect, our head *and* our heart.

At its best design takes the materials, forms, and habits of the place and distills them. Returning to the Talmudic perspective, design creates places that are "new pages," where a new text can be read and interpreted in a variety of ways. The essence of the "page," the landscape, is in the discussion, in the experience of landscape.

LANDSCAPE LANGUAGE has a vocabulary. In Israel this vocabulary is materially rich and symbolically resonant. The building blocks of the Israeli landscape architectural vocabulary are the basic landscape elements of stone, water, plants, and the shaping of space, practiced within a distinctive and evolving culture of use, a framework for human activity. These foundations form a continually evolving language, a living and slowly maturing means of communication created by professional designers and the public. These elements embody ideas and are laden with meaning and weighted with history. The primary elements are found in a rich variety of "natural" sites, but they are also found in the most "human" constructions. They constitute a continuum from the native and raw to the more manipulated, controlled, or refined.

Stone is the primary material, the foundation of place. Stones mean connection, solidity, permanence. Herman Melville traveled to Palestine in the winter of 1857. His journal records his reaction to a landscape dominated by stone. "No wonder that stones should so largely figure in the Bible. Judea is one accumulation of stones — Stony mountains & stony plains; stony torrents & stony roads; stony vales & stony fields, stony homes & stony tombs; (stony eyes & stony hearts). Before you, & behind you are stones. Stones to the right & stones to the left. In many places laborious attempts have been made, to clear the surface of these stones. You see heaps of stones here & there; and stone walls of immense thickness are thrown together, less for boundaries than to get them out of the way. But in vain; the removal of one stone only serves to reveal those stones still lying, below it.... Everything looks old. Compared with these rocks, those in Europe or America look juvenile." Melville's extreme reaction recognizes the intersection of the geological and the cultural. In this ancient landscape, stones have been altars, foundations, tombs, boundary markers, and building materials. Stone is associated with the most sacred sites of hilltops, shrines, and buildings and the mark of wasteland.

Stone gives Israel's regions their distinct character. Limestone is the basic building block, but there are regional distinctions. Kurkar is sandstone of the coastal

Chapter 3

Stone

Stone is eternity.
—Shlomo Aronson

left: Fields with stone. Carmel.

right: An ancient quarry. Carmel.

Sculpture at Machtesh Ramon, Negev. The Mitzpe Ramon Desert Sculpture Park, established in 1986. A series of stone sculptures were created on a portion of the north rim of the crater. Zvi Dekel was a consultant on the project.

plain; easy to cut and shape it is in common usage. Black and gray basalt is used in the Golan and portions of the Galilee, the only areas with a volcanic history. Unlike plants that can be exotic or naturalized, it is rare in Israel to see stones that are not indigenous. Little is imported. A trained eye can tell which quarry has been the source of building material.

Soil types are the result of geology, climate, and vegetation. In the mountainous areas and the Sharon, *Terra Rossa* (*Hamra* in Arabic), red earth, predominates. In the coastal plain the soils are lighter, while in the foothills and valleys there are deeper, darker alluvial deposits. Much of the Negev is stony with shallow brown and gray desert soils. There are pockets of sand dunes, also found along the coastal plain. Few areas of the country have deep soils. Otherwise stone is on the surface or covered only by a shallow layer of soil. Much of the stone is pockmarked with crevices and hollows where soil and water collect and plants take root.

Despite its solidity one can describe the states of stone. Stone has rich sensory qualities. Stones range in color, an actual palette that goes from black basalt to white marble. In Israel most common are the tans, rusts, and brown of limestone. Stone is textured. Our attraction to it includes attention to surface detail as well as marveling at its massiveness and strength. It is said that stones "speak," but it is the technique of how they are worked and composed which gives them their expression. This is the artistry and skill of the stonecutter and the mason. Stone ranges from that found in its raw, natural state, to that which is excavated and quarried, and then transformed through varieties of "dressing" or "finishing" from that which preserves its rough cut quality, through those where it is shaped into regular blocks for building, to the most smooth and polished. There is variation but there are also conventions, traditional and modern methods of working stone. *Even leket* is rough collected stone, typically joined with mortar inside. *Chami* is cut stone with a rough face. Further gradations described in traditional Arabic terminology go from *tubze* with the roughest surface, to *taltish* and *mesamsam* as the most delicate, while *mutaba* is roughened with a meat hammer. Often roughness is associated with the traditional and old, while smoothness is associated with the modern and new, but this is a false dichotomy, for both old and new employ a full range of expressive possibilities.

top left: Stone workers. Manchat Central Park. Jerusalem. Shlomo Aronson.

top right: Stone detail. Suzanne Delal. Tel Aviv. Shlomo Aronson.

left: Stone steps. Gan Ha'atzmaut. Tel Aviv. Avraham Karavan.

What is especially evocative is the juxtaposition
of stone and plants, growing in the cracks between
pavers or in rock gardens; or the interaction of water
and rock as it cascades over forms and changes its
color and luminosity. While stone may be used in
different configurations it may unite spaces and tie
together disparate elements. The simplest vocabulary, the most commonplace aspect of an Israeli park
or garden, consists of great boulders excavated from
the site infilled with dirt and interspersed with
planting. Almost every landscape design uses stone
in some capacity. Stone functions as surface, support,
boundary, and marker, literally and symbolically. As surface it is ground and pave-
ment; as support it is the structure of walls and terraces; as boundary it acts as edge
and container; as marker it is an indicator, a focus of attention, and energy. In a
sense almost all Israeli gardens are rock gardens.

Many of the country's outstanding landscape designs are rock environments:
the Valley of the Destroyed Communities at Yad Vashem, Ben Gurion's gravesite,
Kikar Levana, Har Herzl and almost every *tayelet* and *mitzpor* (lookout). All employ
stone's structural capacity and symbolic resonance. Similarly the natural landscapes
of national parks sites are overwhelmingly geological.

Gan Hasla'im (1988) in Park HaYarkon by Gideon Sarig (b. 1934) takes the
geology of the country as its subject. In an orchestrated progression visitors pass a
rock which seeps water and proceed through a large, arched, stone gateway
encrusted with ferns. Inside the enclosure are successions of rock gardens that use
stone as both sculpture and geological display. There is a Stonehenge-inspired
amphitheater, a serpentine graveled river bed with a spectrum of stone from
turquoise to red, and a geologic study area where children (or adults) can sample
rocks from around the country.

Sarig calls Israel a "stone culture" and his stone and sculptural sensibility is
demonstrated in his designs on the shores of the *Kinneret* (the Sea of Galilee).
Israel's only freshwater lake is under tremendous pressure for use as the nation's
primary drinking water source, but also for amenity and recreation. Beaches line
its shore, but for much of the perimeter the road hugs the shoreline. To create

top: *Susita Beach. Gideon Sarig.*

bottom: *Circular wall. Zippori. Gideon Sarig.*

usable places in this narrow strand is the dilemma. Kinneret beaches are rocky and beach behavior is active. The water is the desire line and people gravitate to the edge and often park along the roadway. If permitted many would park with their front wheels at the water's edge. Sarig's designs for the beaches respond to the constrained yet dramatic sites, social-behavioral considerations, and the exigencies of very modest funding. The design vocabulary and the form are deceptively simple but strong. Stone is the basic element — smooth, rounded basalt boulders from the Kinneret and Golan. Large ones are used as boundaries, marking roadways, points of entry, and acting as barriers to penetration by the automobile. They are spaced close enough that a car cannot pass between them; that is the key dimension. In long arced lines they have a sculptural presence. Smaller stones are used to create walls of different heights at the edge of parking lots. They allow cars to get near, but not too close to the sea.

At Susita Beach (1981) the upper level is workaday: a fence containing a banana plantation, a dirt road, a line of boulders, a grove of eucalyptus arching toward the sea, and then a wall. The sea is almost invisible, but gaps in the wall are steps to the rocky shore. A few steps down and the sea presents itself, but the wall is now a great concave arc enclosing the beach and also framing the sea. The textures and colors are paramount: the smooth water, the intense sun, the rough beach, the pebbled gray basalt wall, and the branches of eucalyptus arching over the wall. You see similar walls at Ein Gev as Sarig learned from the pattern of that seaside kibbutz. On the western shore he opportunistically built stone terrace platforms between the sea and roadway, reclaiming the seashore, creating small, but significant opportunities for recreational space.

Not all boundaries are sharp. Sarig also creates walls that are sculptural gestures. At Zippori the walls act as boundary, seating, and balustrade and provide a subtle separation between the designated areas of the park and the surrounding landscape. It is a fine demonstration of his formative training as a sculptor.

In the desert the sculptural and space making qualities of stone are accentuated. Maya Shafir (b. 1955), who works as a landscape architect for kibbutzim in the Arava, emphasizes the need to be humble in the desert for it is an unforgiving landscape. She exploits the inanimate materials of stone, ceramic, and metals along with higher building densities, tighter spaces, and a careful attention to microcli-

mate. Her stone compositions on Kibbutz Yotvata and Kibbutz Ketura are demonstrations of these experiments.

With little wood and no steel, concrete and concrete products, block and tiles are ubiquitous building materials. Stone has often been replaced by these more economical hard materials as well as granolit and Ackerstein, a modern, mass produced Israeli material. These materials present great challenges, as well as opportunities, for developing a language around their distinctive properties and characteristics.

above: Kibbutz Samar. Maya Shafir.

left: Stone paths. Tel Dan. Greenstein-Har-Gil. (Doron Horowitz)

F UNDAMENTAL CLIMATIC AND HYDROLOGIC CONDITIONS are reflected in design. Even in the wetter northern portions, Israel is still a Mediterranean country, with an extreme water deficit in summer. This drought situation is true year-round as one moves south into the Judean Desert and Negev. Water is a substance to be carefully husbanded, used sparingly, and in ways that can accentuate its effect. This practice is true throughout the Mediterranean basin, in the arid lands of the Middle East, and in any desert environment. The great historic garden traditions of the Mediterranean and Islamic culture, which have inspired work in Israel, are often described as water gardens not because of its volume, but because judicious use intensifies its character.

There are a series of Israeli water gardens. Each exploits a natural condition and then accentuates its impact, be it spring, oasis, river, or seashore. There are water gardens at Banias and Horshat Tal at the sources of the Jordan River, both national parks. There are the excavated and restored springs at Aqua Bella (Ein Hemed) designed by Josef Segal (b. 1926), Park Canada by Tichnun Nof, and Sataf by Shlomo Aronson (b. 1936), all located in the Jerusalem Forest. In each of these cases, springs whose function was once to irrigate a terraced agricultural landscape now bring popular pleasure. At a grander scale there are pathways along the Yarkon, the nation's largest river that flows year-round to the sea. There is also the celebration of the remaining Huleh wetland, the banks of the Kinneret, and the shores of the Dead Sea and the Mediterranean.

Pools of water are a rare phenomena in the Israeli landscape. At the Sapir Park (1983) in the Arava by Shlomo Aronson the design revels in the opportunity to present a rare desert pool and the sensory richness of refuge from the harsh climate. So does another pool at Timna, a pond in the desert by Zvi Dekel (b. 1929). In Tel Aviv's major parks, Park HaYarkon to the north and Menachem Begin Park (formerly Park Darom) to the south, the designers Tichnun Nof created water bodies large enough for paddle boats while also offering walkways along their shorelines, creating more of a European park experience and sensibility for pleasure and recreation.

Chapter 4

Water

For the Lord your God is bringing you into a good land, a land with streams and springs and fountains issuing from plain and hill.
—Deuteronomy 8:7

opposite: Park Canada. Tichnun Nof.

left: Water channel. Horshat Tal National Park. Yahalom-Zur. These channels were created by the designers to flow through the grand groves of the oak trees.

right: Pool at Timna. Zvi Dekel.

below: The Pond of Tranquility. Huga Gardens (Ein Huga). Beit She'an. (1998 Dr. Ariel and Zipi Tibi. Ein Huga consists of three ponds excavated near one of the large springs in the valley. (Dr. Ariel and Zippi Tibi)

Ordinarily water is used sparingly. The agricultural fundamentals of water source, collection, and distribution are paralleled in landscape architectural design. In the courtyards of the Rockefeller Museum (1938), designed by British architect Austin St. Barbe Harrison, water is collected in pools inspired by the Islamic gardens of the Alhambra in Granada, Spain. Those gardens in turn inspired the courtyards of the Supreme Court (1992) by Ram Karmi and Ada Karmi-Melamede. At the Hebrew Union College (1988) in Jerusalem by architect Moshe Safdie and American landscape architect Ronald Lovinger (b. 1940) the arcaded buildings contain three successive courtyards each distinguished by a water feature, rich paving, and cascading plantings from the surrounding buildings. The water display is inspired by Islamic, Indian, and Judaic sources. There are wall fountains inspired by *sabil* (public water sources found in quarters of the Old City), pools with *chadars* from Mugal gardens, and basins and rills resonant of medieval cloisters.

left: Central pool and arcade. Rockefeller Museum (1948). Jerusalem. Austin St. Barbe Harrison. (Her Majesty's Stationary Office)

right: Courtyard, Supreme Court. Jerusalem. Ram Karmi and Ada Karmi Melamed. The Psalm 85:12, "Truth will spring up from the earth and justice will be reflected from the heavens," was an inspiration to the designers.

Courtyards. Hebrew Union College. Jerusalem. Ron Lovinger and Moshe Safdie.

Suzanne Delal. Tel Aviv. Shlomo Aronson. (Shlomo Aronson)

At the Suzanne Delal Center (1989) in the Neve Tzedek neighborhood of old Tel Aviv the Mediterranean and Islamic affinities are clear. Shlomo Aronson's use of water is directly inspired by courtyards at the Courts of the Oranges (Patios de los Naranjos) in Cordoba and Seville, which were originally constructed for their respective mosques. In these gardens, irrigation channels—whose patterns are derived from agricultural technique—periodically filled pools around the trees. Suzanne Delal further abstracts that idea. The water flows continuously through a grapefruit grove, not actually irrigating the trees. Despite the very small surface area of water the plaza feels inundated by water. The references are also local, recalling Tel Aviv's early history of a city surrounded by citrus groves.

Other designs dramatize water's divergent qualities. Harry Wilf Park is the redesign of Jerusalem's Independence Park. The original park design was the result of a competition won by Richard Kauffmann and executed by Elimelech Admoni, head of the Landscape Department of the City of Jerusalem during the British Mandate. It was first redesigned by Yahalom-Zur in 1960 and again by Shlomo Aronson in 1996. Picturesque braided streams cut across green pastoral meadows, recalling the ancient water collection system of Jerusalem, the sources of the Jordan, and the pools at Banias in the north of Israel. The streams end in long architectonic channels and fountains. The expression is grand, the craft meticulous. The Jerusalem stone language of paving and structure is augmented by a stream encrusted with embedded stones. An orchard grid occupies the lower slope.

top left: Harry Wilf Park. Jerusalem. Shlomo Aronson.

top right: Swimming pool. Residence in Jerusalem. G.E.O. Architects. The pool in this design sits at a symbolic juncture, between a green, treed landscape and a paved "beach." Judy Green (b. 1950) worked for many years as a lead designer with Shlomo Aronson's office in Jerusalem. (Judy Green)

bottom left: Gan Ha Mapal / Gan Landes. Tel Aviv. (1985). At this well-trafficked intersection a sheet of water becomes an urban landmark, acting as the backdrop for a street corner plaza to one side and a neighborhood park to the other. (Haim Kahanovitch)

bottom right: Water channels. Nahal Arugot.

At the Jerusalem Zoo (1993) a water system acts as a central spine of the design. Like the zoo itself, it is a miniature of a larger world. The designers, Miller-Blum, had previously done a safari park in Ramat Gan (1971). The zoo is constructed within a *wadi* that Miller described as a desert with power lines. Mimicking a desert spring, on an upper slope water seeps out of a large uplifted stone and follows a channel until it cascades over a stone waterfall into a lush papyrus-lined basin. It then flows in a stream to a pool at the lowest level, bordered by lawn with islands of waterfowl. Upon entering the zoo the entire sequence is visible and acts as an invitation to traverse the terrain. The qualities combine the human and animal predilection for water, simultaneously recalling oasis, jungle, and watering holes.

Water systems are also an essential part of the nation's history and heritage. Ancient systems have been unearthed, restored, and made accessible, making these remarkable feats of engineering open to modern experience. Jerusalem and Megiddo have tunnels that were excavated through solid stone to provide water in times of siege. They are now accessible to the public. At Zippori National Park the ancient Roman aqueduct took water from springs at the base of hills around Nazareth to the city. Archeologists have excavated the aqueduct and Gideon Sarig's design allows visitors to follow the now dry passage though the original tunnels that are ten meters high. Modern metal stairs and walkways contrast with the original plastered walls. Roman aqueducts took water twenty kilometers from the Carmel Mountain to the port city of Caesarea. In Park Alona along the Tananim River three systems are parallel: the natural river, the Roman, and the modern conduit. In the Jordan Valley city of Beit Shean, Bruce Levin and architect Arieh Rachamimoff designed a linear promenade based on a loose interpretation of the water features that were part of the ancient town (1991). A small aqueduct and fountains follow the pathway and provide a link to the Roman and Byzantine heritage of the site.

Park Alona.
Greenstein–Har-Gil.
The pathway runs along
all three systems and
visitors can walk through
underground portions of
the Roman system.
(Greenstein-Har-Gil)

above: Zippori. Roman Aqueduct during archeological excavation. Gideon Sarig.

above right: Zippori. The aqueduct after excavation. Gideon Sarig. The old and new layers are marked in form and materials, whose languages speak of different times. The archeological excavation and its measured layers are amended by contemporary walkways, trees, steps, and rails.

bottom right: Promenade. Beit Shean. Landscape architect Bruce Levin and architect Arye Rachamimoff collaborated on the promenade design. A contemporary aqueduct and fountains surround Roman ruins. (Bruce Levin)

In the Negev the experiments of biologist Michael Evenari have been inspired by a desire to understand how the Nabateans (and later Roman and Byzantines) who inhabited the desert (2,400–1,500 B.P.) were able to farm this arid region. At his farm at the base of the Nabatean city of Avdat, now a national park, Evenari constructed a series of catchment basins that capture available rainwater, and even dew, and direct it to growing plants. The work was successful in terms of plant growth, but also showed the formal possibilities of agricultural patterns in the desert. Conceived by the Keren Kayemet, *limanim* are groves planted in depressions that act as catchment basins. In Shlomo Aronson's interpretation along roads in the northern Negev they are almost archetypal in their basic form, sharp geometry, and in the minimal vocabulary of tree and shade.

The scarcity of water adds to its significance and criticality. Not to be squandered, its fate and focus mirror the nation's landscape concerns. Much of the water is dedicated to "essential" uses for people and agriculture—the nation's ideological building block—at the expense of water for recreation, habitat (especially for

Evenari Farm. Avdat.

Limanim (1977). Shlomo Aronson. Beginning in the 1950s the Keren Kayemet planted "bays" along roads in the Negev. They were inspired by local Bedouin practice of capturing water within wadis. (Shlomo Aronson)

waterfowl), or other amenities. As the agricultural economy shifts this will impact water use dramatically. Recent planning promises an attention to the nation's more modest and neglected streams whose resources have almost entirely been appropriated for agricultural use such as the Yarkon, Alexander, Soreq, Kishon, and Tananim. These offer great promise as recreational and open space resources.

Seven Orchards

An orchard that laps the foot of a mountain is one orchard.

*An orchard that laps the foot of a mountain and digs under to the stream's bed
is a second orchard.*

*An orchard that laps the foot of a mountain and digs under to the stream's bed
and meets an olive grove is a third orchard.*

*An orchard that laps the foot of a mountain and digs under to the stream's bed
and meets an olive grove and continues to the outskirts of a city is a fourth orchard.*

*An orchard that laps the foot of a mountain and digs under to the stream's bed
and meets an olive grove and continues to the outskirts of a city and surrounds
the plaza is a fifth orchard.*

*An orchard that laps the foot of a mountain and digs under to the stream's bed
and meets an olive grove and continues to the outskirts of a city and surrounds
the plaza and climbs the steps to the ancient castle is a sixth orchard.*

*An orchard that laps the foot of a mountain and digs under to the stream's bed
and meets an olive grove and continues to the outskirts of a city and surrounds
the plaza and climbs the steps to the ancient castle and bores through it into the wall
to find its waters is a seventh orchard.*

—Ze'ev Druckman

P LANTS ARE THE ORGANIC LIFE OF PLACES. In designed landscapes they per-
form their biological functions, moderate climate, and are a primary
mode of shaping space. We delight in the changing qualities of plant growth and
life cycle from seed to mature plants, and the pleasures of fruit, flower, fragrance,
and form. In a natural state plant growth is restrained by requirements of soil,
water, and climatic conditions. Found in characteristic associations with other
plants and animals, plants are intimately connected to and expressive of places, be
it the seashore, among rocks, riparian communities, or the desert. A simple shift
from the north- to south-facing slope, or a change in bedrock, soil type, or moisture will yield dramatic differences.

Plants are the quintessence of nature, yet they are bound to culture. We have
imbued the plant kingdom with multiple meanings and related associations. Plants
have their own history and ideological dimension. Olives, oaks, pines, eucalyptus,
palms, *sabra*s, and oranges all have a particular resonance in Israel. The Bible
describes the land of Israel through its plants. Moses's spies returned from the land
of Canaan laden with great clusters of grapes, pomegranates, and figs as evidence
of the fertility of the land. This was the bounteous country of milk and honey.
Deuteronomy 8:7-8 describes "a good land, a land with streams and springs and
fountains issuing from the plain and hill; a land of wheat and barley, of vines, figs,
and pomegranates, a land of olive trees and honey." These species, agricultural
plants associated with the land of Israel, are appreciated for their aesthetic and
symbolic values as much as their productive worth. History and ritual practice are
intertwined with the seasonal cycle of plants and the agricultural roots of festivals:
priests were anointed with olive oil, oil is essential to the miracle of Hanukah,
bikkurim (first fruits) were brought as offerings to the temple, and the *lulav* (palm
branches) and *etrog* (citron) are emblems of *Sukkot* (Feast of Tabernacles). The
Psalms and *Song of Songs* are paeans to the power of the plant world to evoke the
most profound sense of meaning, from the sensual to the spiritual.

Chapter 5

Plants

Trees are laden with meaning. Each carries a cultural legacy, some specific to Israel, more often part of a deeper historical connections to the world of plants. Certain trees predominate in the Israeli landscape image. They are both native and introduced: the olive groves of the Galilee, the citrus orchards of the Sharon, the pine trees of the Jerusalem forest. There are trees that have a sacred status. Harkening back to archaic and folk tradition, single trees and groves are venerated at tombs and hilltops. Given the country's history of successive periods of deforestation, now all ancient trees have garnered venerable status. Long-lived trees are traditionally associated with strength, immortality, and generational continuity: oak, cypress, carob, olive, and fig. The olive's symbolic connections go back to Noah, but they were Palestine's primary agricultural product during Ottoman rule. The symbol of peace, olives are also now politically identified with the Palestinian and Israeli-Arab population. There are the specific plants associated with the Bible and Jewish ritual. Some exotic plants became naturalized and are now part of a national identity. The eucalyptus was introduced from Australia in the 1880s to help drain swamplands. It became so identified with Jewish colonies that Arabs called it the "tree of the Jews." *Sabra*, a cactus, became the popular nickname for Israelis themselves, as a personification of the cactus's qualities, a prickly outside and a sweet interior.

Near Modi'in is found Neot Kedumim, the Biblical Landscape Reserve of Israel. Conceived by Ephraim and Hannah Hareuveni and their son Nogah, it is more than a biblical garden and botanical display, but a condensed reconstruction of an entire landscape. It began with biblical plants, but expanded to be much more than a botanical garden. Within its boundaries are found concentrated representations of terraced agriculture, groves of date palms, oak hillsides, desert acacia, *wadis*, Jordan River thickets, and vineyards. Designed largely by the Haruvenis, landscape architect Hillel Omer (1926-1991) played a role in its early period,

including the design of a magnificent wall which borders a pathway on one side and forms an amphitheater on the other. Other sites in Israel also address the biblical landscape. At Sataf, in the Judean hills, an ancient spring has been restored and a botanical research area is propagating the precise species of the bible.

Plants are part of a collective environment characterized by distinctive plant communities and associations. The basic plant communities of Israel are Mediterranean and desert with a transitional zone of the steppe landscape of the Irano-Turanian region. Gradations of rainfall, temperature, solar radiation, and their seasonal variation along with topography, geology, soil, and orientation create a complex vegetative tapestry.

These natural plant associations are compounded by others that are the product of human interaction. Oasis, park, *bustan*, *pardes*, forest, and campus each conjure up not simply a plant vocabulary, but a setting and landscape experience. Commonplace types, each has an ideological foundation and associations within Israel.

left: Terraces, date palms, and pond. Neot Kedumim.

right: Wall and amphitheatre. Neot Kedumim. Hillel Omer.

Oasis

In the desert there are natural situations where water occurs in abundance, the consequence of water seemingly and miraculously appearing from the ground to bring life to the land. These places, known as oases, *are* discovered, but they are also created, as the water is collected and distributed. These are bounded places of water, vegetation, food, color, sound, shade, comfort, intimacy, and interaction. The qualities of water, its liquidity, sound, light, and life-giving sustenance all are dramatized by the contrast with the surrounding environment, which is harsh, dry, and baked by the sun. These places surely were the prototypes for dreams of paradisiacal Edens, models for a fantasy of life without privation filled with sensory

Ein Gedi. Yahalom-Zur advised the National Park Authority on Ein Gedi and Nahal Arugot, a parallel wadi *and water source. In both situations the question was how to make the sites accessible in the least intrusive manner.*

delight. In each case it is the contrast of inside and out that is paramount.

The ancient oases of Ein Gedi and Nahal Arugot are parallel *wadis* at the shore of the Dead Sea. Ein Avdat is a Negev oasis just south of Sde Boker. These natural sites have been embellished and extended. In each of these examples an orchestrated sequence takes one from the work-a-day world, leaving the bus or automobile, walking uphill a modest distance through the intense heat, with the gradual awareness of the oasis to come. The progressions are culminated by the anticipated but wonderful shock of water appearing miraculously out of the rock.

At Gan Hashlosha/*Sachne* (Arabic for warm pool), Lippa Yahalom and Dan Zur's design transformed the site into a place which is equally an oasis and pastoral park (1958). At the base of Mount Gilboa is found the Amal spring, Israel's third largest after the sources of the Jordan and the Yarkon. A palm allée leads to a shade-dappled lawn sloping down to the

Sachne. Yahalom-Zur. (Dan Zur)

banks of the formerly swampy pool edge. The stream had been dammed for flour mills, the site's traditional use. Redesigned dams expanded the pool and in the process created a waterfall with a stone walkway across its top. Pathways lead to steps and hidden intimate crannies waiting to be discovered. Sachne anticipated qualities found in more contemporary water play parks, not as an artificial attraction, but in a design which accentuates the site's innate qualities. It is accomplished with such finesse that many visitors are unaware of the site as a designed environment.

Sachne. The walkway across the waterfall. Yahalom-Zur.

Bustan

The *bustan* is a common Middle Eastern garden type that has multiple definitions and rich meaning. The term is used in Hebrew and Arabic, with rich sources in folk culture and the vernacular tradition. *Bu+estan* is a place of fragrance in Persian and related to *bosem* (perfume) in Hebrew. It can be a fruit garden, a garden with a spring or irrigation, or a dense planting of useful trees, palms, fruit, and nut trees. It is notably a garden of both pleasure and utility, a social setting where food is grown. The *bustan* is characterized by an abundant variety of plants, irrigation, and interculture, often accompanied by some modest outdoor shelter. Its form, irrigation, and plants all derive from agricultural technique. It is an environment, however, where the pleasures of plants are equal in importance to their productive value. The multisensory qualities of the *bustan* are paramount, especially the sense of smell, with fragrant fruit trees, vegetables, and herbs.

top: Nahal Siah. Haifa. A twentieth-century bustan, now in ruins, but awaiting restoration.

bottom: Gan ha Yekev (1986). Rehovot. Alisa Braudo and Ruth Maoz. Surrounded by a modern housing complex the garden is built within the ruined walls of a former winery. (Braudo Maoz)

There is a *bustan* aesthetic, which accepts and even revels in the contrast of agricultural formality and vegetative disorder. The connections go deeper, and resonate in story, poetry, art, and folklore. *Bustanim* share these general characteristics, but there is regional variation and diverse types. Thus they are found in the city, villages, and the rural landscape, in the plain, mountains, or desert. The *bustan* shares a kinship with other Mediterranean and desert garden types, the *carmen* of Andalusia, Italian villa, and the agricultural oasis. The combination of production and pleasure and the resonance of its multilayered meaning is critical.

Author Chaim Guri describes a Tel Aviv *bustan* from his youth: "This was a special garden in the northern part of the city. It was a kind of dense, Oriental *bustan*, with citron trees, sycamores, figs, pomegranates, and mulberry... It stretched north and east towards an unknown land. There were parks for shelters, and they got lost in the darkness of the gardens, looking for shelters, loving ..." *Bustan* scholar and landscape architect Alisa Braudo notes how the *bustan* migrated with immigrants from North Africa and became part of Israel's domestic landscape. Unfortunately the *bustan* is largely a landscape of the past, destroyed by modernization and development.

Pardes

The *pardes* is the landscape of citrus orchards of oranges, lemons, grapefruit, and pamelos. The etymology links the work to the ancient Persian *pairidaeza* and the Greek *paradeisoi*, paradise. A British surveyor wrote in 1872: "The splendor of Jaffa resides in its beautiful gardens of oranges, lemons, bananas, pomegranates and other fruits that lie around the town ..." The Jaffa orange, exported for more than a century, has been an icon of Israel's economy. Citrus planting expanded dramatically in the years before the establishment of the state and created a distinctive landscape, especially in the central Sharon region. In 1925 there were 30,500 *dunams* (about a quarter of an acre) of citrus orchards. This increased tenfold in twelve years, and by 1964 it was more than 400,000 *dunams* before a decline precipitated by changing economic priorities and the pressures of urbanization. But the *pardes* is still part of the national scene and psyche and in recent years *pardesim*

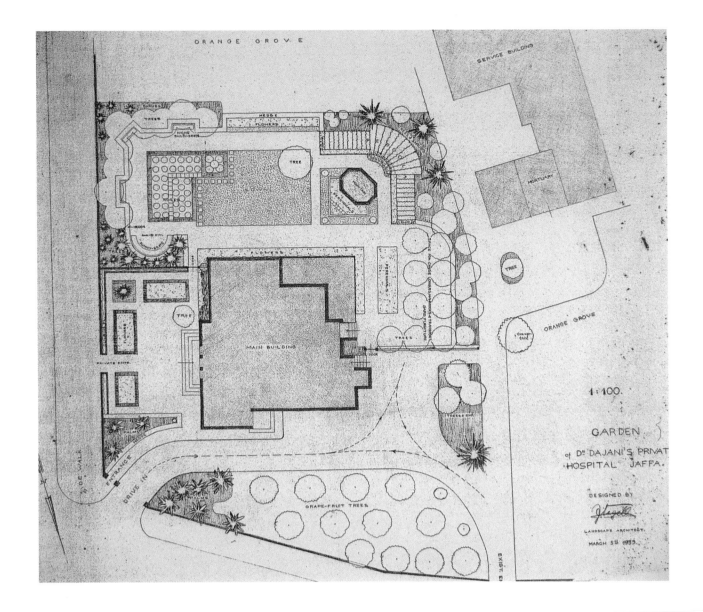

Garden of Doctor Dajani's private hospital (1933). Jaffa. Yechiel Segal. The garden is set within a pardes of grapefruit trees and orange groves. (Yosef Segal)

have even moved to the northern Negev. Most typically *pardesim* are groves bounded by lines of cypress planted as windbreaks. Within this compact planting may be found a pool of water for irrigation. The sensory experience can be overwhelming, the beauty of the glowing orange leaves, the bright colors of fruit and blossoms, and in late winter an overpowering perfumed fragrance.

Pastoral

There is an Israeli pastoral, one that is subtly adapted to its environment. The pastoral is often associated with the English garden, but its heritage is much deeper. What at first may seem like an alien import to Israel is actually akin to a landscape type which is Mediterranean in its foundation. Pastoral design is rooted in pastoralism, the landscape created by grazing animals. It is a landscape of closely cropped fields of grazed grasses, browsed trees, and an association with the seemingly idyllic life of the shepherd. Its origins are in the classical world of Greece

Grazing sheep. Beit Shearim.

and Rome, the landscape of the eastern Mediterranean. The ancient idealization of this landscape and its associations are the roots of modern pastoral design, which reached an apogee in eighteenth- and nineteenth-century Britain and was exported throughout much of its empire, be it a colony or, in the case of Israel, a League of Nations mandate. This legacy is still strong and in the modern mind pastoral imagery equates with park design, leisure, and recreation.

The modern version of the grazed meadow is the lawn, one of the most hotly debated contemporary landscapes. The desire for the color green and a space called the "green" is very strong and demonstrates the power of a landscape ideal, one that is aesthetic, social, and physical. Lawn is found at the core of most of Israel's city parks and a green (a common lawn) is found at the center of every kibbutz, regardless of environment. It frames the dining hall and, in its use as a gathering space and for holiday celebrations, it acts as a green piazza, a commonly shared open space. This desire for a green lawn has deep roots. It hearkens back to more fundamental origins of the pastoral in the eastern Mediterranean and the nostalgic respite inherent in that classical form. Few can deny the pleasures of lying on the grass. It is perhaps the most consistently appealing landscape type. A green landscape is also seen as measure of development and it has an association with being more European. At the same time irrigated lawns consume valuable water resources.

In the Israeli version of the pastoral, the trees are temperate and subtropical, the lawn thick Buffalo or Kikuya grass. Parks such as Jerusalem's Sacher

Lawn. Kibbutz Ein Gedi.

Park or Ashkelon National Park, both by Yahalom-Zur, epitomize an Israeli pastoral. Pastoral parks abound in diverse locations and all environments. Kahanovitch's 1987 Gan HaTsomet (Gan Volovosky), adjacent to Tel Aviv's north bus and train station, is a fine example of an opportunistic design. It capitalizes on the pastoral's association as a place of respite as it provides a green refuge in a site bordered on all sides by heavy traffic.

top: Ashkelon National Park (1957). Yahalom-Zur.

bottom: Park. Tefen. In this unique industrial park in the Galilee the site also functions as an outdoor sculpture garden. Tichnun Nof.

The pastoral has topographic and experiential associations as well, the gentle hill, the vale, the sinuous walk. At Wolfson Park by Zvi Dekel such a terrain was constructed around a preexisting hill, partly to shield the site from surrounding traffic and also to afford a prospect over the city. Surrounding the hill, subsequently crowned by Dani Karavan's White City, are a series of sculpted foothill-like mounds. A promenade lined with benches encircles the hill and plants of a different color mark each point of entry to the park. Water appears in a small vale, a pastoral urban oasis complete with modest waterfall and a stepped walk. Tichnun Nof's Menachim Begin Park in Tel Aviv shares similar elements: hillocks overlooking expanses of water and large lawns and plantings which are a subtropical pastoral, including palms and coral trees.

Gan HaTsomet (Gan Volovsky). Tel Aviv. Haim Kahanovitch.

Forest

Biblical sources and descriptions speak of rich forests on the land, in contrast to Palestine under Ottoman rule at the turn of the twentieth century, a largely treeless domain defoliated by overgrazing and cutting. A "natural" forest, even a grove, is rare in Israel. The emergent forest is the result of the almost century-long afforestation efforts of Keren Kayemet, the Jewish National Fund. In the early mandate period it planted olives and oaks, but shifted to pines and cypress, especially Aleppo pine (*Pinus halepensis*) and Brutia pine (*Pinus bruti*). These monoculture plantations would ultimately dominate the reclaimed forest landscape. As they matured they would be critiqued by some as monotonous "pine deserts," but Keren Kayemet policy has evolved: a more diverse selection of forest trees and more native plantings are now used. These forestlands are culturally precious and an ecological necessity. Only in the Galilee, Carmel, and in the Jerusalem forest are the trees extensive enough to encompass large areas. These areas are carefully managed and more often the "forest" is a "park-forest" of clearly defined large groves that have been thinned and pruned as they matured. These are often open in appearance with little or no understory and often open to grazing.

After 1948 more than 90 million trees were planted in just two decades, with an estimated two-thirds survival rate. Within two generations much of the landscape that was formerly exposed has become enclosed. Each *Tu-b'Shevat* (the "New Year for Trees" celebrated much like Arbor Day) a half million trees are planted. Planting a tree is an almost universal Israeli experience and, in the Diaspora, giving donations for tree planting by the Keren Kayemet is common practice. The Zionist return and redemption of the land and building the state is so intertwined with planting that one could equally speak of *planting the state*. Forests were equated with development as a new landscape was created contrasting with what was seen as desolation.

Tree planting (1981). Galilee. This ceremony is with an ulpan *class composed largely of Russian immigrants.*

Campus

The Israeli campus provides a rich example of approaches to employing this vocabulary in planting design. Tel Aviv University, Bar-Ilan University, Technion, Weizmann Institute, and Hebrew University Givat Ram campus are classic campuses of individual buildings dispersed within a landscape setting that provides the connective matrix. Tel Aviv University and the Weizmann, both by Yahalom-Zur,

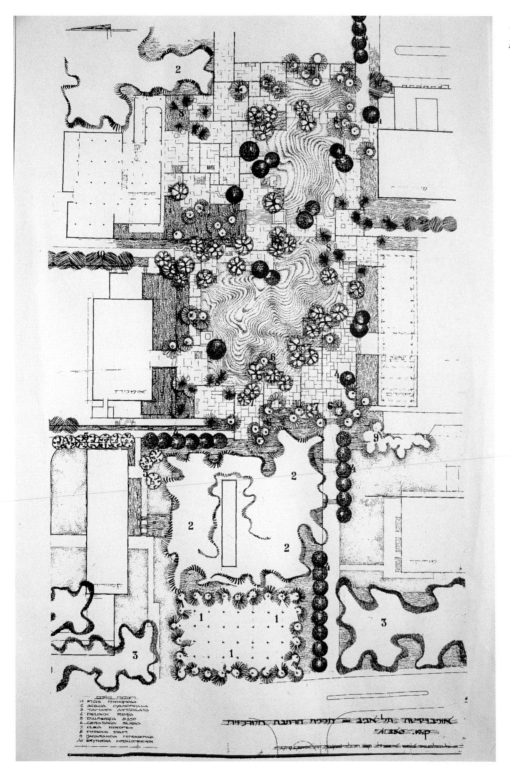

Plan for the central plaza (1967). Tel Aviv University. Yahalom-Zur. (Dan Zur)

top: Aantin Plaza. Tel Aviv
University. Architect Moshe
Atsmon, landscape architect
Moria-Sekely. Winner of the
1993 Rechter Prize. (Moshe
Atsmon)

bottom: Technion. Haifa.
Sunken courtyard. Miller-
Blum.

are pastorals of a sculpted topography of rolling lawns, a landscape of undulation with soft, folded, feminine forms often clothed in turf interspersed with groves of palms and other plantings. The design of Bar-Ilan University was shepaded by Meir Peleg and then Vered Zuta after his retirement. At Technion the canopy of the Carmel pine forest acts as the unifying element. Even in Technion's forested setting the power of grass is present. At the central forum by architects Idelson and Sharon (1958) and Miller-Blum are three attached squares. The lowest—flanked by the library, administration building, and auditorium—is a sunken courtyard with a modular patch of lawn, also the site of the memorial to fallen soldiers. At the Hebrew University on Mt. Scopus—a grand megastructure and collaborative design by architect David Reznik and landscape architects Yahalom-Zur—the protected courtyards are miniature pastorals. At the core of the Hebrew University Givat Ram campus a paved checkerboard plaza melts into a grand pastoral meadow.

After a half century of practice Moshe Blum is succinct in his planting philosophy and evaluation of what is most important. He suggests not using too many different plants or the result is a "Turkish salad." Looking back he would plant as many trees as possible for shade, as places for children to play, and to create an inviting atmosphere, for in housing projects what remains twenty to thirty years later are the trees and shrubs. Blum explicitly recognizes the imperative to reiterate that planting takes time and it is really the next generation that lives within the

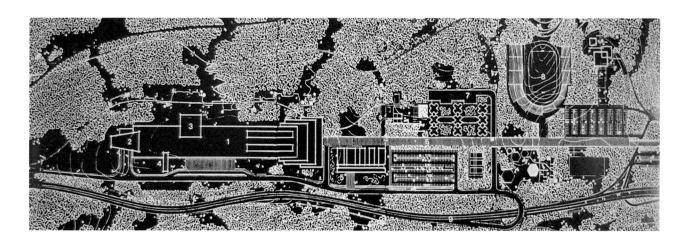

*Plan. Haifa University.
(Miller-Blum)*

designs of an earlier era. It "doesn't depend on what you do, but how it looks in ten years," he says. The best planning, he says, includes the most trees. Time knits development to places. Zvi Miller (1921-1999), Blum's partner, describes their design for Haifa University (1964-77) at the crest of the Carmel as now "married" to the landscape.

L AND HAS A SHAPE. Israel's topography is one of coastal plain, modest mountains, desert plateau, slopes, and valleys. It has distinctive features of *wadis*, craters, and *tels* (a mound covering a ruin). Like potters, landscape architects sculpt terrain out of these raw materials. A honed spatial and topographic sensibility is characteristic of the best Israeli landscape architecture. It is an awareness of the three-dimensional shape of the land and its symbolic properties, and defers to historic integrity, archaic patterns and practices. It is an appreciation of the sensory richness of space. Even when vegetated, the open character of most planting and its minimal height and modest density means that the contours of the land and its surface characteristics, its body-like qualities and its skin, are easily perceived. In turn we look at valleys, slopes, high points, and site planning and structure.

Chapter 6

Shaping Space

*On a day of summer,
hot day, when the sun
is in the sky
The firmament sizzling
like a stove at noon,
When the heart seeks a
corner of quiet to dream—
Come to me, come to me,
tired friend!*

*I've a garden, and in that
garden under a heavy
ailanthus shade,
Far far from the town and
men, there hides a hill,
All wrapped in green, all
speaking God's will—
There we'll hide and rest,
sweet friend!*
—Chaim Nachman
Bialik

*View to Degania, the first
Kibbutz at the southern
shore of the Kinneret.*

Valleys

The *wadi, nahal* in Hebrew (the words are used interchangeably), are the country's natural drainage channels. There are hundreds of miles of these seasonally dry riverbeds. The natural *wadi* has defined edges and a floor of loose stones punctuated by larger rocks. Plants appear in pockets or in a spring efflorescence. *Wadis* vary in scale from modest washes to grand canyons, with variability in width, height, slope, location, orientation, vegetation, and the presence or absence of

top: Wadi Ein Bokek along the shore of the Dead Sea.

bottom: Wadi. Ben Gurion Grave. Yahalom-Zur.

water. Whatever the variation, there remains a connection between the person and an enclosed space. One can walk the floor, follow the periodic course of water, overlook the *wadi* from above, or move up and down its slope. Water, the element that creates the *wadi*, is paradoxically most often present by its absence; but the seasonal patterns of fluvial movement are visible on the ground in soil, stones, and the growth of plants. *Wadis* recall the "dry" gardens of Japan where artistry has shaped and constructed space to imply the presence of water.

Designed by Yahalom-Zur, the entry to the Ben Gurion Gravesite (a national park) at Sde Boker in the Negev desert is an abstract representation of a *wadi*, constructed in an unexpected location, on top of a plateau. The winner of a 1987 competition, it inaugurated a new era in the development of an Israeli design language. To understand the desert Yahalom walked it and its *wadis* for days with local Bedouin. The design is a progression through a space which intensifies the natural forms and materials. The climax is reached at a platform, where the grave overlooks the surrounding desert, creating a dialogue between the wilderness and this constructed terrain. The contrast of the *wadi*, the desert view, and the refined geometry of the flat gravesite accentuates each. To create this spatial drama, 50,000 cubic meters of earth were moved. The exit circles back on the *wadi* garden along the cliff with a continuous view to the desert. It is symphonic orchestration. It is a much-loved memorial, but as Yahalom noted: "Ben Gurion spoke of making the wilderness blossom. I wanted to emphasize wilderness, not to conquer it. I created the *wadi* which seems so natural."

top: Ben Gurion's grave. Aerial view of the site with a view to the central wadi *and surrounding desert. Years earlier Yahalom-Zur had constructed a much smaller* wadi *at the Weizmann Institute. (Dan Zur)*

bottom left: The Ben Gurion Gravesite. Yahalom-Zur.

bottom right: The Ben Gurion Gravesite. View to Nahal Zin.

The oscillation between these realms is apparent in another nearby pathway by Yahalom-Zur. From the terrace of Ben Gurion's tomb one looks out to the dramatic desert of Nahal Zin, the threshold of the Negev that Ben Gurion urged be settled. Directly south is Ein Avdat, a national park, where twin trails lead to a lush oasis hidden beneath its precipitous cliffs. One trail leads up the *wadi*, the entry marked by a sculpted stone map of the park, a minimalist intervention. The path progressively narrows until it reaches the lush oasis. The other trail is a tour-de-force, a dramatic encounter with space and topography. It takes visitors down the almost vertical cliff face along a trail carved from the limestone and supplemented with ladders. Within a few kilometers one experiences the intimacy of the entry to Ben Gurion's grave, the wonder of a hidden oasis, and the adventure and grandeur of the Negev's topography.

The new town of Modi'in, halfway between Jerusalem and Tel Aviv and planned by architect Moshe Safdie, is configured around three green valleys. One valley, designed by Itzchak Blank, is characterized by a central pedestrian pathway

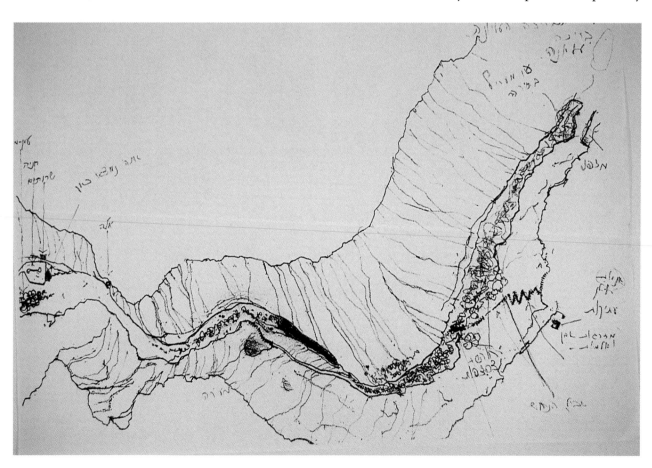

that descends through the valley. At a lower level this dry pathway becomes a wet channel of water bringing the seasonal flow of the *wadi* into the city.

In Kreitman Plaza (1994), the central garden courtyard of the University of the Negev in Beersheva, is a constructed stone "stream" designed by Aronson. This meandering spine is also modeled on *wadis*. In the courtyard the recirculating watercourse has multiple personalities and readings. Its upper level is a path, its terraced edges a social space where people sit, and the lower level a water channel. In plan it also appears as a map, its

scale ambiguous: is it a canyon or rivulet? Aronson has great admiration for the Japanese-American sculptor Isamu Noguchi (1904–1988) and the plaza recalls his California Scenario (1980-82) in the ambiguity of scale and its symbolic resonance. All of this is framed within a larger courtyard bordered by earth mounds, shaded pergolas, and iconic plantings of palms, grasses, and desert vegetation.

At the large-scale *wadis* serve as the backbones of open space systems in Haifa and Jerusalem. Insufficiently protected by statute, they are subject to the threat of

top: Cliff path. Ein Avdat. Yahalom-Zur.

bottom: Oasis. Ein Avdat. Yahalom-Zur.

development and the dangers of encroachment. At Aronson's Gilo Park (1987) in
Jerusalem, the *wadi* is largely protected, as buildings flank its side as they do for
many of Jerusalem's valleys. A park of terraces and a great green bowl wrap around
the head of the *wadi* and frame views down its course.

Slopes

Steep slopes need to be engineered to become habitable or usable. Israeli hillsides have been terraced since antiquity. It sometimes takes a trained eye to discern ancient from modern terraces in the hills surrounding Jerusalem, for the techniques have varied little. Stones and terraces structure agricultural lands, forests, and the urban landscape into an engineered landscape of walls. These vary from those that can be sat upon to grand engineering structures. Walls also make passages and guide one through space, through walks along their bases and upper surfaces. Walls create spatial richness, enclosure, and texture and afford openness and viewpoints from above. Simple stone terraces are found in virtually all parks and gardens, acting as retaining walls and seating. Whole hillside and hilltop communities are built on terraced foundations: Safed, Haifa, Nazareth, Modi'in, and traditional villages such as Pekiin. In Haifa the slopes of the Carmel are covered with unique building types of stepped apartments and houses. At Jerusalem's Israel Museum the sculptor Isamu Noguchi constructed his interpretation of a

terraced landscape with great scalloped arcs for the Billy Rose sculpture garden (1960–65).

Movement in such a terrain necessitates steps, ramps, and switchbacks. Haifa's steep urban landscape is a catalogue of these, a remarkable network of vertical open space with dozens of stairways leading to hidden homes and gardens, sinuous ramps and switchbacks tucked between development. (Many are the product of Zvi Miller's tenure as park's department head in the 1950s.) The city now has a series of signed urban trails on those slopes. Newer hillside communities such as Pisgat Ze'ev, a new neighborhood in the north of Jerusalem, and Carmiel in the Galilee use these pedestrian systems to structure urban open space and to create rich lines of social communication.

In 1909 the Bahai faith began a series of gardens on the slopes of Mount Carmel, where in 2001 they dedicated a new series of nineteen rippling terraces that cascade for a kilometer down the hillside from the crest of the ridge to the restored German Colony. The architect Faribouz Sahba describes the plan as "waves of light" emanating from the Shrine of the Bab at the center of the plan.

above: Terraces. Aerial view of the Israel Museum with Billy Rose Sculpture Garden to the west. Jerusalem. (Albatross)

left: Pathway. Pisgat Ze'ev. Tichnun Nof.

right: Walkway. Carmiel.

Bahai gardens. Haifa. The gardens occupy an entire slope of the Carmel, terracing from the toe of the slope at the German Colony almost to the crest of the ridge. This photo shows the dedication of new terraces of the Shrine of the Báb on May 23, 2001. (Bahai World Centre)

High Points

In Israel, hilltops benefit from the archetypal, biblical, and historic association of high places. There are sacred mountaintops such as Mount Tabor, the site of Deborah's battle with the Canaanites, Christ's transfiguration, Byzantine and Crusader churches, and now a national park crowned by a church. In the Carmel, Muhraka is where Elijah built his altar. One goes up to Jerusalem to the Temple Mount and the Dome of the Rock, the center of the world, the foundation stone, the site of

Shelter with a playground (1985). Bak'a, Jerusalem. Jeremy Epstein. (Epstein-Hazan)

Mohammed's ascension to heaven, and Mount Moriah where Abraham was to sacrifice Isaac. Venerated tombs or remnants of sacred groves are located in high places.

The Hebrew terms *mitzpor* and *mitzpe*, which refer to lookouts and observation points, are often used interchangeably. *Mitzpor* is derived from *tzipor* (bird) and is associated with the bird's-eye viewpoint; *mitzpe* is from *lizpot* (to look over, from above).

Settlements, ancient and modern, have concentrated on hilltops for security and to preserve valuable arable land. This is true at the large and small scale. Until a hundred years ago Jerusalem was a walled city before it expanded to the surrounding hills. It is now struggling to keep its valleys open. In the Galilee, *mitzpim* (compact rural hilltop settlements) have been built to enhance a Jewish presence in the predominately Arab region. There is a link between archaic necessity and contemporary concern.

The historical imperatives of security, from ancient fortification to contemporary exigencies, encourage a spatial structure of sharp definition, and the army's occupation of high points is obvious to the observant. Boundaries are explicitly marked with warning signs, walls, fences, and barbed wire. The messages are not subtle. A defensible-space sensibility, from territorial borders to community design, is part of what Gideon Sarig describes as a "strategic approach to place." Shelters from attack are omnipresent and a mandated part of all construction. Throughout the country it is commonplace for parks and playgrounds to have the superstructure of shelters camouflaged by play equipment or vegetation.

The rare hilltops of the coastal plain became prime garden spots and fortunately many were appropriated for garden use, in actions which protected them from development in Tel Aviv, Ramat Gan, Givataim, Holon, and Jaffa. Gan Ha Aliyah Hashniyah (1952) in Givataim by Meir Victor (1908-1990) is one such hilltop garden. The carefully selected site was the center of a village built at the base

of a small hill crowned by a water tower. The view originally looked west to a developing Tel Aviv and the sea. The park now sits as an island amidst urban development. Each slope of the hillside has its distinctive aspect. To the south is a sloping lawn and terraces. The east and north are planted slopes with shaded pathways. To the west is a now defunct watercourse, a stylized stone stream with walkways that criss-cross the channel. It is an oasis set within a forest.

above: Gan Ha Aliyah HaShniyah. View west to Tel Aviv. Meir Victor.

below: Gan HaPisgah. Jaffa. Avraham Karavan and Hillel Omer.

Located on a hilltop above the ancient seaport of Jaffa, Gan HaPisgah and its adjacent park of Gan Abrasha have a more layered history. The original park section was designed by Karavan with subsequent additions by Hillel Omer and others. It now appears a bit disjointed with a common Israeli collection of park elements. The main view is across a pastoral meadow and amphitheater to the Tel Aviv shoreline. Gan Abrasha is crowned with the arched sculpture and a stone terrace. The park's interior includes shaded pathways, an archeological excavation, and modern sculptural monuments, while its western edge bridges to the restored town of Jaffa.

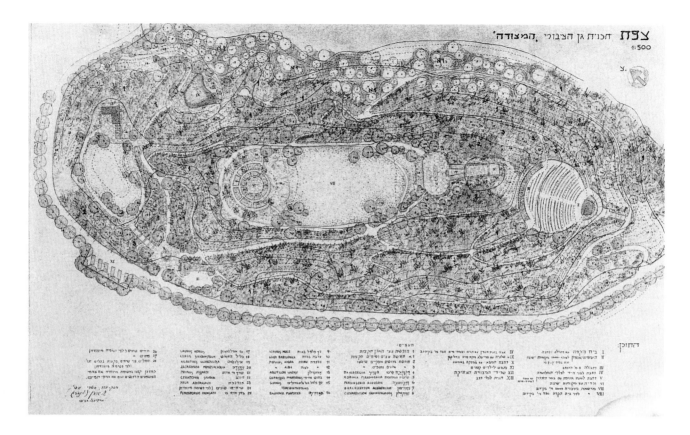

צפון חכנית גן הצבורי ,המצדה.
1:500

[Hebrew plant/legend list below plan — partially legible]

top: Plan. Gan Ha Metzuda. Safed. Shlomo Weinberg-Oren. (Yagur Archive)

bottom: View from below. Terraces. Gan Ha Metzuda. Safed. Shlomo Weinberg-Oren.

In Safed at Gan Ha Metzuda (Citadel Park) (1949) Weinberg-Oren employed a deft mixture of elements. The hill is terraced and densely planted. Pathways lead to the surprise of an open meadow at the top, a formal terrace, and a memorial. Another surprise awaits, a smaller accompanying mount with a spiral path to the top, much like a garden folly. This once finely crafted garden is now partly in ruin and the mature trees obscure much of the once grand view.

Throughout the nation are found scores of viewpoints. At their best they are modest interventions, deferential to the landscape, showing the subtlest use of the vocabulary. Precise in execution, they can have an almost platonic presence: a pathway from the road, a point of arrival at the mitzpor, a viewing platform, a wall suggesting where to stand, a protective edge. Interpretive material is often present, but the spatial character can point the way so subtly that the interpretive material can be superfluous. These are places of minimal intervention and cost but maximum impact. From these observation points the landscape is discovered, appreciated, and monitored.

top left: Mitzpe Lippa overlooking Sde Boker and Ein
Avdat. A circular platform
with a low wall is a gentle
but clear demarcation in the
landscape.

top right: Mitzpe Montfort
(1976). Park Goren. Gideon
Sarig. A set of stone terraced
seats looking out towards
the Crusader fort of Montfort, the mountains of the
Galilee and Nahal Achziv.
(Gideon Sarig)

Ma'ale Ha Akrabim (Scorpion Route) by Braudo, Darel, Maoz (1993). En route
to the Machtesh Gadol overlooking the snaking road which was the site of a 1954
bus ambush. A strenuous path leads to the dramatic overlook. Plaques describe the
events, victims, and their surrounding landscape. (Braudo Maoz)

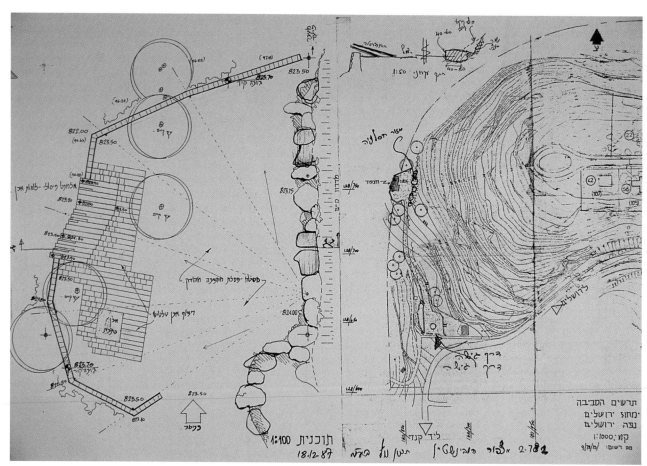

top left: Mitzpor at Tel Dan (1996). Greenstein–Har-Gil. The vista combines a common mix of biblical association, historical archeology, and natural features, in this case the sources of the Jordan. (Greenstein-Har-Gil)

top right: The Rubinstein Memorial (1987) by Joseph Segal with Israel Hadani as sculptor is located in the forest almost opposite David Reznik's more grandiose Kennedy Memorial. From a small parking area there is a view through the woods towards a distant opening with a marking of the edge. Here Segal achieved his effect employing a modesty of means for maximum effect, through a deference to the site's character and conditions, and to the view. The piano "keys" by Hadani are a combination of sculpture and viewpoint, a visual diving board from which one's eyes leap into the Jerusalem Hills.

bottom: Plan and sketch. Joseph Segal. The Rubinstein Memorial. (Tichnon Nof)

Two dramatically different hilltop sites exemplify the quest for a landscape language in their use of stone, water, plants, and space. Ramat Hanadiv is a garden that sits at the southern end of the Carmel at the outskirts of Zichron Yaakov. Here designer Shlomo Weinberg-Oren, in his final work (completed in 1954 just after his death), exploited a remarkable range of spatial possibilities through a series of interconnected garden spaces. The metal gateway leads to an axial entry of grass and stone stripes. The formal entry court then leads to a series of garden spaces experienced in two concentric circumnavigating walks. The orchestrated sequence goes from open to enclosed spaces, with windows from one space to the other. The exterior walk links a terraced garden, rose garden, palm garden, and amphitheater. Expanses of pastoral lawn divide the outer and inner rings. In "The Art of the Garden: What Is Space Perception," Weinberg-Oren spoke of the "inclusion of the surrounding landscape by means of certain openings outward from the body of the garden." Appropriating the borrowed landscape idea from both English and Japanese gardens, the vista from atop the terraced garden across the coastal plain and Mediterranean Sea becomes an integral part of the garden experience. The *mitzpor* is complete with a stone map of the territory below.

This expansiveness has it opposite expression in the intimate enclosure of Baron Rothschild's tomb at the center. This is entered through a dark, densely planted cleft in the rock, which leads to an open architectural courtyard of black and white stone. Here pools of water frame the space and the darkened entry into the tomb designed by architect Uriel Schiller. Weinberg-Oren's ability to play with space and light is brought to the fore. The garden form is both centrifugal and centripetal in character: its grand circle pushes one to the perimeter and the grand views while simultaneously spiraling one towards its center.

Plan. Ramat Hanadiv. Zichron Yaakov. Shlomo Weinberg-Oren. (Yagur Archive).

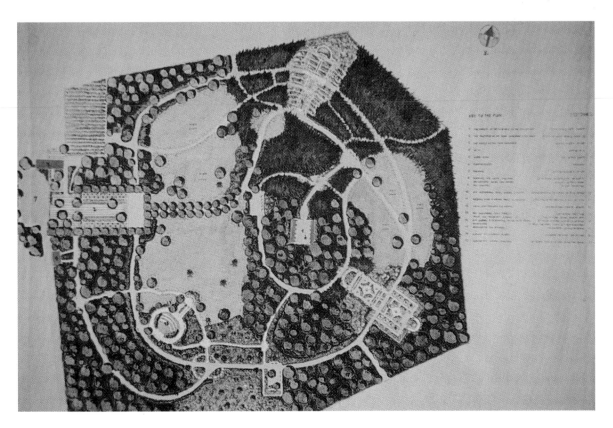

Kikar Levana (White City) (1977-88)
on the hilltop of Tel Aviv's Wolfson Park
resonates with multiple readings of its
dramatic forms. Dani Karavan's quest for
a symbolic language is especially dramatic. He looks locally, and to platonic
form and archetypal sensibility, employing a limited vocabulary of geometric
forms that are invested with cultural
specificity so that it reads and rewards at
many levels. Influenced by the Bauhaus
forms of the city of his childhood, the
design resonates with cubes, spheres,
cones, and pyramids coupled with landscape icons of olive, grass, and concrete.
The pyramid refers to the tents of early
settlement of Tel Aviv, the steps to Jacob's
ladder, the basin to irrigation pools, and
ancient synagogues. As a child in Tel
Aviv, Karavan says he felt things through
his feet. Here he wanted the same visceral landscape connection.   It is an
interplay of positive and negative forms,
ascensions, and depressions. It is a sculpture on a hilltop, an abstracted city
square, an urban observatory, and a
mitzpe over the city, sea, and sky.

above: View from below.
Kikar Levana. Tel Aviv.
Tichnun Nof served as
the landscape architects for
Wolfson Park and collab-
orated with Karavan on
the siting of the project, a
30 × 50 meter rectangle.

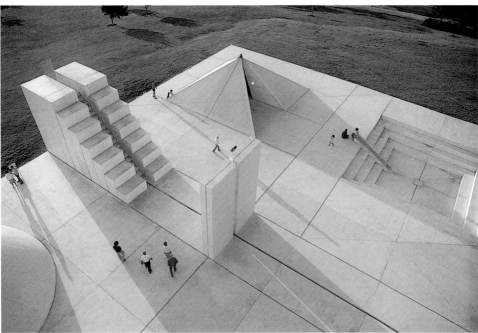

View from the tower. Kikar Levana.

Site Planning and Structure

Site planning is a fundamental part of landscape architectural practice. The questions of the relationship between architecture and landscape occur at multiple scales. One is how buildings sit within the landscape, how they are sited, the sensitivity to orientation and situation, and issues of their mass and composition. The reverse is how the landscape is viewed from a structure. Second, at the more intimate scale are the questions of how the building and ground meet, and the kind of outdoor spaces created as buildings interact with each other, including spaces within structures such as courtyards. Third is the basic connection of inside and outside with respect to which there are rich lessons to be found in the traditional architecture of the region. The rich array of atria, terraces, patios, and open and closed flowing spaces inside and out, not to mention the seasonal use of distinct portions of structures, are too often unheeded in modern Israeli architecture. There is the modest *mirpeset* (balcony), but it is often too small and tight. The classic modernist housing block is raised on piloti, which reserves the ground level for outdoor use, but it rarely includes the intended garden spaces. Many have been appropriated for parking.

Beit Havraa (convalescent home). Zichron Yaakov. Pollack and Fruchter.

There are many exceptions and grand achievements. The Israel Museum designed by architects Al Mansfeld and Dora Gad with Miller-Blum as landscape

architects sits magnificently draped across its ridgeline. Mendelsohn's designs for Hebrew University on Mount Scopus exploited the desert to the east as backdrop, most dramatically at the outdoor theater. At Zichron Ya'akov the Mivtahim convalescent home (1965) by Yaakov Rechter (1924-2001) with Pollack and Fruchter as landscape architects is inscribed just below the ridgeline of the Carmel. Inside is a garden court with waterfalls and garden passages beneath the raised structure to a sloping lawn in deference to the grand view of the coastal plain and the sea. Richly planted stone pathways take one up and down the slope. Beit Gabriel (1994) at the southern shore of the Kinneret by the architect Ulrich Plessner with Miller-Blum as landscape architects is a dramatic structure at the southern shore of the Kinneret. From its elevated location it feels to be embracing the lake. Its outdoor spaces include intimate courtyards and a flamboyant terrace of metal "palms" which echo the surrounding palm trees.

Architect David Reznik collaborated with Yahalom-Zur on many projects in Jerusalem, including Hebrew University and their superb design for the Mormon Church's Jerusalem Center for Middle East Studies (1986). Its highly visible site on the slopes of the Mount of Olives with views to the Old City place it in one of Israel's most magnificent locations. The passage into the building complex is a choreographed revelation of its dramatic situation. Entry is through a walled courtyard. Perforated screened walls open to archways and gentle terraces culminate in a grand belvedere overlooking the city. Stone paths then lead around the building and back up the hillside. Below these public areas are successive terraces of dormitory rooms. The concept was to have Jerusalem enter the building. The dialogue between the designers, Reznik and Zur, resulted in a superb integration of architecture and site, inside and outside, the contemporary and the timeless.

Landscape architects have shown a particular sensibility to those architectural forms that are more temporary and open in character. There is an affinity with the transitory structure of the *sukkah* (temporary structures built during the holiday of Sukkot), tents, beach shelters, and even army encampments, all of which have an orientation to basic comfort, yet display a remarkable inventiveness. A pergola, arbor, or structure for shade is an integral component of almost all outdoor spaces. These provide a sense of shelter and enclosure, yet are simultaneously open. The supporting structure, or the vines which cover it, afford the comfort of shade,

left: Outdoor theater. Hebrew University. Mt. Scopus. Eric Mendelsohn. (1948 photo, Her Majesty's Stationery Office)

right: Beit Gabriel (1993) Ulrich Plessner, architect, and Miller-Blum, landscape architect.

define and enclose space, and provide a covered passageway. As Bernard Rudofsky has noted, the pergola "stands at the threshold of architecture as nature's lobby, or to turn the simile around, as the farthest penetration of architecture into the realm of nature."

There is another aspect of the shaping of space that is as much psychological as actual. Israel's population density now accentuates a challenge Lippa Yahalom describes as creating the illusion of an open landscape in a small landscape, what he calls the creation of "a spacious miracle." This can be accomplished in several ways. One is by the preservation of as much open land as possible; another is creating an illusion of depth to the landscape, especially in new neighborhoods, by leaving areas open, having spaces flowing one into another, and reinforcing their identity through planting. With the exception of the Negev and the western horizon, vast open spaces do not exist, so they are all the more precious. In this spatial challenge the coast and seashore, ridge, cliff, and promontory all need protection as does the boundary between city and country which is becoming less defined as a more suburban zone develops.

above: Sukkah. Kibbutz Sarid.

left: Pergola. King's garden. Netanya. Shlomo Weinberg-Oren.

Kibbutz Yotvata. This shading device for bicycle parking is constructed of metal lattice. Maya Shafir.

LANDSCAPE IS NOT JUST LAND, it is culture. It is impossible to understand landscape architecture in Israel without understanding the Israeli way of life. A product equally of its culture and environment, there are aspects that are characteristic of the Mediterranean and the Middle East, and others that are European and American. The environment and climate sets the parameters of possibilities. Summer is hot and dry, winter is cool and moist, but for much of the country and most of the year life can comfortably be lived out-of-doors. Hot weather means a walk in the evening is a welcome respite and most of the year it is comfortable enough to sit and be outside.

At the prosaic level of daily life people go from home to work or school, to stores, places of recreation, and the synagogue, all within urban open space systems. The small area of Israel means that no one can move far away. People live in their communities and neighborhoods for long periods of time, and associations from school, army, and work are often lifelong. Therefore people are constantly meeting people they know, even in the supposedly anonymous big city. Social life is rich, indoors and out. It is impossible to imagine any substantial project, commercial or public, without a cafe with places to sit. These are at the center of street life, signs of where the action is. At a minimum level, a kiosk with food and drink is provided in even small parks. In natural areas most people tend to go where others go. Places are lively. There is little desire, or opportunity, for solitude.

People walk and people talk. Israel is a gregarious society and a pedestrian one, where for a large percentage walking is also mandated by the prohibition of traveling on *Shabbat*. On *Shabbat* you have two diverse but paradoxically complimentary phenomena. Much of the population is jamming into

Chapter 7

Culture of Use

*And outside,
the boulevards
with a gasp of breath
were filled with bliss,
asked for support,
and the Autumn,
the Autumn carried
a song and a psalm
to its city which was
dressed in a storm.*
—Natan Alterman

left: Men on a bench under pergola. Rishon Le Tzion.

opposite page: Gan Hamoshava. Rishon-le-Tzion. (1952 photo, Museum of Rishon-le-Tzion)

top: Café. Center for a Beautiful Israel. Tel Aviv. Yahalom-Zur.

bottom: Women and children gather on a pedestrian street. Ramat Gan.

their cars rushing to other places; while for others cars remain idle and the street, sidewalk, and pathway come to life with walking, visiting, and sitting. There is a rhythm of walking to and from synagogue, staying close to home, and ritual afternoon walks (akin to the Italian *corso* and promenade of other Mediterranean communities). The religious ritual has a secular counterpart. *Shabbat*, as a day of the cessation from work and rest in modern Israel, also encompasses many forms of recreation. A larger, secular group is simultaneously crowding the beaches, hiking on trails, making *mangal* (grilling) in the parks, or spending the day at a friend's kibbutz. These divergent aspects of Israeli culture put great pressure on places on *Shabbat*, where usage spikes beginning with Friday night. Streets that are filled with cars become quiet, while parks, which lay dormant, bloom with an efflorescence of activity. Most places of business are closed, but they reopen with a flourish on Saturday evening. Places are designed with these activity patterns in mind.

Israelis range from deeply religious to strongly secular, with all shades in between. The face of religion as a cultural and daily force, however, is visible irrespective of personal belief. *Shabbat* behavior epitomizes distinctions among Israel's heterogeneous population. It is a generalization, but religious Jews, secular Jews, and the Arab population each have their distinctive ways of using the landscape, open space in particular. In many situations they will occupy separate spaces or, in an informal but clear code, use the same space at different times. At Sachne (Gan Hashlosha) Saturday is known as a day for Jews and Friday is for Arabs. The proscriptions of modesty mandate that at some beaches bathing areas are designated for religious women. On the other hand, oftentimes parks and gardens fulfill the democratic and egalitarian aspirations of public open spaces and all groups share in the pleasures of the place.

Israel is also a youthful society and child centered. Living at high densities, with most Israelis in apartments, means that children use public spaces. They are always around and seek others to play with. Open spaces surrounding apartment blocks are their territory. The designated play areas are critical gathering places, especially for young children and their parents. Children's activity is fostered by a short

school day for younger children and a culture which allows them great freedom, albeit with the expectation that someone is always watching out for their welfare.

Another significant cultural aspect is the level of group activity. Children and adolescents are part of groups: school groups, scouts, clubs, and *gadna* (pre-army training for high schoolers). They are often seen traveling and hanging out in small packs moving en masse or on organized trips. This is true for both Jews and Arabs. Areas are designed to accommodate large group activities: amphitheaters, shelters, and services. Older and retired persons also frequent open spaces, and areas are often characterized by a single dominant cultural group. For example men will gather to play backgammon or chess. Many areas go through a daily cycle as distinct populations gather at different times.

The beaches are critical gathering places. There, as in parks, most people congregate where others are, at the center of the action. On the land side, most beaches are supported by a strand of services: a promenade along which are found bathhouses, showers, cafes, playgrounds, clubs, and parking. For at least half the year they are places of intense activity, day and

night, again peaking on *Shabbat*. Even in winter walking the beaches of Haifa is a mass phenomena.

The Middle Eastern aspect of park behavior is epitomized by the *mangal*, a habit shared by many in Israel. Groups of family and friends gather in parks, around tables and on blankets, bringing large quantities of food. The locus of activity is a grill, where men cook meat, while women prepare the remainder of the feast. It is an active, spirited event, the opposite of the quiet respite in nature.

Another aspect of the culture of use is that of celebration. The cycle of festivals, religious and secular, are enacted outside, visible in the landscape, and affect open space design and function. Yom Kippur is a day with no cars on the road and a

top left: Picnic. Ein Gedi. Dead Sea

top right: Picnic. Haram esh Sharif. Jerusalem.

middle above: Children playing. Kibbutz Ayelet Hashahar.

bottom: Group on a field trip. Park Canada.

palpable silence. At Sukkot thousands of *sukkah* sprout on balconies, on rooftops, and in gardens; they are strung like necklaces around apartment blocks while great communal ones are erected on kibbutzim. Every settlement had a *hanukiah* (a nine-branched candelabra) lit for the eight nights of Hanukah and an outdoor amphitheater for occasional performances, but especially for commemorations on Memorial Day and Independence Day. At the conclusion of Pesach the Moroccan communities celebrate Mamounia in the park. Activities occur in both designated and undesignated spaces. At Lag Ba Omer it is traditional to build *kumsitz* (fires) and to roast potatoes. It happens in vacant lots, building sites, and leftover spaces.

Design has a political and ideological dimension. Listen to the words of any commentator speaking about Israel or the Middle East. They will speak of trying to understand and get the pulse of what the "street" is saying or how they are feeling in the *souk* (market). These are not just cultural stereotypes. In personifying those places the commentators are demonstrating a key idea: that those environments have social and political functions. A basic function of the modern park and plaza is a democratic space, a place where people of all social classes and segments of society can meet, a common ground. That function is still critical. The street, plaza, and market are classic meeting grounds in all ways, from the extreme of conflict, to demonstrations and manifestations of community. Columnist Esther Zandberg describes the phenomena of the "small parliament," people engaged in spirited discussions out-of-doors. In Tel Aviv this was originally how Rothschild Boulevard was designated with Iraqi immigrants as the discussants. It is now Russians, the most recent group of immigrants, who meet in the same locale. Kikar Malchei Israel, fronting Tel Aviv's City Hall, a traditional site of gathering and demonstration, was renamed Rabin Square after his assassination at the site.

At the more personal level, most Israelis live in apartments, which makes the provision for public open space even more critical. Most apartments have a *mirpeset*, a balcony. It is the immediate, proximate outdoor environment and it is put to use. The *mirpeset* is a place of leisure and play for children and adults. It is a family place where people sit, socialize, and rest. Early apartments were planned to minimal standards and were very compact. Even a modest *mirpeset* offered some relief from a crowded existence. They also are used as places for household work, clothes-drying, and storage places for furniture, books, collections, and food. They are often ornamented and beautified. In short, most of the functions that open spaces accommodate are present here in a very pragmatic, but also imaginative and occasionally beautiful ways. In its inventive multi-purpose approach to this micro-landscape, the *mirpeset* mirrors an approach that is extended at larger scales.

Also underlying the culture of use are the society's core values. Israel is an extraordinarily heterogeneous society with Jewish immigrants from scores of nations and great diversity within those groups. The Arab, Druze, Muslim, and Christian communities are also not monolithic. Nonetheless certain fundamentals are discernible. The dominant founding Zionist-Socialist ideals had a powerful impact on the landscape. At bottom was a return to the land of history, myth, religion, and origin. There was also a personal and community ethos of the pioneering generation (and beyond) which exhalted the collective over the individual, which focused on the public welfare over personal gratifi-

A Shavuot celebration. Kibbutz Sarid.

A demonstration. Francis Hiatt Garden (formerly the Old Knesset Garden). Jerusalem. Jean Pierre Soria, architect.

cation. In the pioneering era work was exhalted and leisure often frowned upon. Esther Zandberg tells of how her parents in Tel Mond didn't use the garden, as it was a sin to sit. Now people sit and use their gardens. Unlike other nations where landscape architects sharpen their design skills on private gardens, most landscape architects here hone theirs on public projects. To this day the private garden is a marginal aspect of professional practice, although that is changing with increased affluence and private home ownership. Israeli design takes for granted that it speaks a language of social responsibility and community obligation, consciousness and concern. The designed landscape is a character in the social life of the nation. It is one's neighbor and friend, part of the extended family. It is there to provide basic needs, to take care of you, to assume its responsibilities.

Five features—stone, water, plants, space, and use—constitute the vocabulary of the language of landscape. Defined by materials, history, and use, a local design language, *an Israeli garden*, is emerging. It speaks eloquently in stone, is frugal with water, uses indigenous and naturalized vegetation, is intimate in scale, and is used intensively. It has modern characteristics and is influenced by a European heritage, but it is strongly rooted in its Mediterranean and Middle Eastern situation. One can describe this as an Israeli style, but it is only the visible manifestation of the variety and complexity of forces that create a place.

PART II

Speaking a Landscape Language

The Lord has singled out by name Bezalel ...
He has endowed him with a divine spirit of skill, ability,
and knowledge in every kind of craft
and has inspired him to make designs ...
to work in every kind of designer's craft and to give directions.
Exodus 35:30-33

Landscapes are shaped by design professionals and policy-makers, but they are created mostly by the gradual accretion of countless human actions. Design is a process and a product, a verb and a noun. Designs represent visions and aspirations, desires and dreams. Designs are the translation of ideas into physical form. The ideas, however, are not always understood or articulated. What is the idea, what is the intention behind a design? How is the language of landscape spoken? What stories does it tell? What themes are expressed in landscape architectural design?

Designs are not only narratives to be received, but they also engage users in such a way that they become actors in the drama. At its best landscape architecture takes the materials, forms, and habits of a place, and then distills them, capturing and communicating its essential quality and character. Good stories exploit the designer's landscape vocabulary with richness and subtlety. When a design can be read at many levels, it means it is telling multiple stories. Some of the finest landscape narratives have the appeal of the best children's tales, where there is joy in repetition, and when tales are committed to memory.

One measure of the depth of the best work in Israel is its ambition, its willingness to engage large themes. These include the relationship between inside and outside; the nature of change; the shape of time; and the nature of the frame. These themes are concerns for landscape architects in all places and situations, though their shapes here are derived from a struggle to understand the complexities of the Israeli landscape.

The way these themes are played out represents the physical and spatial actualization of designers as cultural agents, struggling to give form to society's needs and dreams. It is through the vocabulary of design—stone, water, plants, space, and use—that landscape architects address these themes. The themes all represent a balancing of considerations, the simultaneous response to seemingly contradictory forces. The formal expression of these distinctions are visible in how desert and city meet, how cultivated land and forests intersect, and how the Mediterranean shore is faced.

distant, with its promises hidden from our view. Yet the meaning of "indigenous" is not simple. All landscapes are local, but at the same time have affinities with and make reference to other locales. For example, while the Negev is unique it shares characteristics with deserts everywhere, much as Haifa has much in common with other Mediterranean ports.

In Israeli architectural history one of the central narratives is the quest for a synthesis in the dialectic of "East" and "West," the architectures of the Middle East and Europe. For landscape architecture the connection to place is less symbolic and abstract than actual and concrete. Landscape architecture *grows* from people and the land: climate, stone, soil, water, and vegetation. With landscape architecture this east-west dichotomy is already integral to the physical environment, which is itself such a synthesis. Similarly Mediterranean design draws from European, North African, and Middle Eastern cultures. It is not surprising that Israeli visitors to Spain or Morocco, Italy or Greece experience a sense of deja vu. In landscape architecture the dialectic has been between northern and central European sensibilities and the Mediterranean and Middle Eastern cultures. The former was often seen as cosmopolitan, the later as provincial (and inferior). Another response was more sympathetic, if still romantic: an outsider's eyes seeing an exoticism in a "Oriental" or "Levantine" society. In architecture especially there was a quest for a symbolic and formal synthesis which would incorporate elements of both cultures. The result was an eclectic mix. In more recent years a more distant, but significant American design influence can be felt as well.

Architects have looked to traditional and regional characteristics, including the massing of buildings modeled on the incremental growth of towns and close packing in the desert for climatic adaptation. They have employed courtyards, domes, arches, and ornamentation. Sometimes these devices succeed, but too often they are unintegrated pastiche. How place and people are reflected in their art is a question asked of all creative individuals: architects, artists, writers, dancers, and musicians. For example, the evolution of Israeli music combines *Ashkenazi*, *Sephardic*, Middle-Eastern, and western pop music into a new dynamic amalgam. One measure of the success of Israeli design is how well it negotiates these diverse and complex influences.

This dialectic of inside/outside and local/international is dramatically communicated in the homes of Israel's founders. Chaim Weizmann's home was designed by Eric Mendelsohn (1887-1953) in 1934-36. The landscape architect was Shlomo Weinberg-Oren. In the international style, the home sits on a pastoral hillside originally overlooking the orange groves of Rehovot with a distant view of the Mediterranean. David Ben Gurion's final home, where he retired, was at Sde Boker in the Northern Negev. He chose the location hoping to inspire Israeli youth to join him in settling the desert. It is a modest kibbutz structure set within a desert oasis.

Inside/outside not only means looking to different places, but also to different times. There is a deep pastoral strain to landscape architectural design. This is not just a matter of rolling lawns and clustered trees. It represents a more fundamental desire to retrieve lost landscapes. For immigrants there are the places left behind. For the native, there are those of childhood, of a slower pace and a smaller, more intimate scale, which has rapidly disappeared under the pressures of development. Inevitably the landscape created by the generations of pioneers has become indigenous. Simply put, what was recently new is now a tradition, and so the landscapes of early parks and gardens, kibbutzim, and moshavim exercise a pull on the emotions and the senses. They have become local models deserving of study and adaptation.

Planting Design

The seemingly modest subjects of plant selection and planting design have been the subjects of much controversy. The discussion, at times heated, has really been about trying to define a relationship between people and place. For many years Israeli landscape architects and gardeners have debated the merits of an architectonic approach versus a more natural and naturalistic approach to the use of plants, mirroring commonplace discussions in western garden design since the eighteenth century. At the same time, there have been continuing disputes about what is indigenous and what has been introduced. The

debate is ideological, yet plants also naturally migrate and colonize areas and the biogeography of regions represents the migrations of plant species just as much as animals and people. Like many aspects of the Israeli landscape, this has been exacerbated by the pace of change. New plant species were introduced in rapid succession, quickly changing the accustomed look of the land.

Plant selection is not easy. Some are chosen based on the science of what can grow and survive in particular situations, others for their cultural and historical symbolism, and still others are on personal preferences. Most often plants are selected for their appropriateness, but even that is not easily determined. Plants have botanical requirements *and* cultural connections. Many have been chosen for their affinity from other Mediterranean environments in Australia, South Africa, or California, and these have readily naturalized themselves. A similar approach has been applied to plants adaptable from other desert environments. Many imported species such as eucalyptus or species of palms and figs have naturalized so completely that they now appear native. In this process of environmental transformation Mikve Israel, founded in 1870 by the Frenchman Jacob (Karl) Netter

top: Ben Gurion's house in Sde Boker. Tichnun Nof.

bottom: Chaim Weizmann's house. Mendelsohn designed the circuitous approach with its different views. As an architect he was particularly attentive to site conditions and the landscape frame of his architecture.

Canary palms. Gan Hamoshava. Rishon-le-Tzion. (1910 photo. Museum of Rishon-le-Tzion)

(1826-1882) for the Alliance Israelite Universelie, was extraordinarily significant as both an agricultural school and demonstration site for the introduction of plants to the country.

The formative period of development from the 1920s through the 1940s was characterized by sometimes intense debates over style and materials and plants. Ruth Enis (b. 1928) and Yoseph Ben-Arav have described this in their book *Sixty Years of Kibbutz Gardens and Landscape (1910-1970)*. Everyone was seeking a vocabulary suited to the place and culture. Central European immigrant landscape architects and gardeners brought a range of planting styles and formal languages reflecting European theory and practice. In Palestine, immigrants encountered English architects and their landscape ideas, as well as the influence of émigré Bauhaus architects. Here English romantic ideals often confronted a nascent modernist sensibility.

The native plant and stylistic debate took many turns. There was a desire to diversify the limited supply of plants and make new introductions. At the same time there was a fear that this could lead to a degree of chaos and disorder without knowing how trees would adapt to Israeli conditions. Lippa Yahalom characterizes the schools of thought as personified by Yechiel Segal (1886-1962) and Shlomo Weinberg-Oren (1891-1955). Segal was born in Lithuania and emigrated to Palestine in 1919. He became the first head of the gardening department of Tel Aviv in the 1920s, was responsible for the development of early Holon, and became a key pioneer in kibbutz gardening. Lippa Yahalom recounts a walk he took with Segal in Sharona, the German Templer Colony in Tel Aviv, where Segal pointed and said to him, "This is the garden." It was a natural path, there were blue flowers to one side. While Segal, and later Yahalom, were proponents of native planting, they were not dogmatic in their approach.

Shlomo Weinberg-Oren was most often associated with the formal architectural style, but his ideas evolved throughout his career. Weinberg-Oren promul-

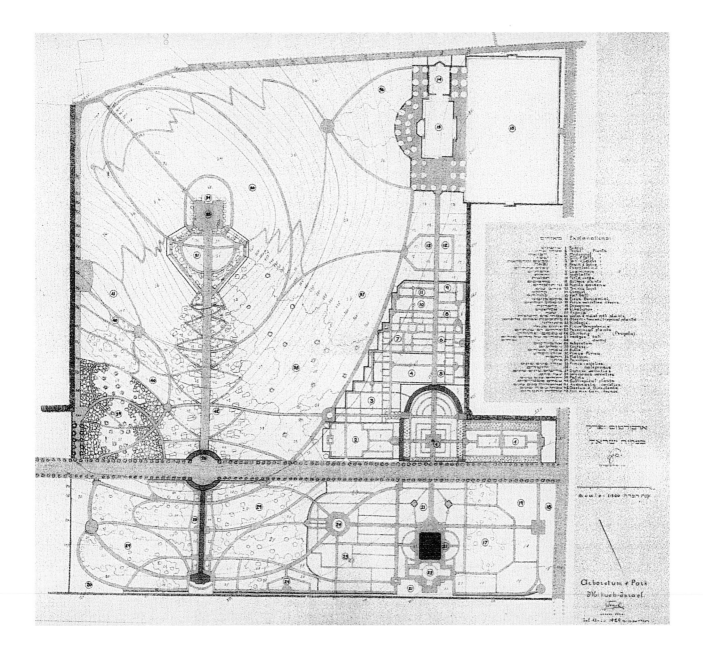

gated what he called the dominant or principle tree idea, which espoused that at least half the trees in a garden be of a single species. This was a reaction to what he saw as haphazardness in planting, lacking structure or logic. Another pioneering landscape architect Alfred Weiss (1909-1971) said that new plantings had created "a mixture of plants, a new green landscape, with a strange and alien appearance: a landscape without a past, without a cultural tradition, and without modesty." It was a "crude-forgery" of the landscape of Eretz-Israel. Weiss saw Oren's dominant tree idea as a bit simplistic. He "demanded that the plants in the garden be suited to the indigenous local vegetation, and that the entire garden be designed only in accordance with the landscape characteristics of the region."

Weinberg-Oren's ideas changed over time. In 1943 he wrote: "if what we want is a landscape-garden, a forest-garden, we have to take a new approach and plant trees in a natural form, and there is therefore not much room for straight-lined avenues." By 1946 Weinberg-Oren wrote: "In the natural garden we aspire to leave the observer with the impression that this garden is not merely man's device but a creation of nature, that man added his decorative feelings to it in order to realize his vision." This personal transition paralleled what was happening elsewhere in the world of design.

Weinberg-Oren was born in Romania. He also studied (as had Segal) at Ahlem, Germany, and at the gardening school at Pillnitz-Dresden. He emigrated in 1925 with his wife Elisheva, also a gardener. In the next decade he taught at Mikve Israel and at Nahalal, the first moshav, and traveled in North Africa. He often collaborated with the architect and town planner Richard Kauffmann, and designed several kibbutzim before joining Kibbutz Yagur in 1936. In later years he would co-edit and write for *Gan Va Nof* and teach at Technion.

Avraham Karavan (1902-1968) also played a central role in this process. Born in Galicia, he spent his first years in Manchester, England, returned to Lvov, and arrived in Palestine in 1918. He worked with PICA (Palestine Jewish Colonization Association), a Rothschild agricultural organization. His son, sculptor Dani Karavan (b. 1930), describes his father as an autodidact, but influenced by English gardens and his mother's love of plants. Eventually he would take a job with the garden department of Tel Aviv under Yechiel Segal and subsequently become head of the department. Like many gardeners and landscape architects, his work was influenced by his relationship with a succession of mayors.

Karavan's accomplishments were many. He characterized the early twentieth-century landscape by saying that nature in Palestine had been eaten by goats and his primary goal was to reintroduce it. Dedicated to enriching the urban landscape, he planted the first palms at the entry to Tel Aviv, was the first to transplant olive trees, and fought to retain the city's native shikma trees. From the 1940s until the mid-1960s he planted trees lot by lot, wherever there was a vacant space on the map. He imagined that it was the task of the next generation to create a style of these materials, although his work was a sure sign in that direction. Since 1971 Tel Aviv has awarded a landscape architecture prize bearing his name. The first was for Yahalom-Zur's design for Sacher Park in Jerusalem.

Gan Meir, named for Mayor Meir Dizengoff (1861–1936), now appears a bit disheveled, but it is still a valued urban open space, ripe for restoration. Tel Aviv's first large municipal garden (twenty-three *dunams*), Gan Meir was the subject of a competition in 1932 won by artist Aharon Halevi. The park however, was not constructed until 1941–1943 by Karavan. By then Tel Aviv was a city of 180,000. The Halevi plan had included more than eighty plants, indigenous and introduced. The plan was a series of meandering paths through dense planting with an axial walkway on the south side. In the final construction the plant richness was retained and in that respect it was an important demonstration project. An ornamental pool was substituted for an amphitheater as a core element, and most dramatically the axis was expanded into a grand promenade beginning at King George Street and terminating at a raised pergola-backed terrace. Lines of trees reinforced the axis, with most of the remainder of the planting informal.

Lippa Yahalom said about Karavan that he was "their university," meaning that for his generation he was the master professor. Tel Aviv's Yad Lebanim, Gan Ha'atz-

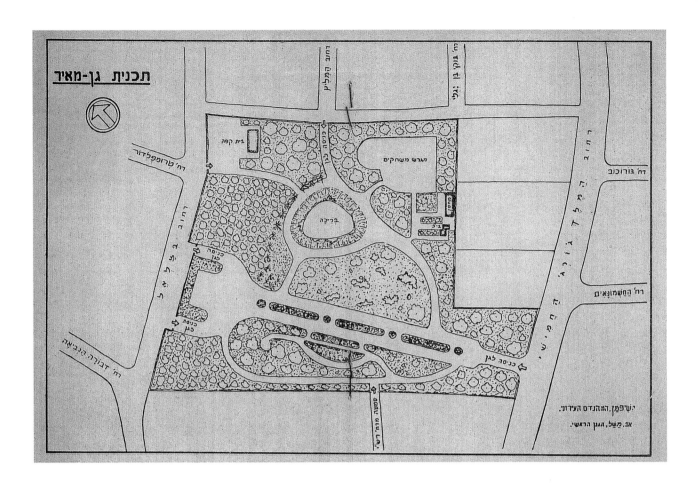

תכנית גן-מאיר

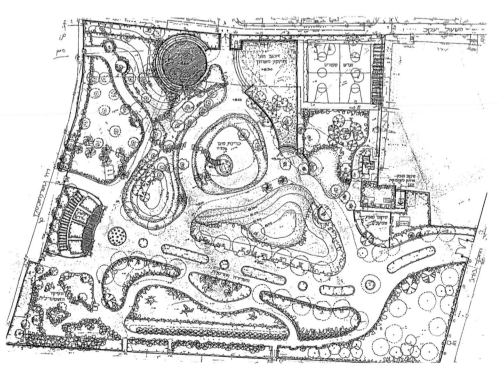

above: Gan Meir. Plan as implemented. (Municipality Archive Tel Aviv)

left: Reclamation plan (1990). Gan Meir. (Moria-Sekely)

maut, Gan Meir and Gan HaPisgah in Jaffa (with later additions by Hillel Omer) all were his demonstration projects of the use of native flora and local materials. Yahalom also describes Yechiel Segal as his "master teacher" with whom he would work with for fifteen years. There were many others who were involved in this pioneering process, such as Chaim Latte (1905–1988) who did research on the introduction of plants, was for twenty years (1950–1970) the main instructor for gardening in Israel in horticulture, and who taught at Technion. His work included the publication of monthly instructions for gardeners and more than 500 articles for *Gan Va Nof*.

All of these early landscape architects knew plants exceptionally well. Most had been formally educated as gardeners, attended agricultural school, or learned through long apprenticeships. They had ample direct hands-on experience and many design decisions were made on site in the field. Through the 1950s this gardening and planting design heritage was very strong, especially in kibbutz design and national parks.

Planting approaches diversified in the 1960s and 1970s. The creation of nature reserves, and the development of sites such as Neot Kedumim and Sataf, reinforced a renewed appreciation and knowledge of indigenous vegetation and the *bustan* as a landscape type. At a larger scale, the Keren Kayemet philosophy began to shift from planting monocultures to richer, more ecologically sound forest plantings. An enhanced awareness of the critical factor of irrigation led to a more refined differentiation among plants: those that require no irrigation, those requiring irrigation to get established, and those that need year-round irrigation. Shlomo Aronson and others explicitly began using a plant vocabulary that has symbolic resonance. Thus, in Jerusalem, at the Sherover and Trotner promenades the plants are a Mediterranean mix with mass plantings of rosemary and sage, along with olives, penstemon grasses, and wheat.

These issues continue to the present day. A half-century ago there was limited plant availability and only fledgling nurseries. New plants were, and continue to be, introduced from Australia, Asia, and South Africa and selections are much richer. The situation transformed from one of scarcity to how not to abuse a new-found richness. Commercial nurseries were expanded. Yahalom-Zur's design for a Center for a Beautiful Israel (1992) in Park HaYarkon offered seasonal displays of planting and exhibits on matters of environmental concern.

In recent years forces are simultaneously moving in opposite directions while remaining dependent on each other. With the expansion of options there has been a rediscovery and resurgence of appreciation of the native landscape. *Ha-aretz* columnist Esther Zandberg quotes Lippa Yaholom as saying, "A rock glistening in the rain and a cyclamen are equal to ten spindly fire prone pine trees." Plant selection remains contentious. There have been recent debates over the appropriateness of planting palms in Jerusalem and each side has marshaled historical and ecological evidence to support its claims.

These discussions and debates are about many things. The seeming simplicities of style represent struggles for authenticity, ways to be true to the character of the land itself, and the desire to find a vocabulary suited to the new Israeli way of life. There are multiple and even contradictory desires. The ideals of aspiring to the

Center for a Beautiful Israel in Yarkon Park, in the north of Tel Aviv. The density of the city suggests the pressures on public open space. Yahalom-Zur. (Albatross)

biblical idealization of a land of milk and honey and creating a Jewish homeland often blinded people to the beauty in the landscape they confronted. There was little appreciation of the indigenous Palestinian landscape. The land was to be conquered and a country created, the desert made to bloom, and local character and time-honored solutions were not always heeded. Yet an Israeli planting style is emerging which is a complex mix of native and indigenous species, a cultural mix of biblical and historic association, and a blend of internationalism and localism.

Sources

"… they shall know the land…"
—Numbers 14:31

There was, and continues to be, a search for sources for design. Where does one look for ideas, inspiration, and insight? The richest projects are deeply connected at the material, functional, ideological, and symbolic level to their immediate sites and cultural context. At the same time they are connected to the practice of landscape architecture as a temporal and spatial art. While connected to developments in contemporary design at the international level, the Israeli context gives local practice a unique trajectory. Landscape architects had to look consciously to Israel's evolving culture, its natural environment, and the materials of the place. They had much to draw upon, but also much to communicate regarding the story of the land and its people.

Landscape architects asked what are the sources and where to look, but within the temporal density of Israel it is also a question of when to look. Many looked for sources in the sense of origins and beginnings, a return to the "roots," and found inspiration in religion, tradition, or culture. Others looked to the land itself and were inspired by designs from selected historical periods. Given Israel's historical geography, this encompassed the full range of Jewish history, including the designs of all who have lived here on the land, from Canaanites to Crusaders, Arabs, Ottomans, German Templers, and British Romantics. Some looked toward tradition, in the landscapes of biblical history, which is the actual geography of the country. Others were inspired by the meaning and symbolism of the biblical landscape and the gardens of Eden and the *Song of Songs*. Some looked to the vernacular, to agriculture, to indigenous practice, and to the bustan.

A striking early example is found in Jerusalem. Yosef Kahaner (1892-1977), born in the Old City of Jerusalem, studied at Mikve Israel and in Montpellier, France. He had advised the Baron Rothschild on moshavot, worked in South Africa, and brought back plant material. In 1930 he built the British High Commissioner's Garden at Government House (Austen St. Barbe Harrison, architect). Along with the Alhambra-inspired courtyards at the Rockefeller Museum, also by Harrison, this is the rare British Mandate garden. It has elements of the English formal gardens of the time, including a semi-circular parterre and a sunken garden. The introduced form is retained, but the plant vocabulary and the stone work are all local. Beyond the sunken garden a series of terraces, like those characteristic of the Jerusalem hills, reaches out toward the vista of the Old City of Jerusalem and the

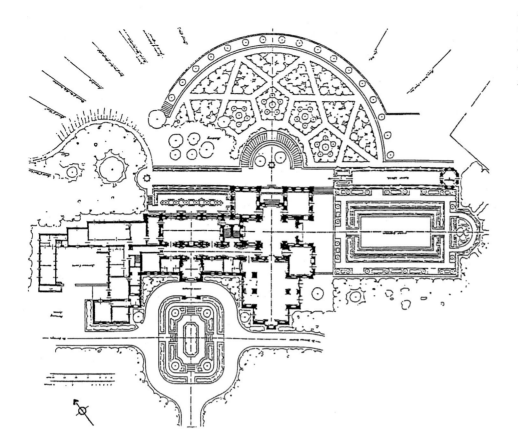

British High Commissioner's Garden at Government House. Jerusalem. Yosef Kahaner. (1948 photo Her Majesty's Stationery Office)

desert to the east. The landscape framed a structure which was part citadel, a symbol on the hill (after 1948 this became the site of United Nations offices), and part protected micro-climate of shade and captured breezes.

As this example makes evident, designers view the landscape as a source, to the look of the land, its formal aspects, actual shape and qualities. The traditional, Arab, largely pre-industrial landscape, often described as biblical, had much to offer. The rural landscape is structured by the patterns and practices of agriculture, the cultivation of plants, and the tending of animals. These not only produce *forms*, but also characteristic landscape *experiences*. Land and behavior are shaped and molded. They are structured into units, from the intimate scale of irrigated vegetable plots to the larger scale of fields and orchards. Steep areas are terraced with stone walls. The agricultural foundation of Mediterranean and Middle Eastern garden practice and pattern is one key to the development of a formal language and plant selection.

There is an Israeli sensibility too, to the Mediterranean iconography of olive groves, vineyards, wheat fields, terraced agriculture, arbors, techniques of drainage and irrigation, and the ditches and canals that direct water. In the desert there are remnants of ancient systems of water catchment, storage, and distribution, notably those of the Nabateans. Traditional agriculture has been the most common source for design, but modern techniques hold promise as well, in the patterns of plastic coverings over furrows and in the geometry of mechanical and drip irrigation. Conversations with landscape architects reveal their personal preferences. Child-

Traditional agriculture. Carmel.

hood nostalgia is common for the fertile valleys of the Emek, the sensory qualities of *pardesim*, the terraced hills leading to Jerusalem, the oases of the Judean Desert and Sinai, the drama of the desert and Galilee villages.

Israel's artists, authors, and photographers have celebrated, documented, and critiqued the landscape and their work has influenced that of landscape architects. Each medium has captured and communicated different qualities. Creative artists are fine-tuned to exploring layers of the relationship between people and place, at communicating experience and landscape essentials. There is the artist's understanding of the landscape, its structure and its spirit. A look at the paintings or drawings of Israel's great artists, Reuven Rubin (1892–1923) or Nachum Gutman (1898–1978), show people and their dwellings embedded in the landscape. Gutman magically captured the spirit of the early history of Tel Aviv and essential aspects of that community. His work has an amazing sense of the phenomenology of the city as he anthropomorphizes its natural and built elements. Tel Aviv appears to emerge from its sand dune environment—a landscape it ultimately obliterated—and the seaside location that it still strives to retain. Anna Ticho (1894–1980) and Leopold Krakauer (1890–1954) display a rare understanding of landscape dynamics and structure of Jerusalem and

Reuven Rubin. The Road to Safed *(1940s). Oil on canvas. (Courtesy of Rubin Museum, Tel Aviv)*

Rehabilitation of the Nesher quarry (February-November, 1971) Sponsored by the Israel Museum, Jerusalem, (©Yitchak Danziger)

its surroundings. There is now a nostalgia for these images and tales, but also an aspiration for the designer seeking to preserve remnants of these landscapes and to recreate aspects of their spirit in new guises. They represent a fundamental desire for that connection to place. Artist Michael Gross said: "Being an Israeli artist ... is to be profoundly linked with the elements of nature, of the light, of the sun we have here, to have a constructive and strong faith in man and nature, man and land, man and water, man and sky."

Certain artists have been touchstones for Israeli landscape architects, notably the sculptors Itzchak Danziger (1916–1977) and Dani Karavan. Danziger studied in the Garden and Landscape Planning Program at the Architectural Association in London (1951–52) and designed several unrealized garden projects. His most influential landscape work was the rehabilitation of the Nesher quarry (1971) just south of Haifa on the lower slopes of the Carmel. This work of earth artistry predates by many years the involvement of artists in environmental concerns and issues of landscape reclamation.

Dani Karavan was imbued with a landscape sensibility by his father, landscape architect Avraham Karavan. Dani grew up in Tel Aviv when he says: "nature was so strong, the buildings were little." He describes his work as "composed of natural materials and memories." Karavan is inspired by actual and nostalgic landscapes, his life experience, the ephemeral and the long-lived. These he distills into forms that have a sculptural presence and at the same time are spatial environments that one occupies.

Writers are a significant source and inspiration as well. Lippa Yahalom says: "all landscape architects need to read S. Yizhar." Yizchar's landscape descriptions are often long catalogues of plants, stones, and colors. Hillel Omer was both a landscape architect and author, renowned for his children's tales and his stories of Kfar Saba. Natan Alterman's poems evoke the life of Tel Aviv. Yehuda Amichai has been a moving chronicler of landscape and its emotional associations.

While this internal inspiration has been primary, there has been a search outward towards other places and times as well. Twentieth-century design everywhere is influenced by modernism, its ideology and formal properties. Israel was especially impacted by the early modernism of the Bauhaus. Refugees, and a few *sabras* educated in Germany, brought Bauhaus principles and modernist idealism to the Yishuv. The Bauhaus did not specifically teach landscape architecture, but its practice of composition and craft were applied. The progressive social principles of European modernism, unheeded in many places, meshed well with Zionism's socialist, communal, and egalitarian idealism. The impact was most dramatic in architecture, so that Tel Aviv has the largest concentration of Bauhaus building in the world. It also influenced community design, as communities were laid out on modernist principles, a rational functionalism with a clarity of spatial organization, with proscribed places for work, housing, recreation, transportation, and services.

At the level of site and project design modernist principles also had a profound impact, especially in urban projects. It is in architectural ensembles—the spaces of courtyards and plazas—that this is most apparent, but again an attentiveness to social needs was primary. Modernist attributes of an open free plan and spaces flowing one into the other and the destruction of classic and Beaux Arts axial organization is found in diverse projects. Despite modernist assertions that it did not represent a style, certain spatial and formal characteristics prevail in an identifiable vocabulary of modernist geometries: angular beds, zigzag patterns, sinuous, curvilinear, free form, and biomorphic forms. "Modern" materials also assert their presence: concrete, metal, glass, and plants used in a sculptural fashion. The work of Miller-Blum exemplifies these characteristics in the use of concrete and modular construction.

The interaction between such disparate sources has made places where the contrasts, which represent choices, give places an identifiable vitality. Cross-cultural interaction is visible in design. At Hebrew University on Mt. Scopus the megastructure of university buildings contains within it a series of elongated courtyards designed by architect David Reznik and landscape architects Yahalom-Zur. The courtyards are paved in stone bordered by dressed and unhewn edges. There is a hard, stone, bright side, and a mounded, green, planted lawn area with clumps of pines, ornamental grasses, and shrubs. The pattern speaks of the specifics of the location of Mt. Scopus on a ridgeline between the desert and forest. This landscape dichotomy also symbolizes Jerusalem and Israel.

in a progressively expanded sense of professional possibilities. The monthly magazine *Gan va Nof* was founded in 1945 by the Israel Landscape and Gardening Association. It continues to play a significant role in educating the public and the professional community in the introduction of plants, landscape practices, design, materials, products, discussion, debate, and critical evaluation. Following on the heels of independence there was a process of professionalization. In their early histories the lines between landscape architects and gardeners were not sharp. In 1948 the IFLA (International Federation of Landscape Architects) was founded, followed in 1951 by the ISALA (Israeli Association of Landscape Architects). The nineteen founding members reflected the diverse backgrounds and origins of professionals in Israel. Almost all European immigrants, they were municipal employees, kibbutz gardeners, private consultants, and educators. Few new members were added in the early years, as going abroad for study was encouraged and a professional degree was requirement for membership. In 1952 the ISALA joined the IFLA. Zvi Miller would serve as IFLA's president from 1982 to 1986 and the federation would hold its Eighth World Congress in Haifa in 1962, a significant professional landmark. The ISALA is again the host in 2005. Official governmental recognition came in 1973 when the profession was recognized officially under the Law of Architects and Engineers of 1953. Landscape architects must legally be part of any design team designing housing or road projects. A generation-long struggle for professional recognition and to educate professionals in the country was complete. By 1999 there were more than 400 officially registered landscape architects and more practicing.

Cover. Gan va Nof. *September/Octpber 1994. (Gan va Nof)*

At their best Israeli designers know where they are. Landscape language derives from places, actual and ideal, real and fantasy, indigenous and imported. Israel imported the cultural language of trees, forest, meadow, and glade from Northern Europe. These intersected with the inheritance of the pastoral and agricultural language of terrace, vineyard, orchard, and field of the Mediterranean. These combined with the landscape language of North Africa and the Middle East, of oasis and courtyard. In this way we return to the Bunting map and Israel's location at the intersection of continents and designs that derive from diverse garden traditions.

Meeting of Gardener's Association, 1943. Note Kibbutz designs on the wall. Zvi Miller is speaking. Shlomo Weinberg-Oren is to the left, David Zaidenberg, who taught gan noi, *is in the center. (Zvi Miller)*

Founding Members of the ISALA. The founders in Netanya at Galei Yam Hotel, March 1, 1951, Gardener's Association. (Zvi Miller). From left, bottom: Elimelech Admoni: head of Jerusalem's landscape department of the municipality under the British Mandate. Moshe Kvashny: born in Israel, studied at Mikve Israel and in the U.S.A., and landscape architect for the City of Ramat Gan. Lippa Yahalom: a student of Yechiel Segel who had an office with Dan Zur from 1946 until 1996 and who won Karavan Prize (1971) and Israel Prize (1998). Yitzak Enovitch: studied at Ahlem, worked as a gardener and as a private consultant in Germany, and later worked for the Municipality of Haifa. Shlomo Weinberg-Oren: immigrated to Israel in 1925, studied at Ahlem, was a teacher in Nahalal-Agricultural School and had an office in Tel Aviv, in 1936 settled in Kibbutz Yagur and ran a planning office there, and was a lecturer at Technion. Roman Feigelson: private consultant who designed many private gardens in Herzelia and Kfar Shemariahu. Meir Victor: studied in Berlin and came to Israel in 1932, worked for the private sector mainly in the Sharon vicinity, was the landscape architect of Yachin-Hekel and from 1947 worked for the government as the garden architect of its offices in Tel Aviv, and was a landscape consultant for the municipalities of Givataim and Bat Yam.

From left, top: Yechiel Segal: studied in Ahlem and came to Israel in 1919, worked for the private sector in Jerusalem and Tel Aviv, and also worked for the municipality of Tel Aviv and public projects in settlements such as Rishon-le-Tzion and many Kibbutzim. Hana Kurz-Huppert: came to Israel in the mid-1920s, studied in Vienna, worked at Kibbutz Alonim and others as a gardener and designer, and lived and worked in Yokneam. Haim Latte: studied in Ahlem, came to Israel by 1923, established a nursery, designed and planted gardens in the Kinneret vicinity (Villa Melchet), from 1930–1950 taught in Pardes Hana at the agricultural school, was an instructor for the agricultural ministry, from 1954–1965 taught at Technion, and was the most prominent writer for Gan va Nof. *Avraham Karavan: head gardener for the Municipality of Tel Aviv who designed many parks. Yaakov Nitzan: had a nursery in Tel Aviv and was head gardener in Hedera and Netanya. Dov Benayahu: studied in Germany, came to Israel in 1923, and worked in the Galilee for private and public housing projects. Zvi Miller: came to Israel in 1935 and was head of Haifa's gardening department in 1951.*

Not pictured: Adam Shadmi: studied in Czechoslovakia, came to Israel in 1931, and lived and worked in Mishmar Ha Emek as a gardener and a teacher. Yaakov Shur: self-taught gardener and ideologist of the kibbutz garden who lived and worked in Ashdot Yaakov Meuhad. David Zaidenberg: curator of the Mikve Israel Botanical Garden and was trained at the Royal Botanic Kew Gardens in England. Yitzhak Kutner: studied in Switzerland, came to Israel in 1933, for ten years taught at Mikve Israel and worked as a designer for the private and the public sector.

R APID CHANGE has been a constant in Israel's landscape history. This condition presents a dilemma for designers. Landscape architects are agents of change, yet they are simultaneously expected to respect places, their past, and meaning. While admiring the traditional, they are also creating a new tradition.

Designing Change

I think of longing:
a landscape
Out to the very edge of
what's possible.
—Yehuda Amichai

Tradition / Innovation

All design oscillates between these poles. The tug of tradition is particularly strong in Israel, but it is complemented and opposed by a desire to be new, even to the point of willfully disregarding the past. The magnetic pull of innovation, fundamental to the modern era, which Israel's development parallels, is profound. Homage and respect for tradition and its modern interpretation, coupled with inventiveness, progressive ideology, and a search for contemporary expression, are all basic to Israel's ideology.

For Israeli designers the question has been how to understand and respond to a traditional landscape while simultaneously *creating* a landscape tradition. This traditional landscape has not been static. For the nation's pioneers, it was a landscape of Arab villages and their agricultural hinterlands of olive groves, citrus orchards, and fields. It included a few venerable towns such as Safed, Tiberias, and Jerusalem, as well as numerous villages set in a rocky, overgrazed landscape of shepherds and their flocks. Remnants of this landscape persist, but it has largely changed. The early modern twentieth-century tradition, the rural agricultural landscapes of the kibbutz and the moshav, has now acquired traditional status.

The traditional is found in materials, methods, form, and ideas. A central question is how to use these materials in a contemporary way. Perhaps this is easier for landscape architecture than architecture, for the materials of plants, soil, stone, and climate are timeless, while modern industrial materials are more problematic. While they do have a place in the landscape, they are rarely dominant. Concrete

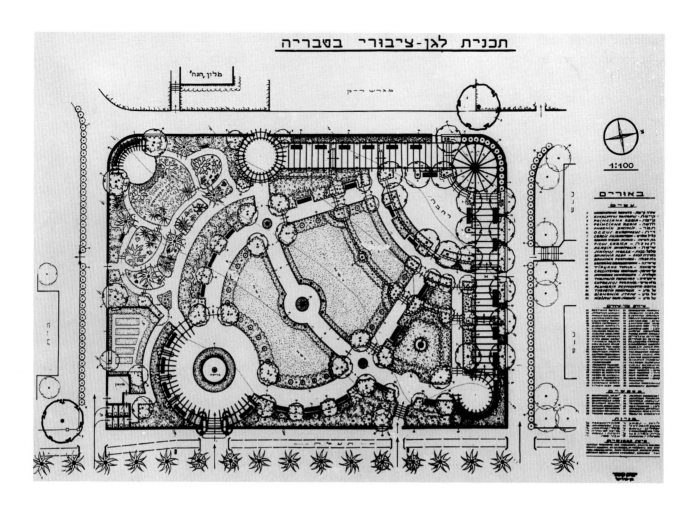

תכנית לגן-ציבורי בטבריה

Plan. Park in Tiberias.
Yitzhak Kutner. (Gideon
Kutner)

would seem to be the dramatic exception, but it is actually a classical material, invented by the Romans, even though it is also seen as quintessentially modern.

There is also a culture of construction, the practices of workers, and their skills. Tradition and innovation apply not only to product, but also to process. For example, some methods of planting and working stone or metal are time-honored techniques. A common approach is to use traditional materials, but work them in a contemporary way. Traditional plantings or stone techniques may be employed in a modernist spatial composition. Sometimes traditional building practice is codified. Israel wisely continued the 1918 British Mandate Ordinance, which decreed that all Jerusalem buildings must be faced with Jerusalem stone. This has not hindered creativity; it has provided architectural unity, not uniformity, to the city.

This is how a landscape design tradition is created. In a rapidly changing environment it is of paramount importance to discover, invent, and learn to speak a traditional landscape language. Such an interaction of imported ideas, forms, and materials with an indigenous landscape yielded the landscape designs of the first generation of landscape architectural pioneers. In the work of Kutner, Y. Segal, Weinberg-Oren, Victor, and A. Karavan, a design language that was very sympathetic to a traditional landscape began to emerge.

Dani Karavan tells a story about his father, Avraham Karavan. It is a lesson about respect for tradition. While building a park the elder Karavan showed his son a wall in Jaffa where he was working. The wall had a niche in it that the Arab builders had built in deference to a tree that was no longer there. Here Avraham planted a tree. The replanting was an act of continuity, a gesture of respect for the earlier design *and* the original wall builders.

These designers were the pioneers at the beginning of the creation of a new tradition. Places such as Tel Aviv's Gan Ha'atzmaut and Gan Meir, and Haifa's Gan Benjamin, combined formal and informal elements in a style that was commonplace in European design at the time. They were all localized by the use of Israeli elements: a native and naturalized vocabulary of plants, local materials, and structures, especially stones, terraces, pergolas, and occasional water features. Coupled with an evolving pattern of use, this represented the beginnings of a new landscape tradition. In the period of early statehood, 1948-1953, great attention was given to open green spaces in older cities and the development of public parks and gardens. Tel Aviv's green spaces increased from 320 to 1,023 *dunams* (Gan Ha'atzmaut is only about 70 *dunams*). Haifa's sixteen gardens totaling 125 *dunams* increased to forty-seven gardens totaling 320 *dunams*.

Gan Ha'atzmaut, designed by Avraham Karavan, is located at the seashore, a transition space between the north edge of the Tel Aviv beach and the city facing the sea. He used huge rough stones of *kurkar* to create a sea-facing rock garden planted

Plan. Gan Ha'atzmaut.
Tel Aviv. Avraham Karavan.

with species tolerant of salt spray and wind. Within the garden are found undressed stones juxtaposed with carefully cut steps, common elements of the country's design vocabulary. On HaYarkon Street the stones and vegetation come right to the sidewalk. The city meets the park directly and one must pass through the stone entry to enter the park interior, a series of protected pastoral glades. The original entry had a square on the street, with a pool and fountain. Begun in 1950, the park opened in 1952, with the north portion added soon after. Unfortunately the park was severed by the construction of the Hilton Hotel which bisected the site.

Gan Benjamin, Haifa's first public garden, is in the Hadar neighborhood, located between the Carmel ridge and the city's port. It was part of a plan for Haifa by the German architect Richard Kauffmann, who formalized the plans of Patrick Geddes for "the Garden Village of the Polytechnium." The idea was to create an *Ir Ganim*, a garden city, under the auspices of the PLDC (Palestine Land Development Company). The Hadar was to have three central gardens, one associated with Technion, which had been designed in 1910 by Alexander Baerwald; Gan Benjamin; and a third which was never constructed. The garden was built between 1924-1927 on the site of an old olive grove and named for Baron Benjamin Edmond de Rothschild who visited in 1925. Designed by the German trained Yechiel Segal in collaboration with Kauffmann, it was a Beaux Arts plan, a terraced symmetrical garden, whose upper level incorporated the olive grove, while the lower was a more formal parterre facing the street. The use of stone and olive trees, as well as the planting of cypress, pine, carob, fig, and casuarina trees within the park and at the edges, served to localize the form. The result was a site specific overlay of materials and use, a prototypical spatial organization that was a cross between a Mediterranean stone terraced garden and a contemporary German design.

The changes to Gan Benjamin are emblematic of the fate of many of Israel's first generation of public gardens, which matured and thrived in their early years, only to be neglected in later decades. A stone wall and a cafe, designed by Baerwald, were added in 1926, followed by a wading pool and public toilets in the 1930s, and play structures and a paved road in the 1940s. In 1956 the upper terrace was truncated by the construction of a theater that ignored the connection to the

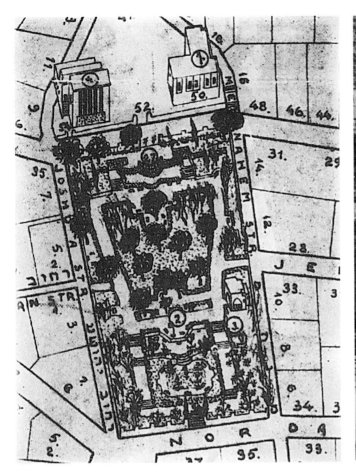

garden. In the 1980s Greenstein and Har-Gil redesigned the lower terrace as a fountain amphitheater to link to the newly created *midrachov* (pedestrian street) of Nordau Street. In the 1990s a poorly maintained garden was revitalized and given new life by the influx of Russian immigrants to the Hadar. Chess games are now a continual year-round happening. In the latest incarnation the upper portion is being redesigned as the new theater entrance and to accommodate underground parking.

left: Plan. Gan Benjamin. Haifa. Yechiel Segal. (Yosef Segal)

right: Gan Benjamin. Haifa. Yechiel Segal. Historic postcard (1936).

The concerns of Israeli landscape architects parallel those of Western post-war landscape architects. Although each nation has its own cultural conditions and landscape architecture in each nation had its own professional trajectory, there were common issues. In the relationship between tradition and innovation the role of modernism was critical. In each case, the complexities of a response to each nation's physical environments within its cultural context determined its distinct response. What Erik De Jong has noted about post-war Dutch landscape architecture ("The quest for a meaningful grammar of design, a workable, meaningful language in a world of upheaval") was commonplace. Professionals in all nations were discussing the relationship of landscape architecture to other arts. They were debating the role of ideology in design. The role of the "indigenous" as either "historical" tradition or "natural" environment as opposed to an array of forces and influences from the "outside" was a widespread issue.

View from a hillside. Israel Museum. Jerusalem. Mansfield and Gad architects, Miller-Blum landscape architects.

The next generation of landscape architects, especially the long-lasting partnerships of Yahalom-Zur, Miller–Blum, and Segal-Dekel, would extend these evolving new traditions. Their work borders on what might be described as an Israeli classicism, a set of informal design rules and the creation of a structure and framework within which experimentation occurs. Their collective work played a significant role in setting a standard of both design and practice. Miller was park director for Rishon-le-Tzion and Holon in the 1940s. Miller and Blum had met at Mikve Israel, where they studied with Kutner and then worked together in Haifa, where Miller was director of parks after 1950. They began their practice in 1960. The firm is now in its second generation, with Amir Blum in Haifa and Yoram Miller in Tel Aviv with an office in Jerusalem as well. Josef Segal, son of Yechiel Segal, and Zvi Dekel founded the Tichnun Nof partnership in 1972. They were soon joined by Uri Mueller and in the 1990s by Shlomo Ze'evy (b. 1958). Lippa Yaholom studied with Yechiel Segal from 1935–1942. Dan Zur, after working on many kibbutzim, began working with Lippa Yahalom after hearing him lecture at a gardener's meeting in 1947. They formed a partnership in 1953 that continued until Yahalom retired in 1992. Zur remains in active practice with an office in Tel Aviv.

The Israel Museum (1961), designed by architects Al Mansfeld and Dora Gad and landscape architects Miller–Blum, offers an instructive response in the intersection of old and new. The designers retained the traditional landscape frame, siting the complex of buildings overlooking the valley and the Monastery of the Cross. The valley was left largely undisturbed. The building complex adorns the hilltop as an acropolis, a modern cubist village, perhaps the best example of where the small, white structure of traditional Arab architecture found a sympathetic resonance in Bauhaus-inspired design. A steady modernist progression of paved spaces leads up to the entry. Water features were added later by Lawrence Halprin, along with Noguchi's design for the Billy Rose Sculpture Garden. The sequence also includes The Shrine of the Book that houses the Dead Sea Scrolls, and constitutes a walled court surrounded by rich plantings. The total ensemble of contrasting ancient and modern landscapes enhances the awareness of each. Perhaps the most modern feature is the road at the base of the valley, which Miller divided in two, diminishing its overall impact.

All design occurs within a set of forces that constrain and limit, as well as those that liberate and offer opportunity. The question is how to be creative within these parameters. Given the predominance of public work in Israel, the larger forces that set these limits are particularly significant. Public policy, planning, funding, and officials all carry weight. In a political system where municipalities have a degree of autonomy, the mayor is a key figure. Mayors Abba Hushi of Haifa and Meir Dizengoff (1861-1936) and Avraham Krinitzi (1886-1969) of Tel Aviv exerted significant influence on the design of their cities. Teddy Kollek (b. 1911), Jerusalem's mayor from 1965 to 1993, is world renowned for his stewardship of the development of Jerusalem after its reunification following the Six-Day War in 1967. Landscape architects especially benefited, for the design of parks and gardens were fundamental to Kollek's vision of the city. Public funds were supplemented by international fundraising for the Jerusalem Foundation that supported dozens of projects. The model is common in Israel, and many fine projects such as campuses, schools, gardens, and *tayalot* were created and continue to be supported by private funds and donations.

Assuming the mantle of civic leadership, mayors often presume themselves to be arbiters of popular taste and have tended towards the colorful, extravagant, and over designed. Like many Israelis they favor a westernized style, which is often eroneously equated with progress. The effusively planted entries to many towns epitomize this phenomenon. While mayors are often conservative in taste, they also desire innovation. It has a political dimension, for most leaders want to be seen as progressive, and have their city appear new, up-to-date, and led by a person who is spending the municipality's money well. It is well known that in any pre-election period maintenance improves and flowerbeds appear overnight.

Government design standards influence the national character. There are national standards for parks, playgrounds, housing, shelters, and roadways, all of which influence design. There is a conventional image of each and it is promulgated. Given the dramatic imperative to construct housing, the work of the Ministry of Housing has a bearing on virtually all development. A change in the Ministry's approach to design was signaled in 1985 with the appointment of Ilana Ofir as its first in-house landscape architect. The goal became to have landscape architects involved in projects from their conception, and this became policy in

The plan for a square for Beit Hillel (1997) in the Galilee by Greenstein and Har-Gil represents the intersection of the valley's agricultural grid with the pattern of the Jordan River expressed as a "river" of pebbles and planting. It is a modest example, but it is extremely sensitive to its site and situation in its formal metaphors, historic preservation (an old water tower was preserved as well), and use of materials.

The traditionalist and classicist seek what is timeless, tried and true, but embedded in the place. In a rapidly changing society this classical urge for consistency and stability is easily understood. There is a deeper resonance as well. Aharon Kashtan, who came originally from Warsaw and taught architectural history at Technion for many years, said that his Zionism had an element of classicism to it, for a return to Israel was also a return to the roots of the classical world of the Mediterranean. There are residual echoes of the ancient conflict between Hellenism and traditional Judaism, the worldly, and the provincial.

As landscape architect Anne Spirn has written in *The Language of Landscape*: "In composing landscapes, humans participate in, and elaborate on, dialects of place, perhaps even choosing to depart from and replace the "rules" with a grammar of a

top: Keren Kayemet in Pardes. Gan Hamoshava, Rishon-le-Tzion. (Museum of Rishon-le-Tzion)

bottom: Gan Hamoshava. Rishon-le-Tzion. Moshe Birchental.

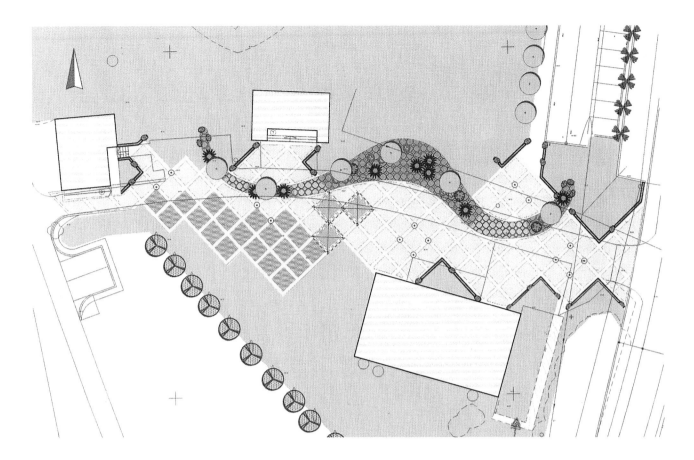

Plan. Beit Hillel.
(Greenstein-Har-Gil)

different place and time, or one simply invented, idiosyncratic. The landscape of
every place engenders expectation. When form deviates from that norm there is a
reason—conscious or unconscious, intended or unintended. Designers who know
grammar break the rule deliberately for the sake of meaning, for the sake of powerful new expression or new relationships. But designers who flout the rule without reason or in ignorance produce, at best gibberish, a jumble of forms and
materials, of meanings that add up to no meaning, like many landscapes today; at
worst potential catastrophe."

The conscious quest for an expressive language continues. It is still a struggle to
root work more firmly in place. A small but growing avant-garde is experimenting
and reworking landscape icons in form, materials, and symbols. The avant-garde
also looks locally and abroad for what speaks of the present and the future, but
often finding different sources and gleaning different lessons. They place experi-
ment and heightened awareness before the comforts of conventional design. The
variety of responses to the *genius loci* includes responding to what is present, but
also willfully introducing a new spirit.

Gan Ha'ahava in Ganei Tikva (1996) by Moria-Sekely (Yael Moria b. 1955,
David Sekely b. 1944) draws from diverse sources, inside and outside the country.
The outside influences are varied: the massive, brightly colored walls and playful
waterworks are inspired by the Mexican architect Luis Barragan, but they also
recall the walls of Mar Saba Monastery in the Judean Desert. A modernistic, blue
pergola stretches along the street and a sunken *giardini segreto* is found on the garden's hilltop, an inversion of a watertower on a distant hill. The requisite stepped

amphitheater is present, but it rises up from the street and looks across to a plaza and water feature in front of City Hall. The whole complex straddles the community's main street with apartment blocks and homes bordering the park.

At the north entry to Beersheva, adjacent to the first housing projects of the city, is Hadassah Park (1996) by Tichnun Nof in collaboration with the sculptor Israel Hadani. Hadani's sculptural environment is playful. A village, or more aptly a camp of conical towers, it consists of a set of stone tents. Built on a former dump, each tent is distinct and built of a melange of materials, a construction yard transformed into an artistic creation of concrete blocks, bricks, pergolas, vines, and glass. One even has a periscope to look out at the surrounding desert. The structures offer shade, a variety of microclimates, protection, and identity. It is also a potential landmark. Illuminated at night it beckons from the roadway.

The pace and pattern of change has been dramatic and not entirely beneficent. Looking back at more than a half century of Israel's development and design practice, Lippa Yahalom, in a mature reflection, said that he yearned for what he called "the wisdom the poor," which is ignored. He was referring to the indigenous landscape and its character, a respect for its qualities, and wished that the transformation of landscape would be undertaken with more deference to existing conditions. What he would do if he were reincarnated, he said, is return to the tra-

top: Gan Ha'ahava. Ganei Tikva. Moria-Sekely.

middle: Hadassah Park. North entry to Beersheva. Tichnun Nof and Israel Hadani, sculptor.

bottom: Garden. Lippa Yahalom.

ditional and indigenous: dig out all the rocks that were brought from the hills to the gardens; rebuild the *kurkar* sea cliffs with a natural landscape, dunes, and vineyards; in the coastal plain remove the green cover and let the sand roam; and remove olive trees from along roads and put them back where they belong. His own work often upheld these values, but belying his critical comments he also offered evidence to the contrary. His reflections were uttered sitting in his elegant garden which combines the modern and traditional. It has native and imported plants, a fountain bubbling in one corner, and a metal pergola overhead.

Preservation/ Transformation

*Until yesterday, we were still standing, our faces towards the future, and swearing
to make the desert bloom. Today we stand, our faces to the future, and we are begging
to stop, and to leave the desert alone. One or two more upward swings and we will
be left without even one desert, not to make bloom and not to keep.*
    —S. Yizhar

*With what past, if that is the case, are they brandishing a threat against you?
With what they call, in their ignorance, love? Do they know what love is? For if
they knew, they would have spared one grove, so we could play hide-and-seek
in her, or one pine thicket, to which we would lead in secret the beloved one.*
    *Or on a roof, without poles and hot water boilers, that we will engrave on it
our names, two by two, male and female, as he created them.*
    —Emile Habibi

Landscape history is embedded in our personal experience, our environmental
autobiography. Israeli adults, and even children, know well the measures of landscape change. Many recall places from childhood, school, or the army—fields,
orchards, oaks, *wadis,* and villages—which were favorite, even secret places, later
turned into roads, housing, and settled communities. Well loved landscapes testify
to a complex set of associations. In these places the landscape speaks directly to
individuals, the story is strong, and the language effective. What does it say?

There is nostalgia for and a desire to preserve at least remnants of the past.
Some characteristics of this landscape have achieved an iconic status: scenes of
pardesim surrounded by cypress trees; villages clustered on hilltops; groves of olives;
and the landscape of kibbutz and moshav, small houses, red roofs, a water tower,
orchard, and fields. Many of these images are part of the traditional Israeli *landschaft* that is threatened. Some of these places, especially Biblical sites, have a resonance reaching back beyond Israel. Others are purely personal. I vividly recall my
first smell of orange blossoms in the Sharon. In Kiryat Shmona a park locally
known as "The Jungle" is part of every child's history in that community. I have
watched children play in the *wadis* of Haifa, building tree houses in places soon
slated for development.

Two extreme responses characterize a designer's relationship to the land. On
the one hand there is a humility and reluctance to transform the landscape, a reti-
cence to introduce anything alien or new. This is borne of a deep respect for the
place. Such restraint should not be confused with lack of initiative. Often it takes
greater imagination and perseverance to resist unnecessary or superficial change.
Such work—in preventing or relocating development in making a site accessible,
or in the subtle framing and orchestration of an experience—may pass unnoticed.
On the other hand, there is bold transformation through dramatic physical or spatial manipulation. This may entail making key decisions in terms of revealing elements of a site, a careful editing of the site, or even removing the soil itself to reveal
what is below. Design can be a way of exposing the true richness of a place,

allowing people to see and experience its full potential, leaving it to the users to complete the picture and design through their activity.

The landscape always remains at once the constant physical framework *and* the site of exceptionally rapid transformation. Without a historical perspective it is difficult to comprehend how conditions have changed in a half-century of Israel's statehood. There is a profound and continuing challenge and dilemma of building a modern nation for millions of people. In the 1950s Israel was engaged in a process of nation building. The absorption of immigrants was the primary task. This encompassed the building of shelter and communities, establishing an economy, and feeding a population. Two desires were often in conflict: one was to rapidly build a nation, a society; the other to respond to pressing human needs. A secondary task was to accomplish this as best as possible with an awareness of the nation's future. Zvi Miller says the priorities were clear. First they had to create the normal conditions of life.

The classic expression of this ideological conflict between preservation and transformation is apparent in the idea of making the desert bloom. Poet Natan Alterman (1910-1970) wrote approvingly: "We'll attire you in a dress of concrete and cement." Early settlements were spoken of as "camps" and landscape architects and gardeners spoke of "improving the camp." In retrospect, it provides a wonderful image of giving stability to a place of impermanence. It meant both making a place better and making life function with greater ease, but also with some amenity. They used another idiom, and began to use the term "*noi*" as *gan noi,* which equals ornament. Many landscape architects began as *gan noi,* on kibbutzim. Thus places were improved with trees and shrubs and also kept fresh in the dusty landscape.

A change in priorities came only gradually. The founding of the SPNI (Society for the Protection of Nature in Israel) in 1954 was a key landmark. After the Six-Day War in 1967 there was a period of optimism and energy. Jerusalem was unified and it was a period of tremendous building. No longer pioneering, it was an era of consolidation. As population increased along with modernization, especially mass automobile ownership, the pressures for protection of the land expanded. That these changes have occurred within the memory of most persons accentuates their effect. National Park landscape architect Racheli Merchav noted a shifting, if not universal, change in attitude from a landscape ensuring survival to ensuring the survival of the landscape. Yoav Sagi, chairman of the SPNI called it "nothing less than a fundamental change in the relationship between people and the land: from a culture of conquest to the culture of stewardship." From an era of exalting and honoring the necessity of building and the creation of communities, Israel has entered an era when it needs to address carefully the husbandry of its landscape resources. There are hopeful indicators. The now famous SPNI campaign of the mid-1960s to stop the common practice of picking wildflowers was enormously successful. In 1988 the Ministry of the Environment was created as a cabinet position and in 1994 a portion of the Huleh, the marsh and lake north of the Sea of Galilee that was drained by the pioneers, was re-flooded, a symbolic landmark of the change in landscape values. While it may have outlived its pioneering ethos, the urge to develop and fill up spaces continues like a hard-to-break habit. Israelis (and they are not alone here) find it difficult to understand an "empty" space. Leaving things alone is not easy. There is a continual tension, a dialectic between landscape appreciation and landscape transformation. Israelis take visitors with equal pride to ancient villages and new neighborhoods, to the pristine desert and the desert made to bloom.

Landscape architecture reflects changing ideas about nature as design demonstrates human understanding of our place in nature. The Israel Defense Force's central cultural role is apparent here as both landowner and client. Following the Camp David accords with Egypt in 1979 Shlomo Aronson worked with the army and the Nature Reserves guiding the relocation of bases to the Negev after the Sinai was returned to Egypt. Gideon Sarig performed a similar task in the north. The Nature Reserves, then headed by Avram Yaffe, was instrumental in getting the army to include landscape criteria in addition to military necessity. Accomplished rapidly and under extraordinarily difficult pressure these are decisions that shape landscapes for generations. Ironically, the military is acting as a de-facto preserver of land, especially in the Negev, along the coastline and with their bases even in cities. Land they now occupy may in the future be open to the public. (Access to 30% of the Mediterranean coastline and 55% of the Negev is restricted for security purposes.)

Oftentimes this landscape seems to resemble a *balagan* (Hebrew for a ruckus or messy situation). Like many of its inhabitants this is a landscape without patience. It has been described as a high tension landscape where life is lived within a pressure cooker. On the down side of this *balagan* is an unfinished, messy, always-under-construction quality, places left unfinished with pipes sticking out of the ground awaiting connection and building materials piled or just discarded. It has a certain matter-of-factness, like the bottom of a closet. It is a fragmented landscape, a lot of loose pieces not always knit together, places begun and not completed. The positive side of this *balagan* characteristic is an inventive ad-hoc quality and what cultural historian Joachim Schlor in his book, *Tel Aviv* (1999), calls "the beauty of the unfinished." In the course of time temporary tent communities (*ma'abarot*) became permanent settlements, streets were paved, and de facto open spaces became parks. In recent years it has become necessary to preserve what was only recently established. Development and affluence is eating away at public open space: cars are parked on sidewalks, buildings are constructed in previously protected open spaces, and streets are widened.

Landscape construction. Lavon.

There are few local "red lines" as barriers to intrusion.

Almost universally contemporary landscape architects are voices calling for restraint, understanding, softness, patience, and understatement, in contrast to design and construction which is too often bombastic, insensitive, and out of scale and context. Shlomo Aronson speaks of the need for a "calm" in design as a partial antidote, or at least respite, from the omnipresent tensions of Israeli life. In opposition to much contemporary work that is over-

designed, Aronson seeks "an uncluttered solution" to problems. "Make it simple," he says, "quiet, friendly." His "wish is to provide the simplest approach at this stage; to provide serenity in our frenetic and complicated local."

The physical expression of Aronson's calm is a form of classicism, a respect for time-honored verities of a carefully honed sense of proportion and harmony, that there is a fitting solution and response to a problem and situation. It also implies the creation of a replicable language that can be employed in diverse situations and that is identifiable as part of a larger coherent system. The refinement and elegance and meticulous attention to craft, evident in his firm's work, are aspects of classic quality.

Braudo-Maoz, partners Alisa Braudo and Ruth Maoz (formerly Itzuvim with Tamar Darrel-Fossfeld), has an explicitly "green" attitude, with an acute awareness of the shortage of open space. They see themselves as mediators between the more extreme "greens" and builders, attempting to keep land preserved, open and interconnected. They are against purely cosmetic greening, what Zvi Miller calls "make-up." Like most landscape architects they try to have an input from the inception of a project, to change attitudes. The pressures are very high. Tamar Darrel describes everything as being pocketed and parceled and made into islands. The hinterland is gone, and it is now a question of what do you keep, what do you destroy and build up again? She notes that it was now hard to find a place to build a fire for Lag Ba Omer, a small but telling indicator. At Sukkot people historically cut palm fronds to build a *sukkah*, but to protect their trees municipalities now provide branches. There are few deserted or undeveloped places and the remaining open spaces become even more critical. Yigal Steinmetz, city landscape architect for Rishon-le-Tzion, urges the need for modesty and the necessity to act with more respect towards the landscape.

Different designs reveal diverse approaches to the desire to protect, preserve, and transform. Zvi Dekel and Joseph Segal worked on early national park designs in the Galilee at the water-based projects of Tel Dan and the Tanur. The design for Aqua Bella/Ein Hemed (1963–1973) just west of Jerusalem was literally a revelation of an ancient spring and crusader site. The concept was to recreate a medieval paradisiacal environment, one that existed only in history books. But first it had to be revealed and excavated, for its exact location and configuration were unknown. Dekel and Segal acted as sculptors scraping away generations of soil to reveal the site's foundation, the spring and stream, making the stone and water visible. They carefully terraced the site to make it functional, the gentle slopes acting as a modest amphitheater to the stream and in the process creating places of repose and enchantment. The desire was to integrate and not to impose, a conscious reluctance to introduce anything alien in materials, forms, or character. It is a subtle integration and accommodation of old and new at all levels. The imagery is a mix of motifs. It is pastoral, archeological, and recreational.

Two examples in Tel Aviv of the intersection of preservation and transformation are expressed at Gan Yaakov and Gan Dubnov. Gan Yaakov (1964) was constructed on the site of a small hill crowned by three large shikma trees (*Ficus sycomorus*), remnants of trees once native to the sands of Tel Aviv. When the new cultural complex was built a new garden was constructed around the trees.

Designed by architect Yaakov Rechter (whose father Zeev planned the buildings) with plantings by Avraham Karavan, the character of the intersection is fascinating. At the original grade the huge trees form one canopy over the space. At the same time the entire park is set within the structural grid of the surrounding architecture, a concrete grid that spans the area and is festooned with vegetation. The frame supports climbing wisteria and envelops the visitors. The intersection of concrete, building, grid, and theater (culture in a refined form), over and around the earlier layer of native vegetation (the stylized use of grasses accentuates this aspects) and a garden, provides a welcome respite in the

above: Aqua Bella. Segal-Dekal.

left: Aqua Bella. Segal-Dekal.

city, a lush urban oasis. The pathways are a bit mazelike and the scale deceptive. The added vertical layers make it feel much larger than it is.

Gan Dubnov is a 1990 renewal by Gideon Sarig of an older garden originally designed by Avraham Karavan. Its extensions link a residential area and the new cultural center of the Opera House and the Tel Aviv Museum. The older neighborhood park was redesigned, integrating its mature canopy of ficus and jacaranda trees and connecting it to a new roof garden atop an accompanying parking lot. One garden is residential, pastoral, and informal, consisting of grass and stone; the other is a roof garden featuring concrete, planters, and an iconic planting of citrus, olives, bougainvillea, and grapes. Beneath the trees a wide wavy limestone path describes the garden edges in simple, elegant fashion. Beneath the trees are found a playground area, sitting area and a fountain, and an inverted pyramid with steps leading into a pool with rough vertical slabs as counterpoint. The pool has multiple inspirations: traditional tanks found in *pardesim*, Solomon's pools near Bethlehem, and pools accompanying springs in the hills around Jerusalem and the Galilee. The park integrates high culture, a city

above: Gan Yaakov.
Tel Aviv. Yaakov Rechter
and Avraham Karavan.

right: Pool. Gan Dubnov.
Tel Aviv. Gideon Sarig.

park, and an adjoining neighborhood. On a visit, dogs were romping, children and parents were in the play area, old people sat on benches, couples lay on the grass, and a girl posed in the fountain, all signs of a successful place.

Pathway. Gan Dubnov. Tel Aviv. Gideon Sarig.

At the spectacular setting of Timna National Park (1977) in the Arava, Segal-Dekel employed the lightest of touches for maximum effect. Roads were deftly laid in the desert, deferring to the lay of the land, and stairs and railings were added only as needed. The integrity of the desert landscape is maintained. The basic concept was a semi-loop road with fingers probing the surrounding landscape. The

Trail with railing. Timna. Segal-Dekal.

idea was to have a road that not only provided access, but also offered views and revealed the desert. Zvi Dekel, a desert lover, wanted to reveal the site and have visitors discover a sense of the desert en route. The only plantings are at the entrance, and all services are concentrated in the lake area, a seasonal water body created by a dam from older mining operations.

A place is preserved because it has value. It may be historic, social, cultural, or the maintenance of a natural system. Landscape architects have been instrumental in historic preservation in

Ceasaria. The landscape design in the vicinity of the Crusader walls was by Yahalom-Zur. The recent transformation, including the seafront promenade bordering the newly excavated hippodrome, is by Shlomo Aronson.

Avdat, Shivta, Old Jaffa, Caesarea, Safed, Rosh Pinna, Acco, Peki'in, Nazareth, Ein Kerem, Ziporri, and many other locales. Even the recent past is being incorporated into design. At Gan HaShnaim (1992) in the Ajami neighborhood of Jaffa, Fuchs renovated the first electrical transformer in Tel Aviv-Jaffa and used it as part of the entry plaza for the garden.

The dialectics of preservation and transformation, of tradition and innovation, are accentuated at "historic" sites. Yet that *all* sites are historic is the premise of the best design work. The existing is often an unknown situation, only to be revealed when the site is excavated. Construction is often halted and designs modified when archeologists are brought in to determine the significance of a find. At the Suzanne Delal Center in Tel Aviv a well was discovered during construction and then immediately incorporated into the design.

Avdat. This national park site in Negev was first a Nabatean and then a Byzantine city.

Reclamation and restoration is a particular kind of transformation that brings back a previous condition, but into a changed context. Often it represents a change in philosophy or ideology or the "discovery" of the hitherto unseen possibility in a place. In Israel's brief modern history attitudes have shifted or at least become more ambivalent. The desert is thus a place to be made green *and* to be preserved and appreciated. The Huleh swamps were drained, to be partially restored by a subsequent generation. Recent conflicts between "greens" and developers are only the politicization of the battles between preservation and transformation.

Covered trail in the Huleh swamp. Gideon Levinger, landscape architect for the Nature Reserves Authority.

Givat-Aliya Beach (1991). Jaffa. Israel Lederman. The design leads down to the sea, and its terraces, steps, arched viewpoints, and details pay homage to the traditional architecture of Jaffa.

There is a growing recognition of both heritage and resources. This includes the realization of the significance of the landscape and designs created by Israel's pioneers, the appreciation of *recent* history and heritage. Areas such as Tel Aviv's Neve Tzedek or Florentine and Haifa's Hadar are being rediscovered and, in cases, gentrified with its attendant problems. The beach has always been a place of paramount importance in Israel, and the urban waterfronts of Acco, Jaffa, Haifa, Ashkelon, and Ashdod are slowly being reclaimed for people. At the local level it is the street which is reclaimed. The Dutch concept of the *woonerf*, a street, which mixes people and cars, recreation and living space with primacy given to the pedestrian, has found a welcome home in Israel. The nation's first *woonerf* was in Ramla by Gideon Sarig and Arie Rachamimoff. It was part of a program of neighborhood rehabilitation. They were subsequently incorporated into new community designs in Ramat Hasharon, Raanana (1980), and Kochav Yair (1982).

Much of the experience of community happens as pedestrians walk from place to place. This activity is celebrated in the *midrachov*, a form of street reclamation, which has had much success. The pedestrian street has dual sources. The first is found in the traditional town. The historic cores of Jerusalem, Safed, and Jaffa were all walking cities and they can barely accommodate modern automobile traffic.

top: Ben Yehuda Street. Jerusalem.

middle: Ramat Gan. Sderot HaYeled.

bottom: View of the surrounding landscape from Tefen.

Second is the desire to recapture the street from the onslaught of the automobile. For example, Jerusalem's Ben Yehuda Street was redesigned as a *midrachov* (1983). In Ramat Gan Sderot HaYeled is a grand, shaded link that connects parks. Ben Gurion Street in Haifa, which runs through the center of the historic German Colony, is now a pedestrian promenade that is a grand entry to the Bahai Gardens on the slopes of the Carmel.

At the grander scale there is a relationship between traditional landscape structure, materials, and use and the emergent landscape. Tefen is an industrial and research park in the Galilee designed by Tichnun Nof (1983). Its core is a series of structures linked by an arcade surrounding a grand pastoral meadow and rocky outcrop. The buildings house the imaginative combination of incubator industries and an art museum. The entire site also acts as a sculpture garden. As one looks out from Tefen's hilltop location, the traditional landscape gives the character and flavor, but it is transforming as the economy and the methods of agriculture change. Landscape architects can use and learn from what is appealing and resonant in that landscape, in the texture and character of much of the rural and village scene. A type of landscape is passing, but its qualities need not be lost. The scale of walls between fields, the grids of olives and oranges, the dense shade of the *pardes*, the smell of blossoms, the changing colors and palette of the earth as it is plowed, the remnant stones in a field—these qualities are part of both the more traditional settlements of Arabs and Druze and the modern settlements of kibbutzim and moshavim. Their imagery of the water tower or dense settlement surrounded by a ring of orchards or fields is now part of modern Israeli imagery and collective memory. The question is what designers can

Ben Gurion Street (1998). Haifa. Here the historic buildings were preserved with great attention to making places for people. (Drawing, Greenstein-Har-Gil)

do with this in a time when the craft of landscape has transformed. In the construction of a new community one can't miss the scale of machinery and landscape transformation. Hillsides are carved like clay into terraces, giant stones are extracted and transported. Equally remarkable is how quickly the brutality of the process is ameliorated. As places become habited, a different scale rapidly emerges as people occupy places, planting and personalization occur, and daily life enlivens the scene.

Midrachov. Rishon-le-Tzion (1987). Moshe Birchental.

N ISRAEL time is thick and deep. Culture is layered over millennia and is contentious. Nature here is both primordial, a *nof bereshit* (landscape "in the beginning") and the product of human intervention since recorded history. The past is
palpably present in the double meaning of the term: it is now and it is here. The
landscape is, in Kevin Lynch's terms, a rich temporal collage, an expression of different times in an overlay of spaces and land uses.

Time has a cultural dimension. The forms, scale, and characteristics of materials
that distinguish landscape design—soil, rocks, water, plants, and sky—have temporal dimensions. The skill and artistry of landscape architecture lies not only in the
manipulation of landscape space, but also in the design of landscape time. There is
an artistry, both bold and subtle, in the reflections in a pool, the welcome shade
found beneath a tree on a hot summer day, seasonal floral displays, and the slow
maturation of a grove of olives.

The goal is how to make these varying temporal scales visible and to reveal the
interconnections. Sensitivity to the Israeli clock and calendar is essential. The daily
rhythm follows Mediterranean patterns. The work day begins early and the school
day ends early, especially for younger children. A mid-afternoon rest or nap is
commonplace. Shops close and reopen in late afternoon and remain open into the
evening, enlivening commercial districts. Until recently most people worked a
six-day week and schools still adhere to this timetable. In the agricultural sector,
on kibbutzim and moshavim, the traditional schedule is still maintained. Yet as
home and work have become more distant and air conditioning has become commonplace, a 9–5 schedule is gradually becoming the norm.

The ritual cycles of Judaism, Islam, and Christianity are embedded in Israel's
calendar. Each faith's time is etched in the landscape. The movement of people,
what they are doing, where activity takes place, and what is proscribed, encouraged, forbidden, or demanded are influenced by this calendar. Only when Israelis
spend time outside of the country do they realize their unique situation.

Chapter 10

Shaping Time

*We're a country that
has no time for time,
the future is so close.*
—Gideon Sarig

*opposite page: Beit Shean.
Moria-Sekely. Tichnun Nof
did the original plan, pre-
excavation. Yael Moria is
now the landscape architect.
The interpretive experience
is choreographed and the
harsh climate acknowledged
in deftly spaced areas for
gathering. The multiple layers of Neolithic, Roman,
Byzantine, and contempo-
rary worlds are signified in
form. (Moria-Sekely)*

The Jewish calendar is dominant. Abraham Joshua Heschel has noted that Judaism is a religion of time and that Jewish ritual is an architecture of time. This is reflected most dramatically in the weekly continuity of *Shabbat*. A definable *Shabbat* landscape begins Friday afternoon as people leave work early, do last minute shopping, and flower sellers and their stands appear in abundance. On *Shabbat* the pace changes in a dramatic demonstration of divergent landscape behavior between the more secular and more observant communities.

At the opposite end of the temporal scale, an awareness of the stratigraphy of time is basic to comprehending the Israeli landscape. Any section through the landscape can be a revelation. To the conventional analysis of design in Israel one must add the archeological. Archeology, a popular passion, acts as an inspiration. It is the historical record, and its methods and sensibility are part of the vocabulary of design. The archeological excavation, so commonplace in Israel, epitomizes this process. As excavation proceeds successive layers are exposed: the uppermost strata is documented and then destroyed in the process

top: Buying flowers for Shabbat. Mahane Yehuda Market. Jerusalem.

bottom: Archeological excavation. Zippori.

of revealing lower layers. Everything in Israel is built atop something else. Excavations expose cross sections of strata, which knowledgeable readers can interpret. There are always questions of how to intervene and design within a historical context. The boundary between old and new is everywhere, as is the issue of site interpretation, access, and integrity. The Antiquities Act of 1978, under the auspices of the Ministry of Education, authorized the protection of historic and archeological sites before 1700. The date itself is problematic, for it places subsequent sites, old by the standards of many other parts of the world, in jeopardy.

Landscape architects have employed an array of design strategies in their presentation and interpretation of the past. The use of traditional materials and forms are acts of continuity, the transmission of a legacy, and the question of when and how to introduce the contemporary as counterpoint or connective tissue is basic. Elements can be preserved, retained as much as possible in their original condition and location, or they may be restored, brought back to a moment in time. Time can be recovered, displayed, and interpreted with plaques, maps, routes, guides, and text, but the past can become integral to design in more subtle ways as well. Historic qualities and character can be sources of inspiration: embodied or symbolized in new forms and places, a spirit or quality captured and reinterpreted.

Dead Sea lines on the road between Arad and the Dead Sea. Shlomo Aronson.

Map. Sherman Park. Jerusalem. Shlomo Aronson.

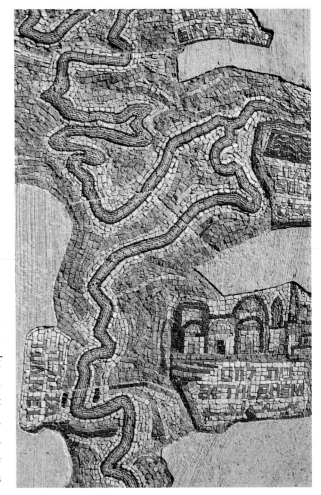

As the first phase of a possible Lowest Park in the World Project, the roads from Arad and Jerusalem to the Dead Sea have a series of sea level markers visible from the roadside, designed by Shlomo Aronson (1996). Each of these takes the form of a terraced stone wall with a blue-tiled stripe running across its length. They are hundreds of feet long and sit on the contours of cliffs and as along the roadside. These are maps at a one-to-one scale and they dramatize the descent to the sea. The markers are the first step towards a design language for the park which Aronson notes may later use salt. (The markers have an added resonance, for in Israel lines on the land and borders of all kinds are critical: frontiers, red lines, green lines.)

At the Castel, located just off the entry road to Jerusalem, Shlomo Aronson preserved the military landscape which was a key part of the battle for Jerusalem in the Independence War. Atop the hill overlooking the ruins of trenches and the historic battlefield is a map of troop movements cast in concrete. Sherman Park in East Talpiot, Jerusaelm, also by Aronson, is a modest neighborhood park with rolling lawn. A terraced belvedere sits over a Second Temple aqueduct marked on a large mosaic map. One can stand atop it and trace its course as the view of the landscape unfolds towards Herodiun and Bethlehem to the south.

top: *Christian pilgrims at Ceasaria.*

bottom: *Taghba. The north shore of the Sea of Galilee, the traditional site of the miracle of the loaves and fishes.*

Designs confront all ages, but all times do not carry equal weight. Prehistory is represented in the caves of the Carmel, and sites of Roman, Byzantine, Christian, Crusader, Ottoman, Arab, and British occupancy and rule are all given their due. Israeli landscape architecture, however, reflects its own priorities. The emphasis has been on the landscape of the Bible, the linkages to Jewish history, and the representation of the continuity between land and people. Biblical sites embody the great import of what took place here. This became vivid to me during my first Hanukah in Israel where the letters on the *dreidel* (the top spun at Hanukah) referred to *Nes-Gadol-Haya-Po*, a great miracle that happened "here," versus *Sham*, "there," that appears on all Diaspora *dreidels*. Only in Israel is the Bible also a travel guide, especially for pilgrims and tourists.

It is worth noting that Israel's tourist industry is sustained by pilgrims, half of whom are Christians who visit sites from the New Testament and seek literally to walk where Jesus did. These sites all have an accompanying landscape expectation: the Sea of Galilee, Nazareth, the hills of Galilee, and the Via Dolorosa through the streets of Jerusalem. The text engenders the hope that the modern landscape will look like its ancient description: a land of shepherds and their flocks, villages, olive groves, vineyards, and date palms, the whole set of places and landscape elements described in the Bible. As Israel has become increasingly modernized, that landscape, which did have a remarkable continuity over millennia, has largely disappeared. It has now become an object of preservation, made the more difficult as the traditional ways of life that sustained it have become more marginal. Landscape preservation and planning have an added impetus, for the significance of protecting and preserving places correspond not just to an historic record, but also to sacred texts.

In the 1980s and 1990s all the archeological national parks were redesigned: Beit Shean, Masada, Caesarea, Zippori, Beit Guvrin, Avdat, and Mamshit in collaborations among landscape architects, architects, archeologists, and the staff of the National Parks Authority. More sites were made physically accessible and their stories dramatized. Park Service landscape architect Racheli Merchav describes this as a period when more attention was given to preservation and the desire for designs which were "humbler." The question was how to respect and honor the

Beit Shean. Moria-Sekely. Tichnun Nof did the original plan, pre-excavation. (Moria-Sekely)

spirit of the place and allow its story to be told. These efforts were directed at particularizing each site and at the same time creating a more coherent national system. Outside intrusions were avoided and careful attention was given to a regional plant vocabulary. Practical considerations go hand in hand with more lofty goals. Parks were transformed to accommodate larger numbers of visitors and their added desires and demands for access, parking, picnicking, and more sophisticated interpretation. Treating these needs with equal quality elevated the significance of these aspects of the sites, so that they too are part of the landscape experience. At the archeological national parks interventions deftly choreograph the visitor's experience, and the choice of shape and material interprets the site.

David's Garden, adjacent to the Jaffa Gate of Jerusalem, was one of the first projects completed after the reunification of the city in 1967. Zvi Miller speaks of trying to create a "timeless" quality, especially through the use of stone. But what is meant by timeless? It means that the site's character is not bound to the present moment, but spans to the past and links to the future. This is an elusive but laudatory aspiration. Another Jerusalem site by Miller–Blum took a different approach: not timeless, but to freeze a moment *in* time. Ammunition Hill was a border outpost and the site of a key battle for Jerusalem in the 1967 war. The design concept was to preserve it, as much as possible, in its condition as a battlefield. After siting a museum on the hill and the requisite amphitheater for commemorative assemblies, the landscape was preserved largely as it was: the topography, trees, and most

Cardo (1983). Jerusalem. Aronson's first decade of work centered on the Old City of Jerusalem. He worked as landscape architect in the restoration of the Jewish Quarter and in integrating the newly excavated Roman Cardo to accommodate modern function. Aronson with Peter Bugod and Esther Niv-Krendel.

importantly the lines of trenches looking across what was a "no man's land" between Israeli and Jordanian territory. The current contrast between this battle-field and the surrounding housing blocks is striking.

Haim Kahanovitch's design for the Museum of Eretz Yisrael (1983) was an example of a more explicitly didactic landscape design. Built on the site of a *Tel Kassila* of Jewish and Roman settlements, the *tel* was integrated into the design. Working with the architect and the museum staff, Kahanovitch incorporated a portion of an excavated Roman road, a rebuilt aqueduct to run a mill, agricultural terraces, and an oil press in a series of outdoor exhibits.

*Museum of Eretz Yisrael.
Tel Aviv. (Drawing, Haim
Kahanovitch)*

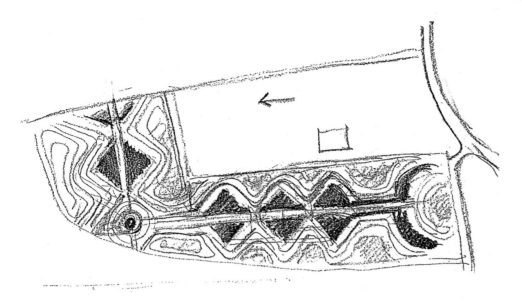

A more symbolic tactic is Dan Zur's design proposal for the main park of Herzliya. This is a historical narrative. The winner of a design competition, Zur's idea is to show the history of Herzliya through the park, using symbolic plantings and spaces representing the progress from a native landscape of oak groves to a moshava and *pardes* to a modern city.

Memory

The little park planted in memory of a boy
who fell in the war begins
to resemble him
as he was twenty-nine years ago.
Year by year they look more alike.
His old parents come almost daily
to sit on a bench
and look at him

And every night the memory on the garden
hums like a little motor:
During the day you can't hear it.
　—Yehuda Amichai

The landscape is both a repository of memory and a site for memorialization. These are part of the landscape's essential civic and public functions: sites for remembrance, ceremony, commemoration, and honor, and places that offer a setting for the most private and most public of emotions.

In *The Texture of Memory* (1993) James Young writes: "Israel's overarching national ideology and religion—perhaps its greatest 'natural resource'—may be memory itself: memory preserved, restored and codified." The Jewish imperative to remember the dead, expressed in the recitation of the Kaddish and memorial plaques on the walls of the synagogue, has a landscape counterpart. Memorials and memorial spaces are ubiquitous at all levels: personal, local, and national. They are located at virtually every school, community center, and kibbutz. They are found in parks, forests, and along roadsides, paying homage to those who have given their lives to the nation or the Jewish people. There are memorials to individuals and to groups. They commemorate events tragic and heroic. There are plaques, stones, sculptures, and always names. Young notes: "Over time these markers recede into consciousness, as part of an inanimate cityscape, but continue to function as the coordinates of daily life in Israel, even when unrecognized."

In places the landscape reads as a walk through *Yizkor-book* (a compilation of the deceased), a narrative of the imperative to remember. The memorials have become naturalized. As Young states: "By themselves, monuments are of little value, mere stones in the landscape. But as part of a nation's rites or the objects of a people's national pilgrimage, they are invested with national soul and memory ... They [memorials] suggest themselves as indigenous, even geological outcroppings in the national landscape; in time, such idealized memory grows as natural to the eye as the landscape in which it stands."

Any place can act as a mnemonic, recalling past experience, but some are explicitly designed as such. Surely these address the most intense and strongest of emotions. Their design necessitates care, the best and most thoughtful attention, and perhaps constitutes the most profound challenge to a designer's skill. The design should have a symbolic vocabulary accessible to visitors, but one that carries layers of meaning. Ideally it fosters a response which is intellectual, emotional, and, at times, even visceral.

The cemetery is a sacred ground, but even here there are new traditions. This is most apparent in the design of kibbutz cemeteries. In their intimate scale, materials, and plantings there is a lack of anonymity. A genuine sense of the collective family emerges. Visiting is like researching in *kibbutz* archives, which is more like walking into a family album than going to a library. In the memorial at Kibbutz Daphna (1981) by Haim Kahanovitch the desire was to create a space that was both intimate and open, set within the kibbutz, but also separate from it. Tributaries of the Jordan River run through the kibbutz. The water is diverted and creates a frame for the memorial, a moat, and a fern-encrusted wall that appears to weep and has within it memorial plaques. A planted earthen berm separates the memorial from the kibbutz proper and creates a small amphitheater facing the wall.

Sculpture is a traditional monument, but there are also sculptural environments where the boundary between the sculpture and the landscape is ambiguous. Enveloped by the sculptural space the spatial and kinesthetic experience is equal to the visual. On a hill north of Beersheva is Dani Karavan's Negev Memorial (1963–1968), a work of sculpture, architecture, and landscape. Constructed around

top: Memorial.
Kibbutz Daphna.
Haim Kahanovitch.

bottom: Cemetery. Kibbutz
Sde Eliyahu.

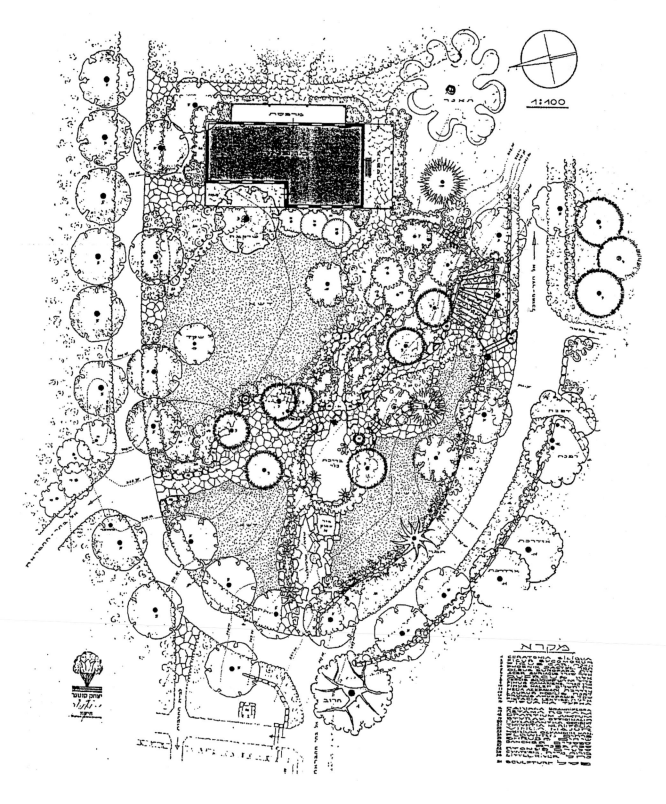

חניתה, גן-הזכרון

Memorial Garden (1959). Hanita. Yitchak Kutner. (Gideon Kutner)

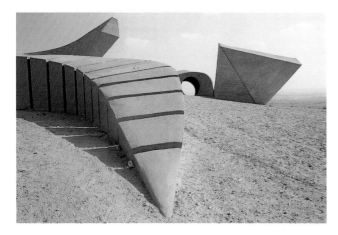

top left: *Negev Memorial. Beersheva. Dani Karavan.*

top right: *The Memorial for Intelligence Corps Fallen (1982). Ramat HaSharon. Architects B. Baruch and J. Salamon. The memorial is in the form of a maze. The competition-winning design is a sandstone labyrinth of walls with the names of the fallen. It is set within a grove of eucalyptus that interpenetrates the site. The contrast of geometries, materials, colors, and association is striking.*

left: *Yahalom-Zur with Y. Yanai (head of the National Parks Authority) placing salvaged armored vehicles along the road to Jerusalem as a memorial to those who fell to keep this passage open in the War of Independence. The use of actual vehicles, but painted, in the actual location of the battle acts as a mute and daily reminder of the sacrifice (1954). (Dan Zur)*

Memorial site to Rabin in Tel Hai College (1997). Tali Tuch and Tami Weiner Saragossi. The mature carob trees were already present at the site. The crushed basalt ground plane, ribbon walls, and basalt sculpture were introduced. (Doron Horowitz)

a narrative, it tells the story of the Negev Brigade from the War of Independence. The historical events are inscribed in the concrete forms of the monument, but these also construct a language, one unique in Karavan's oeuvre. The design crowns the low-rise hill overlooking a landscape that Karavan felt looked the same as it did in Abraham's day. At the summit the sculptural forms of the monument rise out of the ground. They create their own archetypal architecture of passage, cave, tower, dome, and undulation. The primary elements of the desert prevail: the sharp focused light, the contrast of sun and shade, a line of water, a lone tree, and the sound of the wind.

Zvi Dekel of Tichnun Nof and Dani Karavan's collaboration in Hadera is a deft combination of a memorial to the fallen and a commemoration of the founders of Hadera. The design subtly tells the community's history. A central axial path follows a line of palms that date from a planting by Aaron Ahronson that had been obscured by subsequent vegetation. This axis unites three areas. The first is a civic plaza which fronts the library and the *Yad Lebanim* (memorial for fallen soldiers) which Karavan built around an olive tree. The plaza also has pillars of iron inscribed with names of the fallen. The path then leads through an area of sand, the material underlying the city, and a swampy area with huge eucalyptus trees and a monument to the founders who had drained the swamps to create the city. Beyond that is a *pardes* evocative of the next phase of the area's history. The entire site is hedged, and perhaps appropriately fronts the city's recent history, a shopping center.

There is landscape of martyrology. Jerusalem's Mount of Remembrance and its paired hillsides of Har Herzl and Yad Vashem, like the paired holidays of Yom Ha Atzmaut (Independence Day) and Yom Hazikaron (Memorial Day), are physical embodiments of this duality. It is the twinning of martyrs/victims and heroes, destruction and redemption. These are among the most powerful landscape designs in Israel. The processional aspect of each is critical, as the emotional drama and collective weight of tragedy and history are compounded as one progresses through the series of monuments and spaces.

Garden of the Founders and Memorial Park (1993). Hadera. Dani Karavan and Zvi Dekel. (Tichnun Nof)

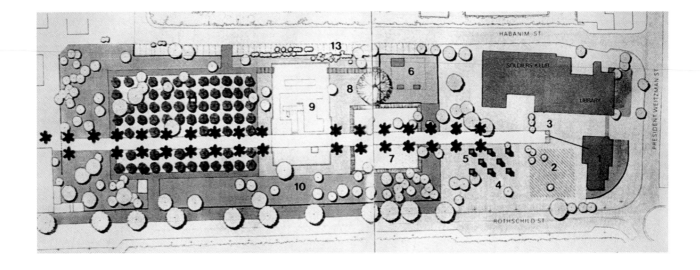

A 1950 competition for the design of a Tomb for Theodor Herzl and the surrounding park was won by architect Joseph Klarwein. The final design evolved over time under many hands, including landscape architects J. Nitzan, Y. Kahaner and Avraham Yehuda. On the slopes of the hill is the national military cemetery with the Herzl's grave and those of presidents and Zionist leaders on the hilltop. A national shrine, the tomb's spaces have an intimate quality. The design builds in

left: Har Herzl. Jerusalem. Graves beneath a forest canopy.

below: Har Herzl. Jerusalem. Overview. 1968 photograph.

increments. The mount has been terraced and densely planted. The canopy of trees, stone work, steps and the uniform military grave sites unify the individual graves and designated memorial areas into a profound sense of collective identity.

Historian Saul Friedlander has written: "one of the most explicit arenas where the mythic pattern of cosmic evil and redemption, of death and rebirth, is enacted in the construction of sites dedicated to the memory of the Shoah." The National Memorial Authority Act of 1953 mandated construction of Yad Vashem, Israel's national memorial to the Holocaust. Since then a succession of memorials and museums have been constructed on the site. The entry to Yad Vashem is a walk down an allée of trees known as the Avenue of the Righteous Gentiles. Each tree is planted in honor of a gentile who saved a Jew during the Holocaust.

The Valley of the Destroyed Communities has taken its place as a culmination in the sequence of spaces at Yad Vashem. The designer team, Yahalom-Zur, won an invited competition in 1978. The project took fourteen years to complete. While the valley is in memory of those who died

top: Har Herzl. Yitzak Rabin's grave. Jerusalem. Design of gravestone by Moshe Safdie. Since Rabin's assassination his grave has become a pilgrimage site.

bottom: Avenue of the Righteous Gentiles. Yad Vashem. Jerusalem.

in Europe, it is constructed in a landscape language (a spatial form and use of materials) that links the dead to Israel, both to the land and the nation. From an upper terrace visitors look down towards the valley. It is like an aerial view over a miniature canyon. A path snakes down to the walled entry. Excavated out of bedrock the memorial is a passage through a constructed maze of stone walls ten meters high, with the only exterior view up to the sky with vegetation just glimpsed atop the walls. Yahalom-Zur said the memorial should not be a garden open to the sky. The walls are stone blocks which frame and support tablets (or scrolls) of the names of 5,000 communities.

While it is a unique design, it does draw upon other places and that is part of its power. Multiple sources of inspiration were filtered into the design and speak to Yahalom-Zur's effort to create a place of importance. The valley resonates at many levels, communicating to visitors at different octaves of emotional and intellectual experience. It recalls *wadis* and canyons in the Judean Desert and the Negev. The stone walls speak symbolically and as markers, echoing the Wailing Wall, ancient quarries, headstones, catacombs, sacred tablets, and the ruins of a city. In contradistinction to monument tradition, which rises up, Yahalom-Zur elected to go down into the earth, like Maya Lin's Vietnam Memorial in Washington, D. C. The story is embodied in space and material and a litany of place names, all in the original languages of destroyed communities, transliterated into Hebrew and English. The story is told even in the subtleties of type. The valley image was not part of the competition brief, but the designer's conception. For Yahalom and Zur, the valley's story has connections that run as deep as the prophet Jeremiah and his images of desolation and the Valley of Slaughter, and they were inspired by the vision of the Valley of the Dry Bones of the Prophet Ezekiel: "The hand of the Lord was upon me, and carried me out in the spirit of the Lord, and set me down in the midst of the valley which was full of bones." Yahalom-Zur used an indigenous landscape vocabulary, but only by creating a landscape like no other did they feel they could have the impact they desired.

The Yad Vashem authorities had wanted the holocaust story told in more didactic terms. Yahalom-Zur brought the noted artist Menashe Kadishman with them to convince Yad Vashem officials that the names alone were sufficient. The effect of the names has a biblical resonance. They are the opposite of the "begats," the litany of the telling of the generations. These are the reverse, the *erasure* from history. In Yahalom-Zur's original scheme the passage through the valley was to have ended with the path rising out of the valley to an overlook across the Jerusalem forest to a resurgent Jewish people.

left: View. The Valley of the Destroyed Communities. Yad Vashem. Jerusalem. Yahalom-Zur.

right: View. The Valley of the Destroyed Communities. Yad Vashem. Jerusalem. Yahalom-Zur.

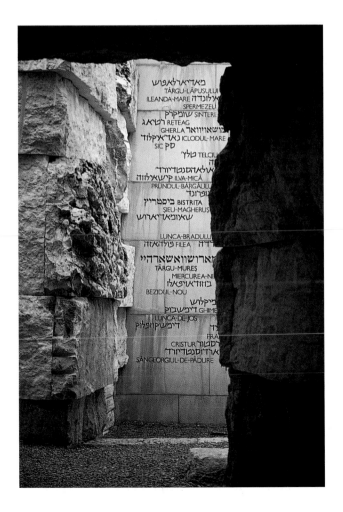

Competition drawing. The Valley of the Destroyed Communities. Yad Vashem. Jerusalem. Yahalom-Zur. (Dan Zur)

friends on kibbutzim where they visit, spend holidays, attend meetings, have picked fruit at harvestime, or stay in guesthouses.

The utopian aspirations of the kibbutz have stabilized into a unique, but still evolving alternative community. In kibbutz design the landscape framework and organizational structure communicate the ideology. There are clear divisions between the world of work, community, and domestic life. As its more extreme communal aspects have faded, kibbutzim have adjusted to meet contemporary ideals and conditions. The kibbutz itself has an oasis-like quality. This is most dramatic in the desert, but even in other regions the physical separation and distinctiveness, even isolation, of the kibbutz landscape is an important part of its character. Far more than other "garden cities," these *are* garden communities, with life lived in a park- or campus-like environment. Life on a kibbutz has much in common with life in a traditional village. Early kibbutzim had all their functions ordered around a single courtyard. As the kibbutzim matured a prototype developed which was then modified to particular circumstances. Most inhabitants also work in the kibbutz, where work and residence are carefully separated. At the core are the shared facilities of a dining hall and commons, a lawn for formal and informal gathering that is the symbolic center. In concentric fashion around this core are the children's houses, places for the elderly (as kibbutz members have aged in place), housing, work, and fields. All of the kibbutz zones and functions are woven together through pathways, outdoor corridors that are the skeletons of the community. The concentrated density makes them largely pedestrian with minimal traffic.

Kibbutz Ein Gedi. An oasis located at the shore of the Dead Sea.

Ruth Enis notes that kibbutz design in the 1920s and 1930s was characterized by an "architectural style, which was adapted to the straight lines of the buildings and the geometrical avenues. They made use of clipped hedges, designed flower-beds, straight terraces—all in a style that was well known to them from the countries of their origin." These formal lines strengthened "the architectural structure of settlement." This form derived not only from classic geometry and a Beaux Arts design sensibility, but also from local precedents found at Mikve Israel and from agricultural colonies founded by the Templers and Baron Rothschild.

In a 1992 speech Joseph Segal described the mutual relationship between the kibbutz and the pioneering landscape architects of the 1920s and 1930s:

"Those small number of landscape gardeners, as they were then called, would not have been able to survive and would have changed occupation had it not been for the kibbutzim. There, a group of people busied themselves in the first years of settlement with keeping the grounds clean; removing "*kotzim*" (thorns), planting groves of trees and creating future tree-covered walkways. Those later on became planned intensive tree planting projects.

"There is no other example in the world where a small group of people "pushed" a collective to collaborate with landscape architects when all the odds were against them. The ground was barren, the surrounding environment hostile, water scarce and in some cases they had no support at home. Soon a wave swept the kibbutzim. The camp was to be engulfed in green. All of the functions and services were to be integrated in a parklike setting."

Segal is clear about the significance of these designs when he noted that, despite rapid social and physical changes, "many kibbutzim retain a special good quality of life expressed in the trees, which by now have become like a container within which life takes place, alongside public lawns and flower beds gracing homes." Specifically he notes the contribution of five individuals: Shlomo Weinberg-Oren, Yitzhak Kutner, Alfred Weiss, Yakov Shur, and his father Yechiel Segal. In 1943 Weinberg-Oren wrote: "Though I trained as a garden architect, I didn't come to Israel as one, I became one through my social commitment. The first social assignment to be fulfilled came from the Kibbutz settlement movement." A 1944 survey of sixty-six of Palestine's 125 kibbutzim showed that fifty-nine had plans done by landscape architects.

top: View to the center. Kibbutz Goren.

bottom: A ficus garden. Kibbutz Sde Eliyahu. Itzhak Kutner.

opposite page:

top: Kibbutz Yodfat. Shlomo Weinberg-Oren. (Yagur Archives)

bottom: Children's area. Kibbutz Beit Alpha. Shlomo Weinberg-Oren. (Yagur Archives)

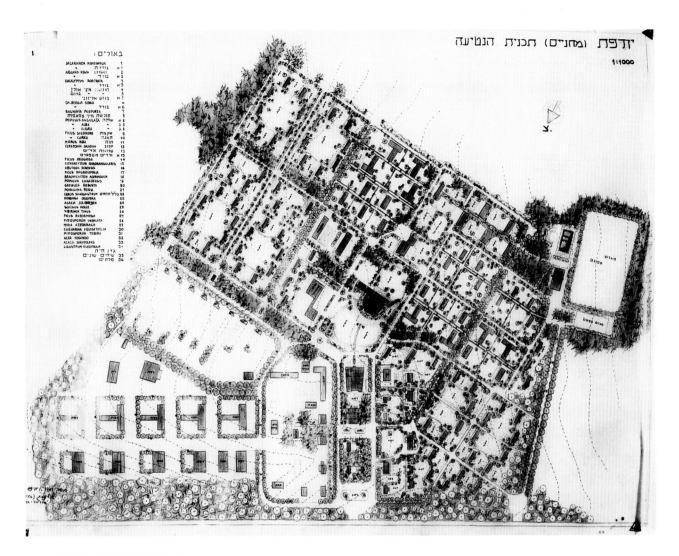

יודפת (מחנים) תכנית הנטיעה

1:1000

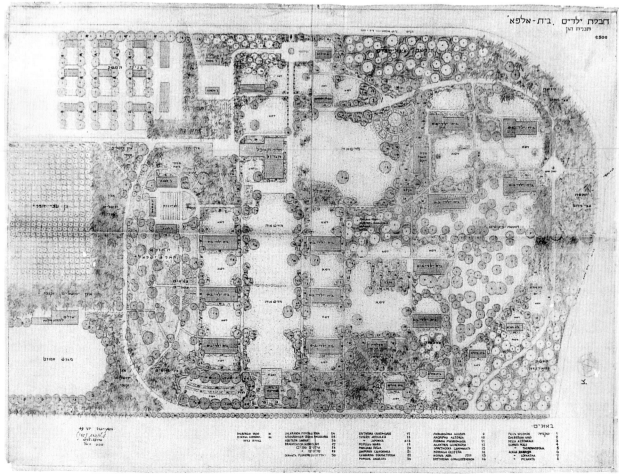

חבת ילדים ,בית-אלפא'
תכנית הגן

1:500

Kibbutz Nir David.
Richard Kauffmann,
planner. Adam Shadmi.
The extensive plantings
modify the extreme climate
of the Beit Shean Valley.

As the Israeli landscape matures and as new neighborhoods housing thousands are built, the kibbutzim represent a tie to the recent past, the early pioneering history of the state. They have become places in nature, free from cars, traffic, and the pressures of urban life. The architecture of kibbutzim, with the exception of dining halls and common facilities, is intentionally modest in accordance with their traditional egalitarian ethos. The kibbutz garden is, in a sense, the entire kibbutz. The gardens, in keeping with the anti-materialist ethos, are neither luxurious nor pretentious, but that does not mean they are not places of beauty and substantial comfort. In the kibbutz, perhaps more than any other community type, there is the essential recognition that the landscape demands monitoring and maintenance over time, and the realization that the physical design of houses, gardens, and places of work communicates something of the inhabitants and their ideals. Each kibbutz has designated gardeners who give their community a distinctive stamp. The relationship of the individual to the collective community is acted out in the gardens of kibbutzim. All lands are held in common, but small dooryard parcels are allotted for individual use. On some kibbutzim the kibbutz gardeners foster this activity and provide advice to members. The personalized gardens become part of the collective personality of each community. On kibbutzim the value of stewardship is self-evident. Landscape architects who have worked with kibbutzim express their love of working with people over time compared to the anonymity of designing neighborhoods for a more impersonal client. Kibbutz Mishmar HaEmek is still being designed by the third generation of a landscape architecture firm: first Yechiel Segal, then Joseph Segal, and now Tichnun Nof.

top left: A garden adjacent to the dining hall. Kibbutz Ayelet Hashachar.

top right: Kibbutz Ayelet Hashachar. A kibbutz garden.

left: Kibutz Mishmar HaEmek. Lippa Yahalom, Hillel Omer, Joseph Segal, and Tichnun Nof. A spatial continuity up the hill, overlooking the Emek. Trees provide clear spatial definition.

Parks and Open Space

"Meir Garden in Tel Aviv"

If we are fortunate and the fleeting time
Will not tell us suddenly: Gone in a flash!
We will continue to walk my friend
Along the paths of Meir garden, leaning on canes, as evening falls …

… and young girls who once walked
Many years ago at twilight time
Will sit by the gilded light
And knit socks for their grandchildren …

… and all around are other young girls
Seedlings cracking open seeds …
Because one generation after another passes by in the garden
And the garden thickens and grows.
    —Natan Alterman

Landscape architects are park-makers, instrumental in park design at all scales, from playgrounds, neighborhood spaces, and city parks to national parks, often linked together in a systemic fashion to create open space systems. The profession of landscape architecture evolved internationally in the nineteenth century from the world of garden art. This tradition of artistry and skill was coupled with a sense of social reform and led to the creation of the first public parks, sometimes called "people's gardens," a democratization of the landscape spaces of the elite and powerful. Parks were often defined as land that contrasted with the city, as an antidote to the worst effects of industry, urbanization, and modernity. In the nineteenth-century industrial city, the park was intended to create a "*rus en urbe,*" a facsimile of rural nature, with the objective of bringing its qualities and values into the city. But open space is not merely a reaction or a leftover; it is an assertion that proclaims its positive meanings, as places of nature and the out-of-doors, where people are afforded opportunities to fulfill the full range of human desires, from reflective solitude and contemplation to collective celebration and even recreation.

While often seen as a respite, parks are among the most densely populated and intensely used spaces. They are places to get away from the city and its congestion, atmosphere, and pressure, and yet they are also *of* the city. Hordes of people will gather on *Shabbat* for weekly celebration, *mangal,* and festivity. As much as the built forms of streets and architecture, green open spaces are the scaffolding that frames the daily life of households, neighborhoods, and community.

Park Raanana on Shabbat (1994). Gideon Sarig. The central park of Raanana caters to the complete variety of park users. It includes playgrounds for all ages, sports facilities, a zoo, sculpture gardens, a promenade, and an amphitheater. It is so popular that it has become a magnet for people from surrounding communities.

Open space is required at every scale, from that close to home, to great green urban lungs, to the nation. Park system planning pays particular attention to how to tie these components together. Where "natural" connections do not exist, they can be created in boulevards or pathways. Even sidewalks can provide essential linkages. In examining Israel's cities one would expect Haifa's open space to defer to the ridge lines of the Carmel that finger to the sea and the *wadis* that penetrate the city; that Jerusalem would be built upon its hills and the valleys remain green; that Jaffa and Tel Aviv would orient to the sea; that Ramat Gan would preserve its hilltops; and that Mitzpe Ramon would defer to the rim of its crater. In each of these examples open spaces are appropriate responses and dramatizations of the city's setting. They become the defining elements that provide an order, a recognizable image, a framework that defines, locates, and limits development. They also need constant defense against encroachment.

During the British Mandate, a time when key aspects of the physical form of the state of Israel was being envisioned, there was compatibility between Zionist/Socialist and Garden City ideals. The latter had their origins in Britain but had great influence on German planning. These ideals were coupled with the influence of the Bauhaus's modernist faith in the power of physical design to effect social change. The German architect and planner Richard Kauffmann (1883–1958) came to Israel in 1920, invited by the Palestine Land Development Company (PLDC) to head its building department. He received significant support from Arthur Ruppin (1846–1943), the first director of the Zionist Organization Palestine Office. In the 1920s Kauffmann's contribution in establishing norms for kibbutz, moshav, and neighborhood design was seminal. His concentric plan for the moshav Nahalal (1921), with its communal core and radiating spokes of family homes and agricultural plots, became an international icon of Israel's community design, despite its uniqueness.

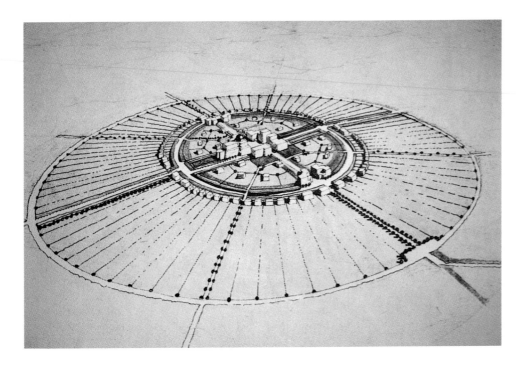

Nahalal. Drawing, Richard Kauffmann.

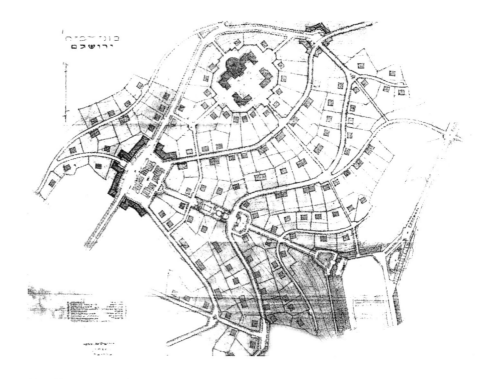

Beit Hakerem plan.
Jerusalem.
Richard Kauffmann.

Kauffmann was also instrumental in involving landscape architects in the design of diverse community open spaces. His neighborhood designs on the Carmel in Haifa (1921–23), Rehavia (1924), and Beit Hakerem in Jerusalem are sometimes seen as the most "Israeli" of places. (He also did plans for the Jerusalem garden suburbs of Beit Vagan, Talpiot, and Kiriyat Moshe.) What is it about their character that makes them such desirable addresses? Partly it is their scale and landscape qualities. They are garden communities, modest architecture set amidst trees, which offer a sense of comfort and repose. They are a reminder of the most basic temporal processes of landscapes: they change, especially when compared with the built forms of architecture and engineering. New buildings are dominant, but within a generation the buildings retreat to being structures within a vegetated landscape. This is not simply a cosmetic softening of the scene, but a vital way of connecting the built to its environment. These pioneering places, which only a few generations ago were new and modern, now feel like well-worn clothing that fits with perfect comfort. Like the *halutzim* (pioneers) who created them, they have aged well and with some pride.

Fragments remain of other early ideas. Laid out in anticipation of development, Tel Aviv's Rothschild Boulevard was the first piece of an urban vision. Late nineteenth- and early-twentieth century European cities built boulevards through their old quarters and on the sites of newly demolished city walls, while in the United States the boulevard guided development, a situation more akin to Israel's new communities. The first segment of Rothschild Boulevard was in Ahuzat Bait, perpendicular to Herzl Street, the main street of the neighborhood. On this intersection was Tel Aviv's first kiosk and children's playground. Built on land unsuitable for buildings, the boulevard was originally planted in 1910 with 1,000 trees from Egypt, but they died in a 1915 locust plague and were replanted predominately with *Ficus retusa* (Indian Laurel) and *Delonix regia*, striking trees which give the corridor a dense, dark quality. Sa'adiah Shoshani, head of the City Gardening Department, was responsible for the early plantings on the boulevard and other Tel Aviv streets. Originally the boulevard included gardens and water pools that have since become places and repositories for public art projects. In the modern, fast-paced city this linear park feels like a rural remnant, that rare place where the dirt and sand that underlie Tel Aviv lie beneath one's feet. The scale and quality of these grand mature trees structure pedestrian and vehicular space and provide a green wall for adjacent apartment blocks, offering precious shade from Tel Aviv's sun. Rothschild and Tel Aviv's other boulevards offer a compromise between the automotive city and the pedestrian world, as they supply needed open space and direct urban development.

Elements of Garden City inspired plans for Tel Aviv by Kauffmann (1921) and the Scottish planner Patrick Geddes (1925) exist as a palimpsest within the modern city. (Geddes had first visited Palestine in 1919. Kauffmann said that he "came to Palestine to continue the work of Patrick Geddes.") Both plans deferred to Tel Aviv's fine seaside situation with strong east-west axes linking city and sea. In Kauffmann's plan, a promenade paralleled the seashore with a garden city behind. Geddes's plan envisioned urban blocks linked by pedestrian ways that he imagined covered with roses and vines. East-west links were strengthened with planted boulevards, which

top: Rothschild Boulevard in 1912. Tel Aviv.

bottom: Rothschild Boulevard today. Tel Aviv.

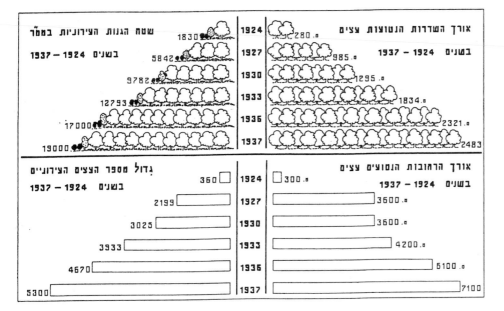

Tel Aviv. Chart of the area of urban gardens and the length of planted avenues (1924–1937).

also connected districts. Geddes's attention to ascending scales of open space was most critical, in connecting each dwelling to open space and movement, to block, district, and city. The plan recognized the primacy of the waterfront, the Yarkon River as an amenity and boundary, green connections to the sea, and the boulevard as a way of defining areas and affording connectivity. Only portions of either plan were instituted, and those were destroyed or fragmented by subsequent development. In recent years their wisdom has been rediscovered and attempts have been made to recapture their vision.

Tel Aviv's Park HaYarkon is the nation's largest urban park. Originally the park was the northern border of Tel Aviv and known as the *bustan*. It became the city's "central park," but it now serves a metropolitan region and is supplemented at the city's southern edge by Menachim Begin Park. It offers a case study of the spectrum of urban park functions. For those living by its substantial borders it is their local park; for others it is a special trip to see one of the many attractions. (Unfortunately, to sustain the economic viability of the park, user fees have been added to pay for attractions, threatening the park's public status.) Tichnun Nof served as the original planner (1967) and since the mid-1980s Gideon Sarig has had the primary responsibility. The work of these designers epitomizes an essential aspect of Israeli landscape architecture. Involvement with projects is over a long term, designers revisit projects, and are often called upon by the client to make modifications to their work in response to changing circumstances. Tichnun Nof's design set the basic frame of the park, its dimensions and grand spaces of water, woods, and meadows. The park surrounds the river and the creation of a large lake amplifies its aquatic character. A long linear open space, the park's dimensions range from only a 150 meters to 1,500 meters wide. The park is zoned into a series of distinct districts with an exhibition grounds and museum. (Early plans even included a drive-in movie!) At its western end the river is flanked by sports facilities. To the east are a series of themed garden attractions with cactus, stone, and tropical gardens. The basic framework is pastoral and almost every pathway acts as a promenade. The park encompasses places for solitude and space for gathering. A gigantic wooden play structure resembles a beehive on Shabbat with its inordinate density of children and parents. Movement is constant. Rental pedal carts move along, accompanied by baby strollers and joggers, while others watch from cafes. There is an exceptional range of users and uses: walking, sports fields, *mangal*, and dancing; individuals, families, clubs, and youth groups. Celebrations and birthday parties are common. The feeling is like a great family picnic or reunion, not an anonymous modern city. As water quality has improved since the mid-1980s, there has been a return to the river as a focus, with boardwalks and overlooks. Studies by Arye Rachamimoff of the Yarkon River basin highlight connections to its largely seasonal tributaries and the entire watershed. Currently, most of the water that should flow to the sea is diverted to other purposes, especially agriculture. Improved water quality is imperative to allow it to be a river park, as is the case for all of Israel's small but precious rivers. Plans propose a greenway connection from the Yarkon's source at Rosh Ha'Ayin passing through all of the northern metropolitan region of Tel Aviv, the core of the park, to its exit just north of the port of Tel Aviv, which is also being renovated. This system would then connect to the open space system linking the entire waterfront of Tel Aviv and Jaffa.

Drawing of the plan for the Yarkon River watershed (1996). Arie Rachamimoff, architect, and Yarkon River Authority.

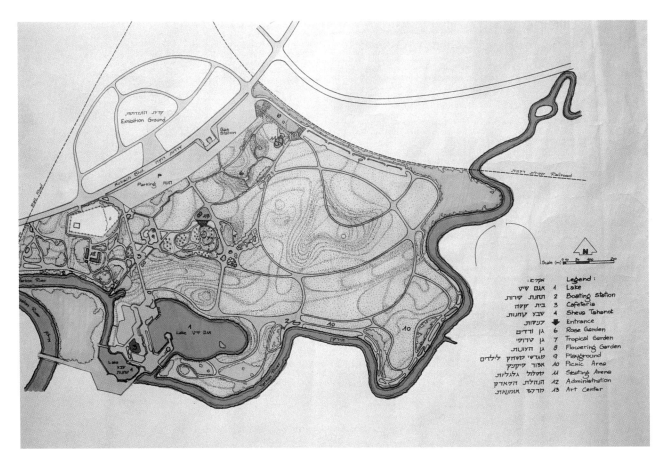

Legend :
1 Lake
2 Boating Station
3 Cafeteria
4 Sheva Tahanot
↓ Entrance
6 Rose Garden
7 Tropical Garden
8 Flowering Garden
9 Playground
10 Picnic Area
11 Skating Arena
12 Administration
13 Art Center

Plan. Park HaYarkon.
Tel Aviv. (Tichnun Nof)

Park HaYarkon. Tel Aviv.
Pathway. Gideon Sarig.

Park HaYarkon. Tel Aviv.
A play structure. Gideon Sarig.

Nation Building

There is a strong connection between planning at the national level and the work of landscape architects. The first national plan was in 1949, and planning is institutionalized with well-established procedures. Priorities and methods are subject to continual debate, however, and bureaucratic log jams are common. Landscape architects have played a role at all scales, from the formulation of policy to the implementation of objectives, through site specific design, directly and indirectly supporting national planning objectives.

A set of well-defined planning goals was instituted during the state's first decade. These were part of the program of nation building, similar to that of other countries that won their independence in the post-war period, although Israel has perhaps been the most successful in the realization of its goals. Israel was clear and direct in its formulation of policy. It included the absorption of immigrants; the provision of defense and security; population dispersion from the nation's center and the metropolitan regions of Tel Aviv, Haifa, and Jerusalem; the development of the country's economic base in terms of agricultural self-sufficiency; and the hus-

The National Plan, 1950. The plans are the physical manifestation of ideas and aspirations for the future; they show population distribution, industry, agriculture, the national water carrier, and national parks. Most of these were instrumented. Left, planned agricultural regions. Center, the National Water Plan. Right, national parks. (Arieh Sharon, Eldar Sharon, architects and town planners)

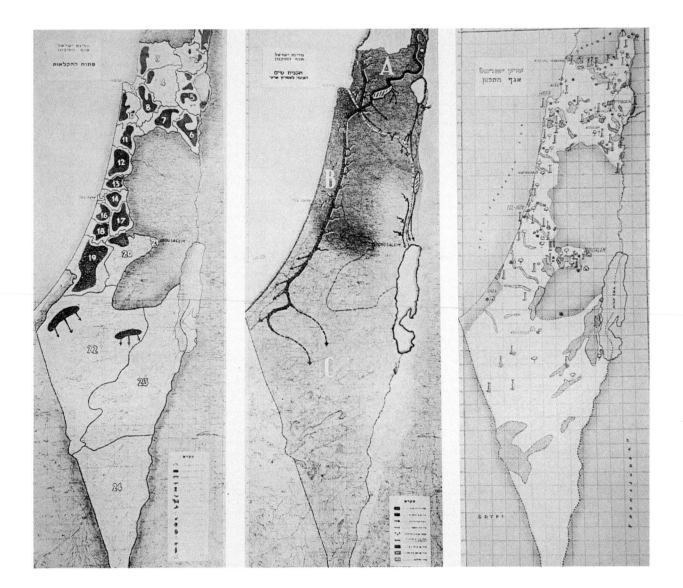

bandry of its resources, especially water and agricultural land. Each of these policies had significant physical manifestations. Most dramatic was the construction of a hierarchy of settlements, including more than thirty "Development Towns" (new communities which attempted to respond to all of these goals); the creation and expansion of several hundred kibbutzim and moshavim; and the institution of regional planning. These new settlements were often located at the nation's borders and frontier regions for security and to establish a presence on the land. In a nation where 92% of the land was under the jurisdiction of the Lands Authority the government had the ability to regulate practice.

Many of these goals were successful, although as the planning context shifted, both internally and externally, so have the objectives and the means to accomplish them. Until the late 1960s these initial priorities held sway. After the Six-Day War attention shifted from rural to metropolitan areas, and especially to a newly reunited Jerusalem. In addition, the culture of the rural pioneering ethic of early Zionist-Socialist idealism was changing. The nation had achieved remarkable success in terms of material development and needed to respond to other social demands and desires. Throughout Israel's history, planning and building were accomplished under great difficulty, under the strains of military defense, mass immigration, economic uncertainly, and pragmatic necessity. Planner Moshe Hill described this as "planning in turbulence." Despite those conditions, there was an awareness of the need to husband and conserve resources, including land, although the conflicts between development and preservation are ongoing.

In the 1940s Alexander Klein (1879–1961) of the Keren Kayemet was instrumental in bringing landscape architects to Israel and using their services. Klein promulgated town-planning schemes based on certain principles. Towns were to be of limited size and population with fixed boundaries, open space systems were to be a central component with a separation of vehicles and pedestrians, and there was to be a centrifugal layout with public facilities at the core. These basic principles persisted in subsequent planning, or at least a struggle to conform to them did. Klein would later become Technion's first professor of town planning and he brought Weinberg-Oren, Zvi Miller, and Chaim Latte to teach landscape architecture. He also prepared the first plan for Technion when it relocated from the Hadar to the Carmel.

Housing was and still is the nation's prime building project, typically constructed under government sponsorship. In the 1970s Israel was building more housing per capita than any other nation. In the 1990s 700,000 new immigrants, largely from the former Soviet Union, were housed. These are the landscapes of *aliyah* and absorption, providing shelter and economic development. Each period had distinct issues. For many early immigrants their first housing was in *ma'aberot*. These gave way to the first generation of *shikkunim* (housing projects), often the basic community building block. For landscape architects, planners, and architects the key challenge, after providing basic shelter and habitation, was to create a viable open space pattern. Housing was constructed rapidly and under great pressure, and too often the architectural imperative dominated, squeezing out needed open space. In this pioneering period the countryside was still near and it may have been difficult to imagine a population that would increase so dramatically.

The early period proved to be the most influential in the setting of basic patterns. As Aviah Hashimshony has noted, the period from 1948 to 1955 "shaped the character of Jewish population centers in town and country in places where nothing had existed." These early projects embodied a "sense of public responsibility, and a relentless search for proper solutions to the country's unique building problems." The subsequent question became how could landscape design ameliorate some of the standardized, minimal aspects of housing, and offer amenity and a quality environment while working within the bureaucratic framework and restrictions of the *Misrad ha-Shikun* (Ministry of Housing).

In 1953 Artur Glickson became head of the planning unit of the Department of Housing. He promulgated the neighborhood scheme as well as key innovations in regional planning. The neighborhood idea, where services could be found at the local scale, had great influence in creating definable zones and areas in new town planning. As communities grew incrementally, each new area had a basic set of services, institutions, and commercial enterprises. Following a hierarchy of open spaces and development from housing units to complexes, neighborhoods to town was the ideal. However, typically there was less attention to open space connections between neighborhoods.

Kiryat Meir (1936). Tel Aviv. Architect Arieh Sharon was educated at the Bauhaus in Desau, Germany. The landscape plan is by Yechiel Segal. This middle-class urban worker's housing complex featured an entry square leading to a central green. Houses were perpendicular to the green and each looked out upon a more private open space. (Yosef Segal)

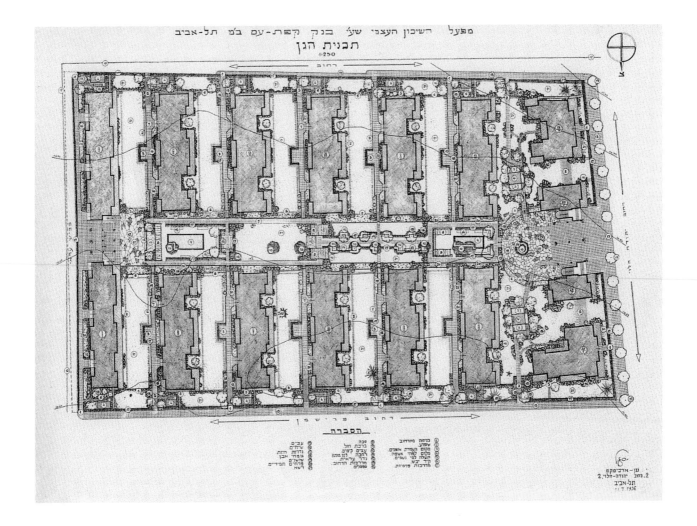

Gan Avraham (named for
Avraham Krinizi, the first
mayor). Ramat Gan.
Moshe Kvashny.

*below: View from the top of
Gan Avraham to Sderot
HaGiborim with adjacent
housing. Ramat Gan.
Moshe Kvashny.*

In many places a framework is now in place. It is not always ideal, but the skeleton is often there, sometimes in need of care, but sometimes lovingly maintained. At best, attention was paid to comprehensive community designs, including open space networks, to structure and guide development and offer the full range of garden and park possibilities. Such systems are found in the towns of Ramat Gan, Kfar Saba, Ashkelon, Arad, Carmiel, Modi'in, and Beit Shemesh. There are other examples, but these represent all regions of the country and work accomplished over the past five decades.

The one-time Tel Aviv suburb of Ramat Gan, now at the core of the Tel Aviv metropolis, built its parks around one of the rare hills in the area: Gan Shaul crowns one hilltop and Gan Avraham adorns the other and connects to a memorial overlook across the terraces of Sderot Hagiborim. These were all designed by city landscape architect Moshe Kvashny (1908–1973), under the auspices of a farsighted Mayor Avraham Krinizi. In the 1970s Ari Armoni extended this early system, with a rich array of tree-lined pedestrian pathways connecting center-city open spaces at Kikar Rambam and finally by the Sderot HaYeled

midrachov linked to the King David Garden, also originally designed by Kvashny (as the King George Garden in 1932, later remodeled by Miller-Blum). In recent years Rachel Assaf has been progressively restoring the early landmarks of the system.

In the mid-1970s, city architect Joseph Kolodny, working with Yahalom-Zur as the landscape architects, deftly extended earlier plans for Kfar Saba's open space system. Kolodny retained the grid structure from previous plans and integrated the small neighborhood gardens into a marvelous woven system of open spaces. In the process a new city grid, a "green grid," was created. It has many scales of open space. The civic center of city hall, cultural center, memorial and commercial spaces has

generous park and plaza spaces. These link, via walkways, to neighborhoods and housing clusters. Local services of school, synagogue, and recreation are found along shaded pedestrian ways. Recent extensions of the system include a taleyet parallel to a roadway linking an older, poorer part of the community. The open space system seamlessly links all aspects of community life, and as new projects are constructed they amplify the system, such as an open-air shopping mall by archi-

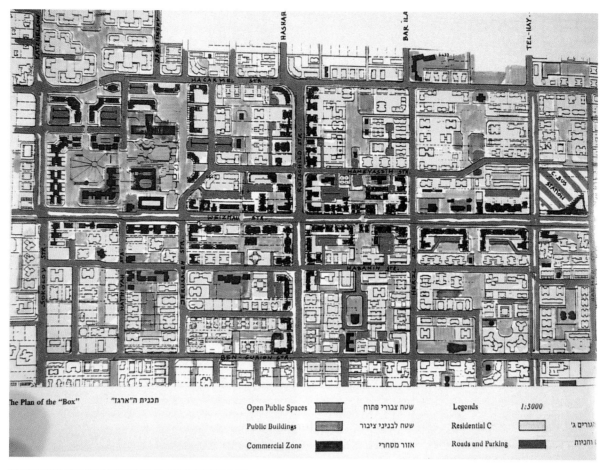

top: Kfar Saba. Plan of open spaces. The Green Grid. Joseph Kolodny. (Municipality of Kfar Saba)

left: Walkway. Kfar Saba.

bottom Ashkelon. Afridar area. The public landscape structure includes wide sidewalks, a central square, and a grand park leading to the Mediterranean.

tect Moshe Tzur. Landscape architect Tamar Darel-Fossfeld, speaking as a resident and working mother, says of the system: "It backs me up."

The northern Negev city of Arad is 640 meters above sea level and was originally built to house Dead Sea workers. The design responds to the harsh desert conditions and the exposed site. The buildings are clustered around courtyards, with narrow passageways to provide shade and protection from strong winds. Cars and pedestrians are separated, and schools and commercial areas are placed along

pedestrian axes that connect to the topography of the *wadis*. In the morning the walkways are filled with children going to school, but later in the day it is the parking lots that are lively. Much of the city is built on hard rock and to plant any trees holes were drilled. Planting itself was carefully controlled so as not to adversely effect asthma sufferers. Zvi Dekel was a member of the design team and received the second Karavan prize for the design of the Avishur Neighborhood in 1973.

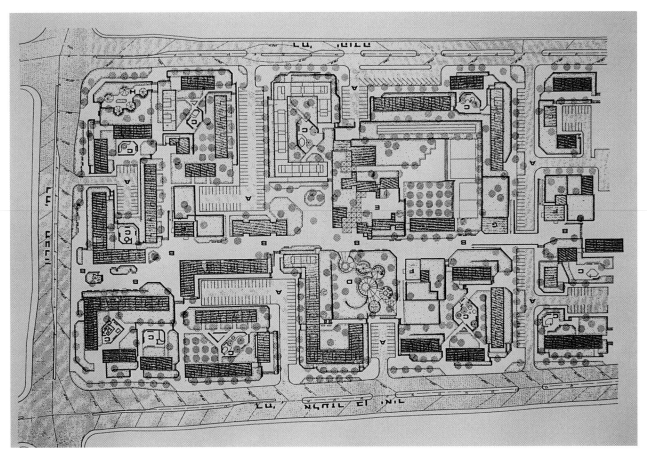

Carmiel is the major development town of the Galilee. Its open space system shows a diversity of responses to site conditions and a variety of housing types, from courtyard houses on pedestrian ways to the inclusion of zones of private homes. At Carmiel, as in all of these towns, the pedestrian system provides linkages to the town center and a plaza ringed by commercial businesses and civic structures. Portions of Carmiel are built on modest slopes so a system of stairways as an essential part of the open space network.

In the 1990s two major cities were created in the nation's center, halfway between Tel Aviv and Jerusalem: Modi'in and the expansion of Beit Shemesh. The open space system of Modi'in, a city projected to have a population of 250,000, was planned by Gideon Sarig in collaboration with the architect Moshe Safdie. Beit Shemesh was master planned by architect David Reznik and Shlomo Aronson. In the first residential area Braudo-Maoz designed more than thirty gardens, instantly enhancing the residents' quality of life. Modi'in is built on the ridges and terraced slopes surrounding three open valleys, which terminate at the city center. Each of the valleys is designed by a different landscape architectural firm: Studio (the office of Paul Friedberg and Dorit Shahar), Shlomo Aronson, and Yitchak Blank. Each narrow valley is about one kilometer long and bordered by a planted boulevard. All roads and pedestrian ways lead into a valley. Each valley accommodates hard and soft spaces—schools, synagogues, recreational facilities, pathways, and adjoining commercial activity—and the character of each is distinctive. Blank's design takes as its theme the *wadi*, and the main pedestrian path acts as a dry river bed that transforms into a water feature at its lower course. Aronson's includes a rock garden and latticed pergolas. Studio's has a grand turfed amphitheater bowl at the center that links to the next valley. The entire town opens to a more wild landscape and a more natural valley, Wadi Anaba, being designed by Gideon Sarig. It begins at the planned central train station and as it moves down the *wadi* will gradually revert to a more natural pattern. Beit Shemesh also anticipates a rail connec-

tion to its urban center. Existing and proposed forests, along with preserved agricultural land, act as the framework for urban development and fingers of parkland penetrate the community design. The designers speak of a desire to create a green city, one that changes one's mood.

Recent development is often overscaled with high-rise apartment blocks, yet a primacy is still given to open space planning. In Rishon LeTzion, the landscape design helps ameliorate the scale of construction and creates distinctive areas. In the neighborhood of Kiryat Ganim, designed by Haim Kahanovitch, there is a central green axis and water garden leading to areas each with its own gardens, schools, and mixture of low- and high-rise buildings. A large community park is at the edge.

There are other kinds of systems. They need not all be continuous and physically connected. A matrix of open spaces can act as a catalyst for development and as concentrated points of a community's identity. Numerous interventions— some smaller scale and some not so small in scale—can reinforce and change the life of a city. Moriah-Sekely has been employing aspects of this strategy in its open space scheme for Jaffa, which capitalizes on its historic fabric and is opportunistic in its use of vacant parcels.

Jerusalem

Jerusalem, as always, is a special situation. The city speaks to the nation, as well as to followers of three world religions. The focus of attention is the walled Old City. It is only 215 acres (about 900 x 900 meters), enclosed within the sixteenth-century walls of Suleiman, but its impact radiates like a stone dropped in an urban pond. The city only began to grow beyond the walls in the second half of the nineteenth century. Under the British Mandate there were a succession of plans for the city: 1918 (William McLean), 1919 (Patrick Geddes), 1922 (C.R. Ashbee), 1934 (Holliday), and 1944 (Henry Kendall); then, for the divided city, plans were made by Israelis in 1948 (Rau) and 1959 (Shviv) and by Jordanians in 1964. They all tried to preserve the character of the Old City and paid particular attention to its landscape setting, the adjacent valleys, and hills. Greenbelts and preserves of varying dimensions, and restrictions on buildings surrounding and inside the Old City, were the essential components. Plans for the entire city, done shortly after independence, extended much of the British thinking, and greenbelts encircling the entire city were proposed. The plans capitalized on Jerusalem's topography,

which suggested a natural solution, the valleys between the city's hills being designated the central components of a network of parks and open spaces.

After 1967 and a reunited city, a team led by architect Arieh Sharon was placed
in charge of planning. A special zone that broadly encircled the Old City was the
focus of attention. Within this area a national park of 2,400 *dunams* (600 acres) was
designated, hugging close to the Old City walls north and west, and to the east
and south encompassing the Hinnom and Kidron valleys, the City of David, and
the slopes of the Mount of Olives. Only six weeks after the Six-Day War, National
Park landscape architect Arye Dvir produced a landmark drawing, which showed
the areas surrounding the wall. Not all of this vision was created, but it set a stage
for discussions and subsequent designs. The Jerusalem National Park concept has
been incrementally developed and has influenced designs beyond its jurisdiction.
The basic concept respects the historic and sacred viewshed of the Old City. It is a
series of concentric rings of open spaces encompassing all of the area found at the
base of the walls and that of the surrounding valleys, hearkening back to the long
lineage of greenbelt schemes.

The resulting parks are a coordinated collection of singular designs, which act
as a frame for the Old City. They are multifaceted and function as circulation,
educational space, archeological park, interpretive zone, backdrop for the walls and
vistas, local recreation, and even as land for grazing animals. Each of the open

*Open space plan, 1944.
Jerusalem. Note especially
the preservation of open
spaces around the walls of
the Old City and a pro-
posed Mount of Olives
Nature Reserve to the west.
(Her Majesty's Stationery
Office)*

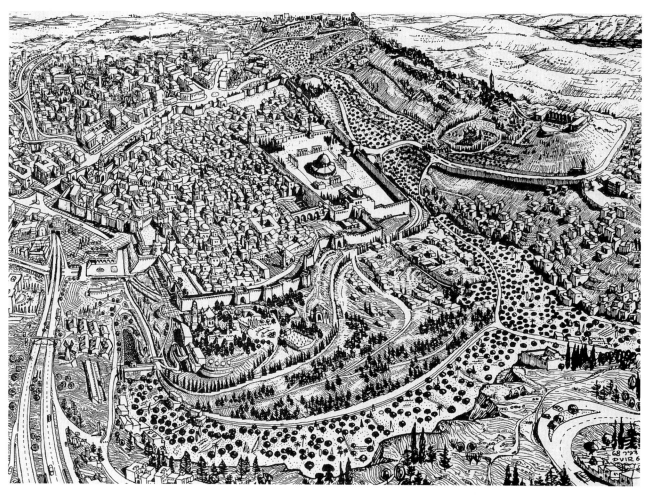

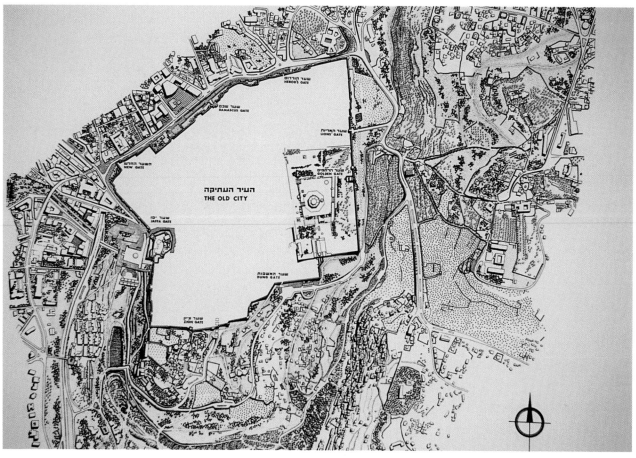

שער הורדוס
HEROD'S GATE

שער שכם
DAMASCUS GATE

השער החדש
NEW GATE

שער האריות
LIONS' GATE

שער יפו
JAFFA GATE

שער הרחמים
GOLDEN GATE

העיר העתיקה
THE OLD CITY

שער האשפות
DUNG GATE

שער ציון
ZION GATE

spaces adjacent to the walls has a distinct character. Much of the periphery acts as an archeological and historic promenade, with views to the walls and surrounding sites and vistas. Miller-Blum did David's Garden, a stone plaza fronting the Citadel (1967); and Aronson's Beit Shalom Park (1978) along the city's south wall became a site for archeological tours and children's play. The historic gates are critical. At the Damascus Gate (1980–1985) Peter Bugod and Eunice Figueriedo constructed a staircase which is also a grand amphitheater and forecourt for the gate and for the Old City's main market street. The entry bridge crosses over archeological excavations of the Roman city and its gateway. Gan Ha Choma, by Moshe Margalit, is series of pools and palms that follows the north wall towards the New Gate. The Jaffa Gate has an accompanying terrace that overlooks the Mamilla district (architect Moshe Safdie, landscape architect Ron Lovinger) and the next ring of open space. From the higher levels the ground slopes down through the Mamilla Valley Park (1993) to the Sultan's pools (1980) located between the walls and Yemin Moshe. Here Arie Rachamimoff added platforms, stairs, and walls to create a space for performances and as a buffer around the city walls. It is difficult to discern the modern additions from the ancient stones. The topography wraps around the city's eastern wall to the Mitchell Garden and Wolfson Park, by Yahalom-Zur at the head of the Hinnom Valley. Wolfson's arced green terraces abut the ancient walls and caves of the valley, and gradually give way to the distant view of the desert. It marks and accentuates the transition, the ecotone that Jerusalem straddles, from Mediterranean landscape and forested hillside to stark, treeless desert.

opposite page

top: Jerusalem National Park (1967). (Drawing Arye Dvir)

bottom: Jerusalem National Park plan (1969). (Arye Dvir)

Beit Shalom Park. Adjacent to the Dung Gate. Jerusalem. Redesigned by Shlomo Aronson. (Shlomo Aronson)

Damascus Gate. Jerusalem.
Peter Bugod and Eunice
Figueriedo.

Gan HaChoma. Jerusalem. Moshe Margalit.

Walkway and lookout to the Kidron Valley and its collection of tombs and the Mount of Olives. Jerusalem. Arie Rachamimoff.

top: Mamilla Valley Park. Jerusalem. (Drawing, Ronald Lovinger)

bottom: Sultan's Pool (1980). Jerusalem. Arie Rachamimoff.

Wolfson Park. Jerusalem. Yahalom-Zur.

Mayor Teddy Kollek was determined to make Jerusalem into a city of gardens and his Jerusalem Foundation (founded in 1966) funded scores of projects grand and small, as the city almost tripled in population from 1967 to 1997. Exacerbated by the city's rapid growth there is renewed attention to open space plans at the metropolitan level. There is a danger that urbanization will destroy the landscape framework, the hills, ridges, and valleys that are part of the Jerusalem experience and landscape image that has existed for centuries. The best designs have accentuated these topographic characteristics while judiciously preserving or adapting portions of open land for modern use. The worst have obliterated these distinctions. Recent plans by architects Reches Eshkol and landscape architects Amit Segal and Itamar Raayoni (1995) focus on the edges of the city, its ridges and valleys, and the multiple roles that open space has to play in each of these situations. (As the nation's capital, Jerusalem is also the site for national grounds and collections, government institutions, and sites of ritual and remembrance, places such as the Israel Museum, Jerusalem Zoo, Botanical Gardens, Yad Vashem, Knesset, Supreme Court, and City Hall.)

More than 2,000 years ago Mediterranean authors wrote about the classic relationship between the city and country. The Roman author Horace wrote of common wisdom in "The Town Mouse and the Country Mouse," which most of us know as a children's story. While Horace satirizes his characters, his lesson was that both ways of life have their virtues. These worlds which may seem in opposition to each other are also interdependent. Cities exist within hinterlands that support them economically and socially, and the countryside is equally bound to the city. In Israel this relationship takes on distinct forms. North of Beersheva, with rare exceptions, one is almost always within sight and easy distance to the city. Viewed from the opposite direction one is equally close to a non-urbanized landscape, but

Botanical Garden (1979). Jerusalem. Shlomo Aronson. The first botanical garden by E. Aig was built at Mt. Scopus in 1931. A new botanical garden fills the wadi *adjacent to Hebrew University's Givat Ram campus. The pathway takes one through a succession of terraced miniature landscapes, each depicting distinctive geo-botanical regions. A watercourse through the* wadi *leads to a pond and pavilion. (Albatross)*

this relationship is imperiled as the sharp distinctions between urban and rural are changing.

Until recently Israel's cities maintained strong boundaries between city and country which accentuated the spatial clarity of the Israeli landscape. Most land is owned by the state and leased to owners. The government's statutory policies of land-use planning define its function and extent. At the landscape scale there are clear divisions between forested Keren Kayemet lands and the concentrated nodes of settlement surrounded by agricultural land. This historic policy was to prevent urban sprawl and preserve agricultural land, but it has an ideological component

as well. The link to the land and the landscape of pioneers is through the agricultural and rural landscape of kibbutzim and moshavim. What was once distant now sits at the edge of the metropolis in which development has begun to sprawl beyond. Much land is lost already, and without prompt action a rare chance to shape the metropolitan landscape will be lost. Unfortunately recent planning practices responding to the pressures of urbanization and the decline of the agricultural sector jeopardize these qualities. History presents unique opportunities not to be squandered for short-term returns.

The Wohl Rose Garden begun by Meir Victor as a park for presidential receptions. Neglected under the Kollek administration, it was revived as a rose garden designed by Meir Victor and Josef Segal. Its most dramatic features are the water channels and pools that were part of a reclaimed quarry. The garden is a central piece in an emerging governmental zone that encompasses the Knesset, Supreme Court, and government offices.

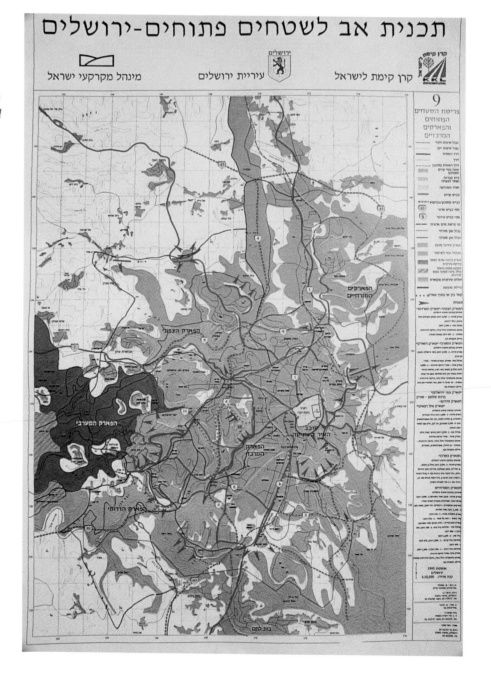

Jerusalem open space plan (1995). (Reches Eshkol & Segal Raayoni)

National Parks

The building of a new nation for a new type of Jew was paradoxically rooted to the past. National historical and archeological parks were part of the program of Zionism, for a return to the land was also a return to a Jewish history that was rooted in those places. At an ideological level, national park planning helped codify the already rich symbolic landscape of the nation. Visiting these sites—on school trips, on *Shabbat*, with the army or scouts or Society for the Protection of Nature in Israel (SPNI), or as a tourist—became part of the modern pilgrimage.

The National Plan of 1950 identified areas for national parks that exploited existing landscape features, nature reserves, and historical sites. In 1955 a department was charged with the preservation and restoration of historic sites and sites of natural beauty. Its task included the layout of national parks and picnic grounds, constructing access roads, restoration and site improvements, the creation of observation points for outstanding views, and a program of signage. Yan Yanai, the initial head of the National Parks, wanted small efficient areas. In this early period a great opportunity was missed to acquire more land for the designated sites. The National Parks and Nature Reserves Act of 1963 established the National Parks Authority and Nature Reserves Authority, which were combined into the Nature and National Parks Protection Authority in 1998 as part of the National Parks, Nature Reserves, National Sites, and Memorial Sites Law.

Landscape architects were involved in national park designs from the outset. The first generation of designers did an admirable job. Arye Dvir (b. 1933) was

Beit Shearim (1956). Yahalom-Zur. Note the intense plantings that frame the ruins and graves at the core of the park. (Dan Zur)

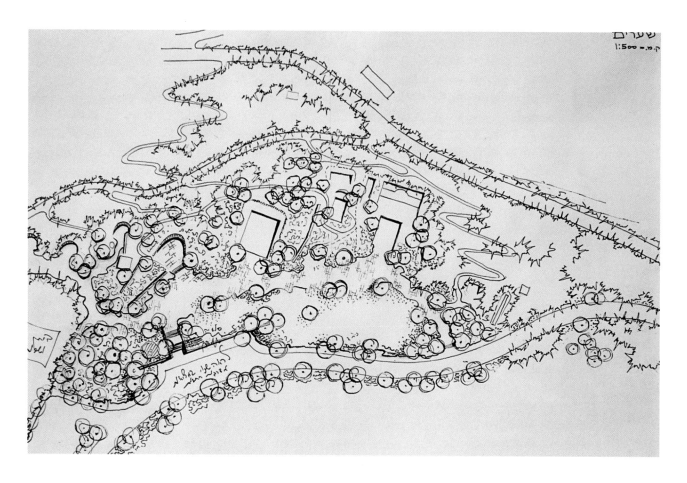

שערים
ק.מ. 1:500

Beit Shearim plan.
(Drawing, Dan Zur)

chief landscape architect and planner for the National Parks from 1963–1987, succeeded by Racheli Merchav (b. 1957) from 1990–1999. They designed, and also coordinated the work of others. Lippa Yaholom and Dan Zur (Beit Shearim, Ashkelon, Ceasaria, Beit Shean, Sachne, Horshat Tal, and Ein Avdat) and Joseph Segal and Zvi Dekel (Ein Hemed and Timna) did much of the early design work, setting the tone for both national parks and kibbutzim, establishing a standard in quality, especially in planting design. Many of these parks have been discussed and illustrated earlier, for they are exemplars of the nation's language of landscape design.

At a regional scale, Park HaCarmel (the only Gan Leumi called a park), the largest national park (8,400 hectares and seven million visitors per year), is indicative of park functions in a more natural setting. The original plan by Miller-Blum (1966) was overly ambitious, even including lakes. Since 1975 Gideon Sarig has been the landscape architect for the park. The park surrounds the Druze villages of Usafiya and Dalyat el Carmel and Kibbutz Beit Oren. Inside its boundaries are found campgrounds, fields, orchards, nature reserves, historic and archeological sites, restaurants, picnic areas, and an extensive system of hiking trails.

Beaches

Israel's beaches and shorelines are deserving of special attention as the nation's prime open spaces and recreation areas. The bulk of the population lives within a half-hour of the Mediterranean. The beaches are used intensively half the year and are visited year-round. Points of access to the water, places for gathering by the shore, promenades, and the provision of services (including showers, bathhouses, and food) are found in every city and community that touches the sea, from Ashkelon and Ashdod in the south to Nahariya in the north. Adjacent to dense metropolitan areas, the shoreline offers the prospect of open horizons and expansive space. The seashore is, however, under enormous pressure for new marinas, high-rise housing, and commercial development. Each of Israel's four shorelines is distinctive: the Dead Sea, the

Tayelet. Ein Bokek.
Tichnun Nof.

circumference of the Kinneret, the Gulf of Eilat, and most importantly the Mediterranean. The entire coastline of the nation is only 273 kilometers with 188 on the Mediterranean, where large portions are under military control and off limits to the public.

The Dead Sea shoreline is *suigeneris*. There are few places else like it in the world. The lowest place on Earth, it is 400 meters below sea level. The seashore itself is a unique and delicate habitat, large portions of which are protected as a nature reserve, while modern resort development is concentrated in human-made oases at Ein-Bokek and Ein Gedi. At Ein Bokek a walkway along the seashore by Tichnun Nof, and another at Ein Gedi by Haim Kahanovitch, have been constructed, offering views to the sea and pockets of shaded protection.

The northern shore of the Sea of Galilee, the Kinneret, is a prime recreational area and the site of some of Christendom's holiest sites, Taghba and Capernaem, places of pilgrimage for tens of thousands annually. It is at these waterfront sites where, according to scriptures, Christ performed some of his miracles. The most dramatic sites are very modest.

The beaches of Eilat comprise the nation's rare touristic waterfront, where the beach is typically part of a vacation experience (except, of course, for Eilat's residents). The city has a series of pleasure palace hotels, each a controlled fantasy replete with gardens, fountains, and pools. Most border the promenade along the Gulf of Eilat or encircle the lagoons, a key element in Shlomo Aronson's 1989 master plan. Yahalom-Zur designed the original south promenade, and new hotels are now redesigning the frontage. Uri Mueller of Tichnun Nof has designed several of these. At the Royal Beach Hotel (1993) he created a modern oasis with palms as a continuous canopy across a series of terraced lawns overlooking the hotel's pool. Bruce Levin's design for the Dan Hotel (1994–1996) is particularly subtle in its articulation of the overlapping parallel zones along the beach. Fronting the hotel, palm trees not only line the tayelet, but also bridge the hotel garden and the upper edge of the beach. Palms are planted within a sinuous weaving line of grass that yields to the sand and sea. (Run-off from the grass is trapped into sewage treatment so as not to harm Eilat's precious coral.)

*Beach front. Eilat. Dan
Hotel. Bruce Levin.*

At Bat Galim (1977) in Haifa, Miller–Blum made an early attempt at creating a seafront walkway that broke from established models. Between the coastal neighborhood and the sea is a promenade bordered by grand stone slabs. These break the waves, but also act as viewpoints and platforms for fishermen. Unfortunately, poor maintenance and additions mar its current condition. At Hof Dado in Haifa's southern edge, Miller–Blum and Iris Tal, collaborating with architect Perla Kauffmann, concentrated intensive development in the long, narrow strand between the coastal highway and the Mediterranean. Parking is close by but well screened, and gateways planted with dune grasses lead to the beach. The beachfront promenade is lined with buildings, restaurants, pubs, locker rooms, an amphitheater, a playground, lifeguard stations, and more. The designs are exciting "postmodern" geometries but in the long tradition of playfulness which is part of the beach and holiday experience. It is robust, colorful, inviting, and very popular day and night. At some spots it is even a bit overpowering, pushing a bit too close to the sea and dominating the beach.

*opposite page: Hof Dado.
Haifa. Perla Kauffmann,
architect, and Miller-Blum.
(Albatross)*

National Planning

Land has always been viewed as a national resource in Israel with the vast proportion under some fashion of state control, often in the form of long-term leases. There are multiple jurisdictions and methods of landscape protection. Lands that are most strongly protected with restrictions on development include the national parks, nature reserves, and designated archeological sites, as well as Keren Kayemet land which has its own hierarchy of preservation.

Landscape planning also looks at larger regional systems as a framework for design. The role of the landscape architects in this process is particularly directed at landscape preservation while simultaneously guiding future development. The district plan for the Galilee (1992) by D. Shefer, S. Amir, H. Lo-Yone, and A. Frenkel is based on an understanding of landscape resources of the region. It proposes a matrix of open spaces under various levels of restrictions with the goal of retaining the character and quality of the Galilee landscape. It combines both designated and de facto open spaces, including lands held in reserve for future development and other open spaces in reserve for aquifer recharge, forestry, cultivation, and recreation.

During the 1980s renewed attention was given to neglected portions of the 1950 National Plan, notably the river valleys. These still emerging schemes and ideas are an example of national action that indicate a change in the country's priorities, with huge implications for design at regional and local scales. Renewed attention to the rivers was instigated by the SPNI, then the Keren Kayemet, and finally the Ministry of the Environment, which made the cleanup and rehabilitation of the nation's rivers a national goal. The ultimate goal in any land planning in Israel is a statutory plan, a document which has the force of law. River planning is moving slowly in that direction, but there is great opposition, especially from the nation's farmers in kibbutzim and moshavim, for the plans will surely restrict their newly found freedom of a greater voice in the use of their lands.

In 1956 the waters of the Yarkon were diverted for agricultural use and Israel's largest stream lost its power and quality. In 1988 the establishment of a Yarkon River Authority signaled a change in direction and a harbinger of a renewed attention to the nation's scarce surface water resources. A 1990 master plan for the Yarkon describes it as a "Green Lung," the resurrection and persistence of the fundamental ideal of the international nineteenth-century parks movement. In 1999 a National Rivers Administration, under the Keren Kayemet and the Ministry of the Environment, was created to oversee the restoration of the nation's rivers. The mandate included plans for river rehabilitation which was to function as a catalyst for related projects such as trail systems and park development. Regional river administrations were established to deal with the Lachish, Zippori, Ayalon, Taninim, Hadera, Alexander, Sorek, Harod, and Jordan. Parks already are located along portions of the Lachish, Harod, Hadera, Kishon, and Tananim. Landscape architects, architects, and planners are all involved in doing proposals for the rivers of the coastal plain: the Alexander (Amos Brandes with Amit Segal), Taninim (Greenstein and Har-Gal), Yarkon (Arie Rachamimoff), Yachish (Amit Segal), and Hadera, Kishon, and Sorek (Braudo-Darel-Maoz conceptual plan). Each river project defines a valley, corridor, and viewshed in expanding zones of impact and influence.

An ambitious national plan for 2020 is en route to becoming a statutory plan. A five-person team headed by Shamai Asif and Arie Shachar also includes Eldad Spivak, Shlomo Hason, and Shlomo Aronson, who is responsible for the open space component. The challenges are how to respond to the extreme pressures placed on open space and how to control the sprawl and sub-

Conceptual plan of the Sorek Valley from Beit Shemesh to the sea (1995). Braudo-Maoz. Plans for the river corridor include pedestrian and bike trails along the river and defined areas for preservation, reclamation, and intensive development. Master plan (2001), Tik Projects and Tichnun Nof. (Braudo Maoz)

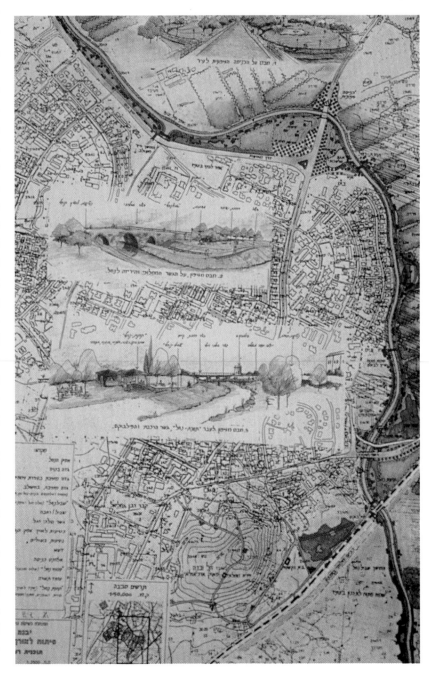

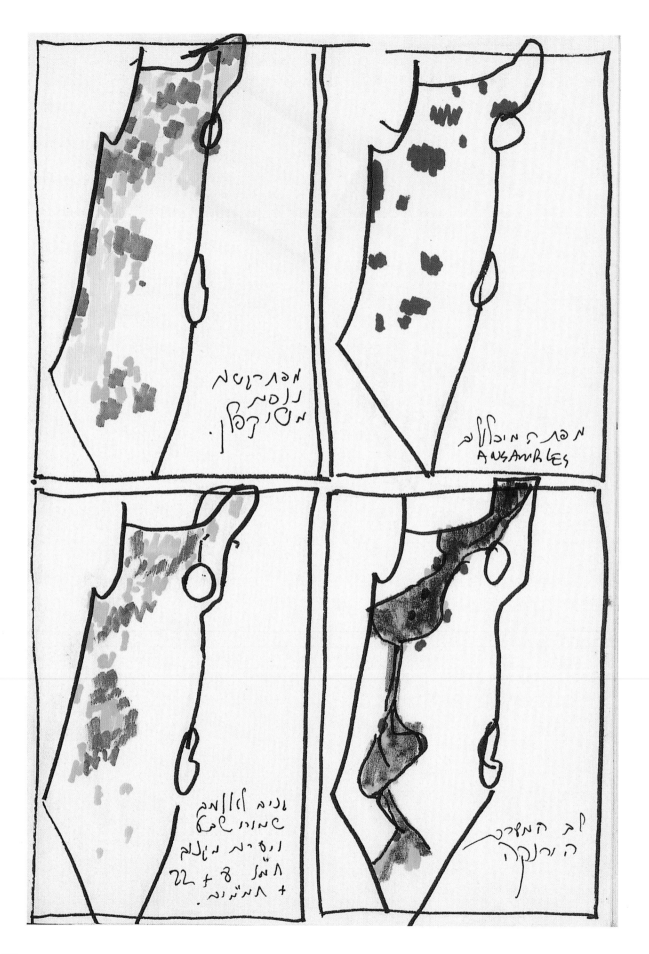

urbanization of communities. The plan has identified several tactics, including the expansion of settlements instead of the creation of new communities; preserving agriculture as open space, with the attendant subsidization; and a new classification of a "visual ensemble area." This last tactic is cultural landscape preservation on a national scale. Twenty-seven areas, equaling about 10% of the land north of Beersheva, have been identified as critical. These areas are not protected as nature reserves or national parks, but still display a landscape integrity. They are typically unspoiled mountain valleys or agricultural zones rich in archeology and history. They include many of the iconic and favorite landscapes of the nation, including the Emek Jezreel, Yavniel, Arbel, Emek Beit Netofa, Lachish region, the north shore of the Kinneret, and the Sharon. The small area of Israel is increasingly fragmented. To work against this fragmentation these visual ensemble areas, coupled with other designated open spaces, are proposed as a "Green Boulevard" running north to south. This is an imaginative extrapolation of the urban open space system idea to a national scale. This series of interconnected north-south units form the warp while the east-west open space connections, especially the river valleys, form the weft. With additional attention to the peripheral areas, a comprehensive open space plan for the nation is in the offing. Of course it will take tremendous political and social will to reach fruition and the forces against it are very powerful.

Roads

For centuries many visitors to Israel have been pilgrims, seeking to experience the places where great religious events and historical dramas took place, and continue to be enacted. The pilgrim progresses through a set of choreographed experiences, landscape rituals, and narratives. Christians visit sites associated with the life of Christ. The Via Dolorosa in Jerusalem and the fourteen stations of the cross are the best known of these. Jews follow the course of ancient and modern Jewish history. Shlomo Aronson is working on a series of projects that are intended to illuminate the landscape for visitors from abroad. He boldly conceives these as among the "veins" of the country, a series of national base lines. These include the Sherover Promenade, Dead Sea lines, the National Plan for Afforestation, and the Cross Israel Highway. Modern pilgrims arrive at Ben Gurion International Airport, the first stop in what for most visitors is an actual transect of the country. There they will be greeted by a garden epitomizing Israel in a series of groves of olives, palms, oranges, and a wheat field, an abstraction of Israel's geography. Most visitors then travel to Jerusalem. A drive of less than an hour takes them on a national cross section that goes from the Tel Aviv metropolis, through a rural fringe of an agricultural landscape of fields, orchards, and vineyards of moshavim and villages, through the terraced hills to Jerusalem, and, if they continue, to the edge of the desert.

At Latrun the ascension to Jerusalem from the coastal plane is marked by a break in topography, Sha'ar Ha-gai, a site laden with historical associations. At this site Aronson relocated a key interchange, carefully moving it away from the break in the hills. He employed the traditional elements of stone terraces and olive orchards as markers and as a transition to the hills of the Jerusalem forest that is

opposite page: 2020 plan. Sketches of the open space concept. Bottom left: National Parks, Nature Reserves and National Forests. Bottom right: The heart of the green system. (Shlomo Aronson)

+33.8

+39.0

AR

+37.6

RAMP

5.4%

+36.6

+33.8

+35.0

EXIT

EXIT

+33.8

WATER FALLS   +30.0

+33.8

SKYLIGHTS

+33.8

STONE PAVING

ENTRANCE BUILDING

directly ahead. In lieu of standard highway landscaping, terraced orchards of more than a thousand olives punctuated by entry palms were constructed on a grand scale. It is a complete design, where the highway and iconic elements of the agricultural landscape work in concert.

The hills of the Jerusalem forest lie ahead. After disastrous fires in 1995 this burnt forest is being replanted. Aronson's restoration scheme is subtle. The ancient landscape was originally reforested by the Keren Kayemet in pines and cypresses, and the experience of passing from open plain through the dark green of the enclosed forest had became a much loved landscape. The replanting scheme respects and restores that pattern with plants that are naturally regenerating. The anticipated result is a subtle combination, and a realization that arbitrary dichotomies between a natural/ecological approach and a historical/cultural approach in design are spurious: both need to be accommodated.

The design of the Tel Aviv-Jerusalem Highway is a reminder in history that roads are among the most persistent of landscape artifacts. As a primary element of infrastructure, roads are bones with the power to shape a landscape. The landscape is most often experienced along a road corridor, be it on foot or from a bicycle, bus, or car. The design of the corridor, therefore, is not solely for transportation; it also has a fundamental impact on people's perception of the landscape. At the national level Mahleket Avdot Ziburiot (or Maatz, the Public Works Department) is the national road building authority. Unfortunately modern road planning is dominated by the imperatives of traffic engineering. Landscape architects (and architects) have had to fight to have input into the design and planning of these most essential landscape components.

The dramatic changes in transportation in Israel have brought road design to the fore. There were only 24,000 private cars in 1960, 80,500 in 1965, 308,000 in 1977, and more than 1.3 million in 2000. Traffic densities are double the average of Western nations. The recent fervent spate of road building accentuates a key aspect of landscape architecture in Israel. Perhaps more than any other aspect of environmental design, roads dramatize the problem of balancing the general and the particular. The road is a supra-national landscape form with a set of standards determined by road and traffic engineering. The question of how to "place" and situate such a landscape form is an exaggerated example of what one confronts as a landscape architect all the time. The strategies are instructive. They range from minimizing the road's impact, to trying to make it seamless with its context, to walling it off from its surroundings and disassociating it from the surrounding landscape. In a few rare circumstances there are designs which try to make it into something that might constitute a distinctively Israeli response, such as Sha'ar Ha-gai or the road north from Carmiel, and the entries to Tel Aviv and Haifa.

Beginning work in 1984, Avinoam Avnon (b. 1953) was the first landscape architect for Maatz. He describes his work as the coordination of "macro-landscaping." The early involvement of landscape architects with roads was largely in terms of planting, but that role has expanded. Beginning in the 1880s eucalyptus was planted along roadsides for drainage. Landscape architects first became involved in the 1960s working on the road to Jerusalem. Planting was also done on the coast road to stabilize the shifting dunes. The mid-1980s brought a breakthrough when

opposite page: The Ben Gurion International Airport Garden (1995). (Shlomo Aronson)

View from the Carmiel-
Tefen Road. (Judith Garmi)

the road connecting Carmiel and Tefen (1989–1993) cut into the hills of the Lower Galilee. Its careful attention to the road cut and replanting became the model for subsequent construction. Judith Garmi was the designer. The goal was to relate to the area in terms of scale, materials, color, and vegetation. The road cuts were treated as a project in landscape reclamation and signs of construction were minimized. The desire was to modestly blend in, to announce the presence of the landscape, not the road.

Each interchange in Israel has a name. They are the decision-making points where people are astutely aware of their position in space. They are especially ripe places for important landscape statements. The Missubim interchange in Tel Aviv (1987) was the first that was intensively planted and irrigated. It was conceived as "a flowering interchange" with an expanded palette of plants, especially Australian species and full-grown trees. The Aluf Sade and Bar Ilan interchanges in Tel Aviv designed by Revital Shoshany were integrated designs of road, landscape, and acoustic barriers. A roadside language is slowly emerging, especially the use of appropriate plantings to characterize areas. The entries to towns act as calling cards that each community sees as a projection of its own identity. Perhaps a holdover from the ancient idea of a city gateway, this concern for the community's image is reinforced by government funding for town entries which has made possible dozens of projects.

Recent trends include Maatz's coordination with the Keren Kayemet in planting hundreds of thousands of trees in right-of-ways, with species chosen to enhance regional and local identity. Avinoam Avnon describes his major success as bringing the system to understand the role of landscape architects. Every project now has a landscape architect from the first stages. Such presence is critical in changing routes, road cuts, alignments, and the shape and size of interchanges.

In the design of the controversial Highway 6 (The Cross-Israel Highway), landscape architects for the first time had an opportunity to play a major role in road alignment, corridor treatment, and interchange location and configuration. Highway 6 is the country's first toll road and the largest construction project since the National Water Carrier, constructed in the 1950s to bring water from the Kinneret to the Negev. The eighty-six kilometer highway goes from the south of Ashdod to the outskirts of Haifa (Hadera) along the eastern corridor of the country. The design has incorporated elements of an ecological approach to ameliorate its potential negative effects. The central goal is to integrate the highway into its surroundings. More than 100 bridges were designed to be unobtrusive, plants were chosen for their adaptability to local soils, irrigation was minimized, and "seed banks" were collected from natural areas. Perennial grasses reflect seasonal changes and are sympathetic with the natural and agricultural areas that now border 80% of the highway. But the highway will surely encourage new development that will challenge the long-term program of sustainable rehabilitation.

Forests

Israel's forests epitomize the evolving relationship to the land. The scene that confronted early immigrants was the complex product of the history of human encounter with the environment. Biblical sources and descriptions describe a forested land. In contrast at the turn of twentieth century under Ottoman rule the land was denuded and desolate, the consequence of overgrazing and cutting, most recently for fuel and building materials for the railroad. However, portions of Palestine at different times in the distant and recent past have been forested. The philosophy of the Keren Kayemet, founded in 1901, molded and reflected ideas about the Israeli landscape. The early settlers and the Keren Kayemet began a program of afforestation and tree planting. It was to create shade and windbreaks, stabilize the soil, produce wood, and also create a green, comforting, and more familiar landscape for European immigrants. It was a way of possessing the land, an act of both reclamation and redemption. Land was purchased, but it was emotionally possessed through the act of planting and working. Planting trees became intertwined with building the state and asserting political control. Yosef Weitz, known as the "Father of the Forest," was the key spokesperson and the architect of Keren Kayemet afforestation policy and ideology. In 1951 Ben Gurion said that "making the wilderness bloom" was "one of the two central goals of the state,"

top: The Aluf Sade interchange. Design by Revital Shoshany.

bottom: Construction along the Cross-Israel Highway (Derech Eretz). Derech Eretz Highways is an international joint venture between Africa Israel Investments Ltd, Housing and Construction & Holding Company Ltd, and the Canadian Highways Investment Corporation. Derech Eretz is headed by CEO Ehud Savion. Landscape architect Tamar Darel-Fossfeld established the ecological approach to the rehabilitation and is managing the landscape design and development. The firms of Braudo-Maoz, Shlomo Aronson, Bruce Levin, and Greenstein-Har-Gil are providing detailed design.

and proposed planting trees over a quarter of the nation. He said: "We must clothe every mountainside with trees, every hill and rocky piece of land which cannot be successfully farmed, the dunes of the coastal plain, the Negev plains east and south of Beersheva—in other words, all the land of Edom and the Arava as far as Eilat." Ben Gurion's green dream was partially fulfilled. The numbers are formidable. In the twenty years after 1948 more than 90 million trees were planted, with an estimated two-thirds maturing. The Keren Kayemet has planted more than 200 million trees in 280 forests on 90,000 hectares of land and still plants 3 million trees a year.

After independence, which saw an end to British restrictions on planting, a massive program of afforestation was undertaken to "green" the land and create forests, which served multiple functions: tree planting provided work for thousands of arriving immigrants, trees were planted along roadways to provide shade and cover for army vehicles, and dunes were stablized. Weitz wrote that in the Negev landscape avenues of eucalyptus along roads and as shelterbelts became "green curtains." Planting also became an act of memorialization. Funded by donations, individual trees, groves, and whole forests were planted as part of the nation's memorial landscape.

A generation later the backbreaking work of the tree planters had begun to reach fruition, but as the trees matured unanticipated objections began to emerge. Monocultural plantings were criticized as "pine deserts." In the 1970s practices gradually changed. There is now an increased awareness of visual quality, ecology, and the multi-functional demands placed on the forests. In the 1980s the Keren Kayemet began to respond to user demands for the forests as open space and recreation. Access roads were built, along with trails, picnic areas, and facilities. The current generation is bringing to the situation an even more complex ecological understanding. A richer and more appropriate variety of trees are planted and the value of forests as living systems emphasized. At one time two-thirds of the plantings were Jerusalem pine, but now a wide variety is planted, including oak, carob, cypress, terebinth, acacia, eucalyptus, almonds, Judas trees, and others. This is a humanized forest, actively monitored, managed, and intensely used.

This is especially evident in the central area, where Tel Aviv and Jerusalem threaten to merge into a single metropolitan area. The designated area of the Jerusalem Forest helped to preserve this culturally and ecologically precious landscape. Forests are now divided into landscape zones in terms of their natural resources and are managed in small units. The Jerusalem Forest is no exception. Here, each valley is a distinct zone. Major and minor roads to Jerusalem lead through the forest, which is intensely used. Iris Bernstein, landscape architect for the Keren Kayemet central district, describes it as "park" forest subject to careful management and maintenance. The Keren Kayemet even hires people to clean up on Sunday after *Shabbat*.

In 1973 Mordachai Kaplan in collaboration with Shlomo Aronson produced a National Concept Plan for the Forests of Israel for the Keren Kayemet. The plan categorized the national forests in terms of use and distinctive characteristics recognizing the various functions and forms of planted forest and the rare, natural forests located largely in coastal and riparian areas. The plan tried to capture as much land within forest boundaries as possible, an important objective for a statu-

opposite page: The Keren Kayemet National Forest plan. (1995). (Keren Kayemet)

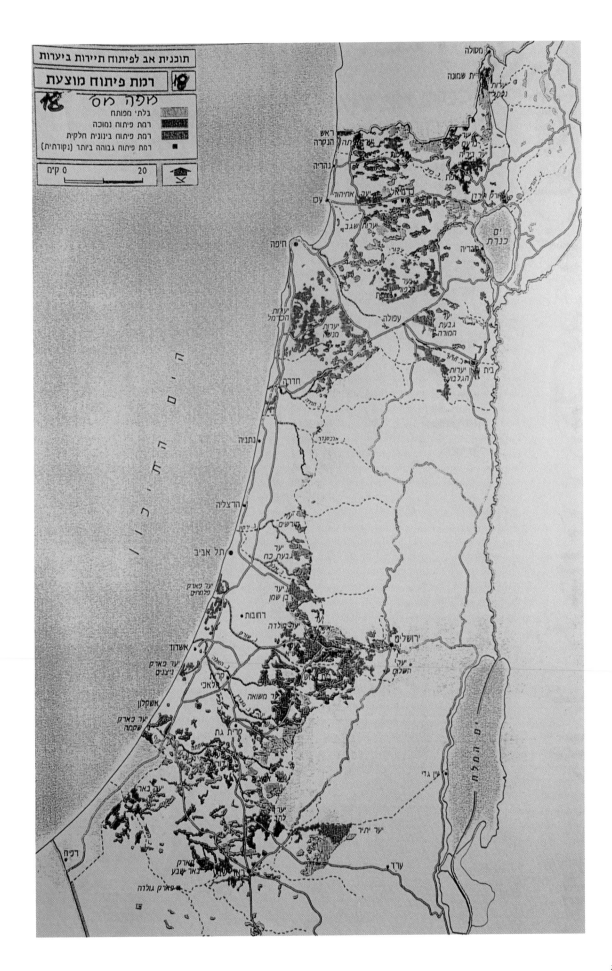

תוכנית אב לפיתוח תיירות ביערות

רמות פיתוח מוצעת

מפה מס

בלתי מפותח
רמת פיתוח נמוכה
רמת פיתוח בינונית חלקית
רמת פיתוח גבוהה ביותר (נקודתית)

0 קמ 20

Drawing of the proposed
National Recreational Trail
extending from Mt. Hermon
to the Yatir forest in the
northern Negev (1993).
(Shlomo Aronson)

ary plan has the force of law. This plan, revised in 1995 by Aronson and Keren Kayemet planners and scientists, led to the statutory National Afforestation Master Plan. The plan designated 1.6 million *dunams* of land, 16% of the land north of Beersheva, as forest. That, coupled with national parks and nature reserves, more than doubled the areas of protected landscapes and amounts to 50% of the nation north of the desert.

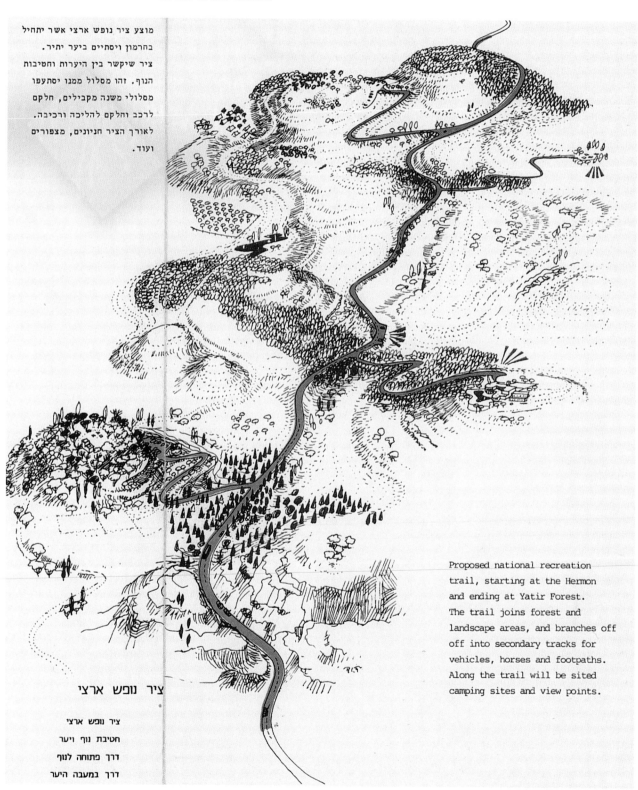

מוצע ציר נופש ארצי אשר יתחיל בחרמון ויסתיים ביער יתיר. ציר שיקשר בין היערות וחטיבות הנוף. זהו מסלול ממנו יסתעפו מסלולי משנה מקבילים, חלקם לרכב וחלקם להליכה ורכיבה. לאורך הציר חניונים, מצפורים ועוד.

ציר נופש ארצי

ציר נופש ארצי
חטיבת נוף ויער
דרך פתוחה לנוף
דרך במעבה היער

Proposed national recreation
trail, starting at the Hermon
and ending at Yatir Forest.
The trail joins forest and
landscape areas, and branches off
off into secondary tracks for
vehicles, horses and footpaths.
Along the trail will be sited
camping sites and view points.

Tayelet

One type of space begins to sum up many of the issues of landscape language, structure, and meaning in Israel. The tayelet is a landscape type that has elements of the Mediterranean *corso*, urban boulevard, waterfront promenades, and garden belvederes. They are grand terraces that connect the built environment to its larger context—urban living rooms—and they are part of daily life, places where people gather and visitors are taken. They are what Gordon Cullen called "the line of life," a linear zone in which the forces which characterize a town are concentrated.

Tayelot are also thresholds to look out from and to look back upon. With their view across horizons, cities, and craters, they address the need for a sense of expansiveness, of openness, which is becoming increasingly rare in modern Israel. As viewpoint and belvedere they afford views to the land, sea, and city. Along the Tel Aviv tayelet are views from the beach towards Jaffa and the city skyline, and from Jaffa a view across to Tel Aviv. In Haifa, there is the vista from the Carmel over the city and across the bay to Acco and the Galilee. In Jerusalem, the view is a panorama from the modern city to the west, across the Old City, Mount Scopus, Mount of Olives, and the desert to the east. At Mitzpe Ramon, the view is to the Machtesh Ramon. Tayelot offer dramatic landscape vistas but there is also the carefully orchestrated path, the strategically placed bench, shaded enclosure, and the amphitheater in which to sit. Each of these exemplifies Jay Appleton's formulation of the archetypal ideal location, a place that is both prospect and refuge, a viewpoint allowing one to scan magnificent scenes within the safety of an enclosure. When high enough such views afford map-like overviews, ways to understand complex landscapes and to place everything in perspective. These are places where people point, identity, and learn the landscape. Each tayelet provides passage and respite. In geometric terms one can think of the *mitzpor*, a lookout, as a point which, once extended, becomes the linear tayelet.

The first tayelet in Israel was Netanya's Kings Promenade by Weinberg-Oren in the 1930s, a planted promenade along the cliffs overlooking the sea. Its stairways to the beach set a pattern followed in other coastal towns such as Herzliya. One of the newest, Shvil Ami (1995) by Tally Tuch and Tami Wiener Saragossi, is found in the rural landscape connecting two Galilee kibbutzim, Kfar Blum and Sde Nehemiah. It follows a channelized section of the Jordan River. Forbidden from touching the river, the path had to be on the upper terrace, with only limited planting allowed on the slope. The design is modest, a pathway which connects the kibbutzim, grape arbors for shade, benches to rest, and deference to the river. Biblical quotations that speak of the Jordan are placed within the pathways.

The Tel Aviv tayelet, by architect Yaakov Rechter, links Tel Aviv and Jaffa. The rippling paving patterns are inspired by Rio de Janeiro's Copacabana Beach designed by Roberto Burle-Marx. The tayelet reclaimed the city's waterfront and brought back the great tayelet of the 1930s, albeit in a different form. It stands between the beach and sea on one side and the frontage road and a wall of hotels, restaurants, clubs, and pubs on the other. It magnetically attracts all and is active in every season. It is a vibrant social space used by a cross section of society mingling locals and tourists, day and night. It links Gan Ha'atzmaut to the north and Charles Chlore Park, designed by Hillel Omer, to the south. At each end it is being

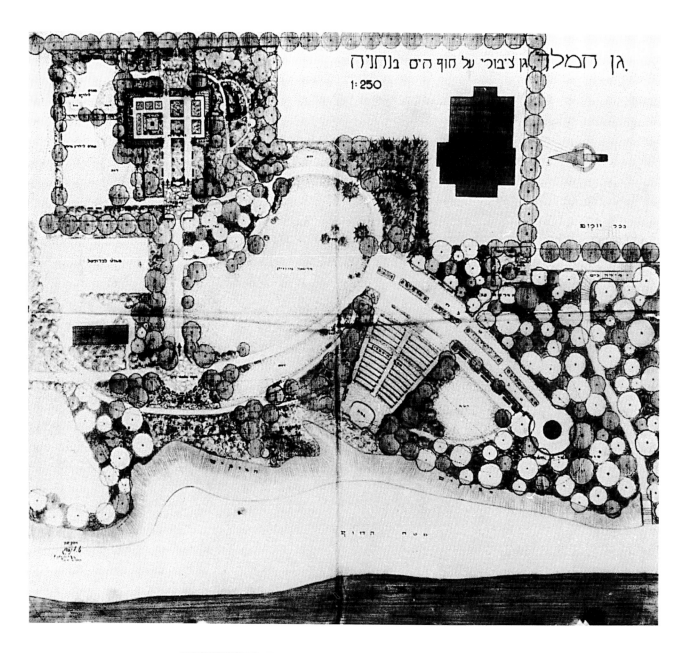

גן המלך. גן ציבורי על חוף הים בנתניה.
1:250

*Kings Promenade. Wein-
berg-Oren's scheme included
a formal entry from the city
of Netanya to a large open
meadow with walkways that
overlook the beach and the
sea. (Yagur Archives)*

*right: Kings Promenade's
amphitheater. Netanya.*

Shvil Ami. Tali Tuch and Tami Saragossi. (Doron Horowitz)

Tel Aviv Tayelet. Yaakov Rechter. (Albatross)

extended to its logical boundaries, to the north linking the port and then to the Yarkon River and park, and to the south to Jaffa.

In 1952 the depressed Yeffe Nof roadway was built at the edge of the Carmel in Haifa. Zvi Miller, then park director, proposed a promenade over the road. More than thirty years later, his partner Moshe Blum would design the Louis Promenade (1993). The promenade itself is a narrow strand, but within only a few meters parallel passages are deftly woven together. The innermost strand is set within pine trees, and backs into homes, hotels, and a park. It is green, intimate, and shady. An intermediary strand is a walkway alternatively moving between trees and then out into the open. It offers surprising private places in small eddies just off the main path and stream of traffic, but with views out across the sky. The outermost strand is a stone promenade, open to the sun and the sky with a view to the city and across the bay to Acco and on clear days to the Galilee. Blum describes the tayelet as a mirpeset, but at the scale of the city instead of an apartment. The material palette corresponds to these strands. Surprisingly delicate, it is unfurled like a stone carpet, which weaves its mosaic-like blocks with the softer materials of soil and planting. Interspersed along the 500-

meter promenade are gazebos, seating, and a stepped amphitheater. It invites people and performances. Funded by private donations, continued maintenance is not done by the city but by a special contract with Miller-Blum as supervisors. At its western end the tayelet ends at the upper reaches of the Bahai Gardens. In their most recent addition these Persian inspired gardens now terrace up the entire slope of the Carmel hillside from the German Colony at their base.

The Albert Promenade in Mitzpe Ramon, designed by Tichnun Nof (1987-1991), sits at

top left: Tel Aviv Tayelet. Yaakov Rechter. People on benches under a pergola which are scattered along the tayelet. (Albatross)

left: Louis Promenade. Haifa. Drawing of a view along the walkway. (Miller-Blum)

above: View down the tayelet. Louis Promenade. Haifa. Miller-Blum.

below: View from the innermost portion. Louis Promenade. Haifa. Miller-Blum.

the junction of the city—a modest-sized development town of 5,000 people—and a grand geological phenomena, the Makhtesh Ramon, a crater forty by nine kilometers. The site gets only sixty-five millimeters of rainfall per year. The new tayelet extends east from the glazed information pavilion along the rim of the crater and ends at a field school. The goal was to integrate the city and landscape. Along the tayelet one can always see the city and also be at the edge of the crater.

It is a simple path beside a kilometer-long stone wall, but its variegated edge gives dramatic views into the crater and of the wall that acts as a protective boundary and a capstone to the rim. It recalls walls found in other dry Mediterranean regions such as Greece and Spain. The passage is punctuated at a few points with walkways to the town and niches to get closer to the crater. The drama of the desert presides. Dekel fought not to make the place green, but defered to the colors of the sky, crater, space, and rocks. The ends of the tayelet are anchored by two mitzporim. To the west is a covered pavilion by architect Yossi Tadjar which, like the bowsprit of ship, reaches out into an ocean of air. Zvi Dekel describes it as the wings of a bird, a glider into space. It also provides much needed shade in the

View of the crater along the wall. Albert Promenade. Mitzpe-Ramon. Tichnun Nof.

View of the lookout. Albert Promenade. Mitzpe-Ramon. Tichnun Nof.

harsh setting. To the east is a sculpture by Israel Hadani. Seven vertical stone slabs like stable sails capture wind and light. Set back from the edge of the plateau they direct one's vision. Zvi Dekel saw the crater's edge as the "seashore" of Mitzpe Ramon, like being "on the beach."

If Shlomo Aronson has a signature project it is the combined Sherover (1989) and Trotner (1990) promenades, which link to the Haas Promenade (1985) designed in collaboration with Lawrence Halprin. (This collaboration completed a circle: while an architecture student at Berkeley, a lecture by Halprin convinced Aronson to study landscape architecture.) The 2.5-kilometer complex is understood as a single entity and known simply as the tayelet. The Haas section is a grand, broad stone sidewalk anchored by a belvedere and cafe. The Sherover section is a pathway through a constructed landscape of olive groves, wheat fields, and grasses (penstemin). The pathway leaves the neighborhood of Abu Tor, passes below the shaded wall of the St. Claire Monastery, and finally links to the Haas Promenade via a grand staircase. This passage features an effusion of Mediterranean plants.

The contribution to the language of design is significant. Ariel Hirschfeld has written that here Aronson is rethinking the Israeli garden. An "elegant ribbon," stunning in its own right, it consistently defers to a distant view and also urges one to attend to the details of construction and the changing aromas of plants. As one winds along its paths or descends its steps the design ties one to the visceral experience of the topography. It is *of* the city, with a view to its sacred core, yet it is *on* the cusp of the desert, where green and sand intersect. It is at the intersection of the ancient and contemporary worlds. The materials speak. The stones ascend from rough lower courses to smooth surfaces. The details are inspired by ancient works, traditional practices, and the designs of the British Romantic period in mandatory Palestine. At one point flint is used, a local stone distinct from the ubiquitous Jerusalem limestone. It is a subtle indicator of the careful attention to the locale.

Aronson describes the progression along the promenade as a series of chapters, but it is more than a simple narrative. The design rises to the level expected of its honored situation. Encompassing one slope of Jerusalem's Kidron Valley, it is a great amphitheater space, a *teatro mundi*, where everyone sits facing north towards

Plan. Sherover Promenade. Jerusalem. Shlomo Aronson. (Shlomo Aronson)

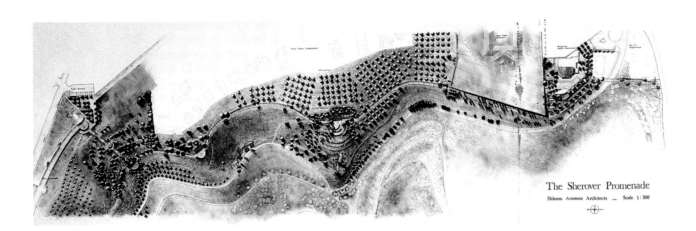

The Sherover Promenade

Shlomo Aronson Architects — Scale 1:300

View of Haas Terrace. Jerusalem. Lawrence Halprin and Shlomo Aronson.

bottom left: View of Haas Terrace. Jerusalem. Lawrence Halprin and Shlomo Aronson.

bottom right: View from Haas Terrace to Sherover Promenade. Jerusalem. Lawrence Halprin and Shlomo Aronson.

The dramatic view down the staircase towards the Old City. Jerusalem. Haas-Sherover Promenade. Shlomo Aronson.

the walled Old City and east to the desert. The grading accentuates the three-dimensionality of the space with deference to historic integrity and archaic patterns and practices. The landscape amphitheater is echoed in the constructed geometry of arcs and curves punctuated by straight axes. Culture and nature meet in a promenade at the edge of city and desert, where the vista encompasses Jerusalem from west to east, green trees and stony desert, modern construction and ancient architecture.

Aronson has called for calm in design, but his calm is tremendously exciting. Like many great spaces there is a repose between the compelling demands of tradition and the present moment, an equilibrium between the challenge of the intellect and the pleasure of the senses. Through a combination of conscious design and serendipity, the weight of history and the fragrance of rosemary have equal status. Here the intersection of the grand, historic vista laden with emotional, spiritual, and political resonance meets the everyday. Adults and children play, residents and visitors stroll, people sip coffee, and everyone monitors the progress of seasons. The place is ancient and modern, preserved and transformed, eternal and ephemeral, universal and precisely of the locale.

The next stage of this project is the Armon Hanatziv Desert Promenade, the Rhoda Goldman Promenade by Lawrence Halprin and Bruce Levin, developed from plans first made in 1975. The design begins at the east end of the Haas Promenade. The new pathway moves progressively from that formality to the traditional terraced walls of the Fellaheen farmers of the villages below. The promenade will pass through a seventy-year-old Keren Kayemet pine forest and below the United Nations headquarters. This was once the British High Commissioner's residence and remnants of Yoseph Kahaner's terraced garden will be restored. The path culminates at a stone amphitheater with views back to the Old City and east to the Dead Sea, Jordan, and the mountains of Edom in the distance.

Goldman Promenade, Armon Hanatziv (1997). Jerusalem. Lawrence Halprin and Bruce Levin. Drawing by Lawrence Halprin. (Bruce Levin)

THE WORK OF Israeli landscape architects has helped shape the nation. The places they have created are part of the new national base map, the ground which will structure future transformations, the framework for design and development. The achievement of the small community of Israel's landscape architects in creating a national landscape is as grand as any in the second half of the twentieth century. In the Israeli landscape of the future landscape architects can play an even expanded role.

Israel's story has been a response to historical imperatives. As these change, so too will landscape architecture in Israel. The past surely shapes the future, but new demands and questions will inevitably emerge. Some will be predictable, others not. The key question for the next generation of landscape architects will be how to respond to cultural and environmental changes. Their work can anticipate and help direct the evolution of the Israeli landscape. It is time for new visions and dreams.

Where is the landscape going? What are the challenges for the future? After a half-century of statehood a new set of conditions confront the society and designers. The list is long and daunting. There have been grand shifts in a half-century. The society has evolved from a broad-based and pioneering agricultural society to a post-industrial, information-based service society. In many ways it has to a large degree bypassed a period of industrialization. Some describe this as a post-Zionist landscape.

There is a major ongoing psychological shift from building the country and landscape to preserving the landscape. Landscape architects have been at the nexus of having to accommodate growth and development, often working with great rapidity on large numbers of projects, with minimal or tight budgets, poor maintenance, and government constraints. They have been at the intersection where pragmatic necessity confronted idealistic vision, one that remains strong despite rising cynicism and revisionism. Nonetheless an examination of their work often reveals places where their decisions were sound. The basic structure and frame-

Chapter 12

The Next Generation

Here in these mountains,
hope belongs to
the landscape
Like the water holes.
Even the ones
with no water
Still belong to the
landscape like hope.
—Yehuda Amichai

opposite page:
Drip irrigation. Arava.

work of open space has sucessfully molded communities. It has not been encroached upon. In its maturation plantings have grown and softened what was once raw and unsightly.

The challenges for the next generation are dramatically spatial. Remnants of open space will need to be preserved and jealously guarded. Signs of the loss of open land are everywhere. Standing at most viewpoints and belvederes one always looks towards development. There are few "empty" open spaces. The sharp boundaries between the city and countryside are eroding and much of the nation is now encapsulated in metropolitan Haifa, Tel Aviv, Jerusalem, or Beersheva. The agricultural landscape has been the basic frame for much of the country and its settlements, but agriculture's role is decreasing. As pressures increase, there will be an enhanced need to protect landscape quality and preserve scarce landscapes, while simultaneously shepherding new and needed development. The role of landscape architects in both landscape preservation and the thoughtful multi-purpose planning of land will become more critical, but the creation and feeling of open space, *a phenomenology of openness*, will also be essential. More places of respite will be needed and the edges that offer the grand view and sense of spaciousness and horizon, the seam between sky and landscape, will be vital.

Israel remains a nation under construction. The population is anticipated to rise to 8 or even 9 million by 2020 and the density to rise proportionally. An almost 30% increase in population in the 1990s and its attendant opportunities and problems was a harbinger of tomorrow. Only 5% of Israelis now live on kibbutzim or moshavim and 44% live in the Tel Aviv metropolis alone. The economy is in transition from a modified socialist system to a free enterprise capitalist society. Previously the government was involved in everything, especially in decisions effecting the landscape. The new economy is characterized by privatization in all spheres, including private sector development. Kibbutzim and moshavim, once pioneering settlements, are now mature communities, even historic sites.

A poor nation has become more affluent. Economic development of the nation is incomplete, but it has been extraordinarily successful. Within a generation a higher standard of living has become commonplace, but the satisfaction of one set of needs creates new aspirations and problems. What satisfied previous generations no longer meets expectations: the once rare dishwasher becomes commonplace, the rooftop solar heater is replaced by the electric version, one car (once a luxury) now must be two, apartments have to be larger, and more aspire to a free standing home and garden. The landscape impacts of these changes are dramatic and they are accompanied by a growing demand for the *open spaces* of affluence: villas, clubs, marinas, offices, hotels, commercial centers, and office buildings. There are more places of commercial recreation and the construction of waterplay parks and wedding parks. More colleges will be designed as opportunities for higher education expand. With economic change the demands of work and the expectations of leisure are shifting. Israeli time is changing. The nation is inevitably moving from a six- to a five-day work week. (Schools are still six days. When they change the shift will be virtually complete.) This changes the patterns of landscape use, especially in terms of recreation. A more typical two-day western "weekend" is emerging, superseding the single day of Shabbat.

In summary, the Israeli way of life and what constitutes the "good life" along with its accompanying landscape manifestations is transforming. Many of these developments—products of affluence and success—are not unique to Israel. The design challenge remains how to *root them* in Israel. Dealing with each of the themes discussed in this book is part of that challenge. The vocabulary and language of landscape design and how it is spoken will change in foreseeable and unforeseeable ways. The traditional skills and craft of using materials, especially stone, are waning. Manufactured materials and processes are becoming more common. The continuing struggle to define places through an indigenous language of plants will become even more difficult as more exotic materials are introduced, and as the meaning and associations of plants change. Retaining an Israeli particularity will become even more difficult.

Water consumption is changing. Agriculture has been the primary water consumer, but as agricultural demand for water recedes (or is rationed) more is made available for domestic and civic use. Perhaps future economies of desalinization will make water more abundant, but continued frugality is the more likely prospect. Israel's few streams and water bodies are already under renewed attention in terms of water quality. Plans and designs that will allow them to reach their full potential as open space and for recreation represent a most promising trend.

The demands on open space are heavy and uses are changing. Sites near population centers experience higher levels of intensity of use and are under significant pressure. Those at the periphery are less vulnerable, but given Israel's condensed geography, almost any place, especially favored recreational sites, are close at hand. Development and technology have changed the space of the nation. Places that were once remote and isolated are now in the core of the country. The periphery is closer. The Negev, the south, has always symbolized Israel's future. The continued question of how to develop and preserve it will only become more paramount.

Technology has radically impacted landscape behavior. When air conditioning was unknown the only comfort to be found was outside on the street, in cafes, parks, and at the beach. With air conditioning commonplace in public places and more affordable at home, the physical comfort of being in the open air changes from necessity to amenity. Television wasn't introduced in Israel until 1968 and cable TV not until the 1990s. Their effect has been dramatic. Television brings people inside, unlike the ubiquitous radio, still always raised in volume for the hourly news broadcasts. This behavior has been recently supplemented by cellular phones, as private, inside behavior moves outside into the public arena. There will surely be additional new and unforeseen technologies and cultural developments that will impact behavior and design.

The move to universal automobile ownership is pronounced, and the consequences are catastrophic. Cars bring pollution, accidents, traffic, and stress—as well as consuming precious land for roads, parking, and services. They alter the pace and pattern of communities. Management of the automobile, attempting to keep it in proper perspective and place (literally), is a central task, one confronting much of the modern world. In a broad sense a pedestrian culture with public transit is changing to a car culture. People drive more, walk less, and extend their home range from neighborhood to the nation. All of this impacts the landscape, from the desire for more roads, to increased internal tourism, to the development of facilities and sites.

One of the most obvious spatial opportunities may be the street itself, which needs to be reconceived not only as a transportation corridor, but also as urban open space. Most outdoor activity occurs on streets, but the streets are increasingly overwhelmed by traffic. What once were wonderful pedestrian spaces are now too often parking spaces. Cars need to be tamed and domesticated, but too often the bullying car is winning. As in many European cities the car inevitably will be stored underground. Density makes mass transit both an obvious necessity and a part of the solution. The nation's already fine bus system needs to be supplemented by railroad, light rail, and bicycles. The proposed extensions of rail travel are promising, but visionary plans have languished for years. The flat coastal plain and mild climate make Israel ideal for a culture of cycling. Multi-use transportation corridors will be the work of landscape architects.

The relationship between inside-outside is in constant flux, as the landscape changes inside Israel and as more powerful outside forces, under the banner of globalization, exert their almost irresistible influences. There is always the need to look for lessons in the proper places. Too often the spacious and affluent United States is viewed as the model, when solutions can be found in other small, densely populated, socially enlightened countries such as Denmark and the Netherlands. There are other significant lessons to be gleaned from Mediterranean and Middle Eastern examples. The nation is becoming more international through communications, travel, and technology. A reaction against the excess of outside influence demands that renewed attention be paid to local character. Many possibilities have not been explored by designers. The local is manifest in many ways, including a rich vein of vernacular and folk practice, wellsprings of form and meaning that heretofore have been largely untapped by landscape architects. There are lessons to be found in an afternoon walk. Thousands of mirpesot display imaginative designs in tight spaces. There are the pruned, arched fig gateways to apartments. The gardens of personal collections, most often found on kibbutzim, are wonderful examples of folk art and sculpture. Israel is the world's pioneer in drip irrigation systems. Fields and gardens are ribbons of brown tubing, especially when plantings are new, but no designer has truly exploited its wonderful formal properties. Here is a chance to draw on the ground.

The cultural richness of Israel's communities—and their artistry, craft, and customs—has not sufficiently penetrated or been appreciated by the world of landscape architectural design. There is inspiration to be found in Yemenite jewelry, Persian carpets, Russian embroidery, the artistry of calligraphy, and diamond cut-

A ficus archway. Haifa.

A falafel stand. Haifa.

ters. There is something to learn from the popular Israeli landscape which is still a bit raw, but very vital and remarkably a rich cultural mix. Landscape architects need not only to look to ancient sites and the great traditions, but also to the noisy, energetic traditions all around them. There is a language of the street and the vitality of the *souk*, beach, bus station, and the gardens of salads found at sidewalk falafel stands. A respite from the *balagan* is not the only answer. There is an aesthetic in the modern, fast-paced, dynamic, and sometimes coarser aspects of Israeli life that can be embraced in all its energy. It is to the next generation to respond to this world.

While Israeli designers have been inspired by the traditional Arab landscape, a great untapped opportunity lies in the human resources of Israel's Arab population. Heretofore landscape architecture has made few inroads into the Israeli-Arab design community, but will surely do so in the future. It is essential that this population is recruited into the professional ranks. These communities have much to offer and can also benefit from the professional services of landscape architects.

The future will also demand attention not only to over-development and large-scale spaces, but also to the basics of design. As space becomes scarcer the need for thoughtful and considered design will be increased. The cracks and openings between buildings, the tears in the urban fabric, await attention. The collective impact of such small gestures will make a difference in this future. At the highest densities urban rooftops await discovery. Building over as well as up offers potential, such as the use of air rights over roadways. Tel Aviv's Ayalon Highway may ultimately become a tunnel, not a gash through the metropolis.

There are vast areas that await reclamation. In much of the world, this is already central to landscape architecture practice. Older, hastily and poorly built projects need to be revisited and reclaimed, restored or transformed. There are despoiled

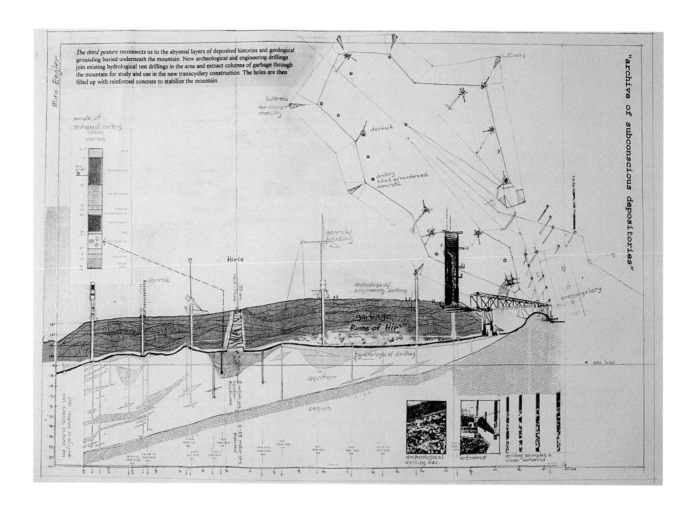

The third gesture reconnects us to the abysmal layers of deposited histories and geological grounding buried underneath the mountain. New archeological and engineering drillings join existing hydrological test drillings in the area and extract columns of garbage through the mountain for study and use in the new transcyclery construction. The holes are then filled up with reinforced concrete to stabilize the mountain.

Design proposal. Hiriya. Tel Aviv. (Drawing, Mira Engler)

derelict lands, industrial sites, beach fronts, and military facilities. Haifa Bay and the polluted Kishon River, quarries, and mountains of garbage await reclamation. The exhibit of alternatives for the Hiriya landfill site at the Tel Aviv Art Museum was a promising first step. Mira Engler's proposal is sympathetic with the Israeli archeological sensibility, only now it is directed toward the waste of the modern city and the mountain *it* has created.

Scientific understanding of natural processes is now fundamental to the practice of landscape architecture. Israel has lagged behind in this area, but is moving rapidly to address ecological concerns. The level of scientific expertise in the country is exceptional and expanded collaboration with landscape architects is inevitable. In the modern city open spaces are fundamental to the preservation of natural systems. Their design can also illuminate and reveal the ecological and natural order of where we live and tell us something about our relationship to the natural world. These are landscape stories waiting to be told.

Landscape architects have a particular responsibility for the preservation and study of their design heritage. There are many older gardens and parks that need immediate restoration. Sadly, visitors to Gan Ha Aliyah HaShniyah see an artificial stream where the water no longer flows; the plantings at Gan Ha Metzuda in Safed are overgrown; the Negev Memorial is strewn with garbage; the water channel of Sderot Hagiborim in Ramat Gan is dry. Care of these sites can be coupled with the growing imperative to preserve the rapidly deteriorating and endangered modern history of the country. As this text has made clear there are lessons in the work of these pioneering designers worth heeding.

The future will also bring the need for international cooperation. Solutions to environmental problems cannot be found inside national boundaries. Confronting issues of water and resource conservation and development is inevitable. All nations bordering the Mediterranean and Red seas share their fates, and tourism will continue to be an ever more significant design and planning determinant. There are hopeful signs, such as the establishment of the binational Red Sea Marine Park with Jordan, part of an agreement on Special Arrangements for Aqaba and Eilat in 1966.

Underlying all considerations will continue to be that of security. During the research and writing of this book the prospects for peace have oscillated from a wary optimism, to deep pessimism, to reluctant realism. Hopefully Israel is moving from being a country at war to a country at peace. The future's most exciting and optimistic prospect lies in a landscape of peace, with open borders and cross-cultural contact. Linkages, connections, and cooperation once only imagined are becoming possible. Israel will be less isolated and more connected to its region. Vast lands in the Negev, along the coast and in almost every community, are under the control of IDF (Israel Defense Forces). These hold much promise. The military may prove to have been a land bank for the nation. Peace could bring a massive tourist influx, affording the stimulus for true coordinated planning with neighboring Palestinians, Jordanians, Lebanese, Egyptians, and Syrians. The interaction of Israel and its neighbors will surely have an impact on design. With the prospects of open borders, more landscape needs may be satisfied outside of the nation. This is already the case in Europe and may be that of Israel and its neighbors. (The Sinai, even after its return to Egypt, is still visited regularly.) There are lessons to be learned between the cities of Haifa and Beirut, Jerusalem and Amman, Tel Aviv and Cairo, Aqaba and Eilat. The opportunities should inspire the imaginations and dreams of the next generation. The prospects are boundless. Imagine the possibilities of rail connections reestablished from Damascus to Cairo with stops at Tel Aviv and Gaza, or the Tel Aviv-Amman Parkway, the Galilee-Golan Greenway, the Dead Sea World Heritage Site, the rebirth of the Nabattean trade route across Sinai and the Negev to Petra and beyond, or a Green Line which is green. Hopefully peace means a landscape of fewer memorials.

The highly emotional and contested relationships between Israel and its Arab neighbors and citizens will continue to be part of the future of design, especially as the Palestinians assert their own claims to landscape imagery and the land itself. For designers the line between being inspired by and even honoring others and the appropriation of ideas and forms is often difficult to traverse and will surely be part of future discussion.

A landscape under continuous construction, in a culture under great pressure, has offered too little time for reflection. Yet landscape architects are well aware of the successes, failures, and limitations of their work. There is a move from a period of building to one of consolidation and renewal. The time is already here to reconsider past projects undertaken in haste, a time to create systems and connections out of discrete projects and parcels, a time to add layers of beyond immediate need, a time to redress social wrongs, a time to readdress the land as the basis for life and society, and a time to add new layers of commentary and meaning. One of the most dramatic impressions of the Israeli landscape in the twenty-first century is the volume of work undertaken by landscape architects. The projects and ideas discussed here represent the work of only a few hundred individuals. As is typical of Israelis, they take modest pride in their accomplishments, but are rarely satisfied. In his eighties, Lippa Yaholom cautions that landscape architects "should have more doubt in their work," and engage in more self-criticism. Responding to the current state of design and landscape is the first step in imagining the future of landscape architecture in Israel. The range is wide, but there are some areas of agreement. The sympathetic character of earlier design eras is often overwhelmed by expansive development that seems to happen spontaneously, and is often ugly, banal, over designed, and bombastic. Many seek a return to modesty, the need for greater simplicity and restraint. Most common is a quest for a kind of ease and comfort. Critic Ariel Hirshfeld suggests not looking for what is original but for what is right, and notes that some of the most significant places were the simplest.

Landscape architecture in Israel is maturing, but it is at a critical juncture. The pioneering professionals enjoyed on-site, hands-on experience which is now rare. There has been the dramatic growth in the number of practitioners educated within the country. Institutionally landscape architects are well positioned in terms of planning, design, and construction. After fifty years of professional effort they now hold key positions in Misrad-ha-Shikkun and Maatz, the National Parks Authority, the Keren Kayemet, kibbutzim, city parks and planning departments, and regional councils. The professional relationships with architects, engineers, planners, and gardeners continue to evolve and more attention needs to be paid to the role landscape architects have to play in collaborative practice. For certain projects it is mandated that landscape architects must be part of design teams, an exceptional accomplishment for so young a profession. The next generation of professionals needs to be more assertive in its role in these institutional situations. Israeli landscape architects have served the society's social and cultural agenda through their professional skill and artistry. It is now incumbent upon them to assume a mantle of leadership and to continue in the field's best visionary tradition, offering direction and even inspiration.

Landscape architecture is an optimistic art. All planting implies caretakers to tend and nurture the garden and sufficient time without disturbance to allow places to reach maturity. Oftentimes designers will never live to see their work as conceived. It is done for future generations. While the contribution of the designs discussed here to Israeli life is immeasurable, they will have even greater value for the future. Landscape architecture is not an instant art, and rarely at its best when first constructed. Now there is a legacy of work and places to study. It will act as a model, precedent, and inspiration for future work, from which one can learn and extend the best of the past. Everything discussed here requires further observation, description, study, analysis, and critique for its value to find a place in future design.

The era of the pioneers is over. New challenges await. The hope is for landscape architects who understand the past, know the needs of our time, and are mindful of the future. The hope is that designers will continue to create places that speak a landscape language that is rich, eloquent, and poetic. The hope is for landscape architects to continue to take the best from outside while learning from within, to be bold enough to respect tradition yet continue to invest it with the vigor of innovation, and to retain a sense of idealism and mission. After a lifetime of work, Lippa Yahalom, now in retirement, notes: "I still dream gardens."

Aliyah – Hebrew for "going up," it refers to the successive waves of immigration to Israel.

Arava – Hebrew for "plain," it is the long, dry region between the Dead Sea and Eilat.

Ashkenazi – Refers to Jews from Central, Eastern, and Northern Europe.

Balagan – Hebrew for a ruckus or a messy situation.

Bereshit – Hebrew for "in the beginning." The first book of the Torah, Genesis.

Bezalel – An arts school in Jerusalem founded in 1906 by Boris Schatz and named for the first artist noted in the Bible.

Bikkurim – Hebrew for "first fruits" in biblical times brought to the Temple at the festival of Shavuot.

Bustan (pl. bustanim) – A garden distinguished by the combination of elements of an agricultural garden and pleasure garden. It is a garden type found in some variation throughout the Islamic world.

Carmel – A mountain ridge which begins in Haifa and goes south for 19.2 kilometers.

Diaspora – Refers to the historic dispersion of Jews in exile from Israel. The term now refers to Jewish communities outside of Israel.

Dreidel – A four-sided top spun at Hanukah with Hebrew letters on each side.

Dunam – A land measure. Four dunams equals approximately one acre.

Emek – Hebrew for valley, it has specific reference to the Emek Jezreel, the Jezreel Valley, the largest valley in the country. It stretches southeast from Haifa towards Beit Shean and the Jordan Valley.

Eretz Yisrael – Hebrew for "the Land of Israel." The meaning of land here refers both to a geographical area and the nation.

Etrog – A citron, traditionally carved during the holiday of Sukkot.

Gadna – Pre-army training for high school students.

Galilee – The northern region of Israel. It is divided into an upper and lower region. It is the most mountainous, wettest portion of the country and the home to the largest portion of the Israeli-Arab population.

Gan – Hebrew for ornamental garden, it also refers to kindergarten.

Gan Leumi – The term for Israel's national parks.

Gan Noi – Ornamental gardening.

Gemara – Commentaries on the Mishnah.

Ha-aretz – A term used synonymously with Israel, meaning the country or nation.

Har – Hebrew for mountain.

Hadar – The downtown of Haifa.

Halutzim – Hebrew for pioneers.

Hectare – A unit of land measure equal to 2.471 acres.

Huleh – A lake and swamp north of the Sea of Galilee. Its size is much diminished as areas of the marsh were drained by pioneers.

Hutz-la-aretz – Hebrew for "outside of the country."

IDF – The acronym for Israel Defense Forces, the army.

Kaddish – The Jewish prayer for the dead, recited by mourners.

Keren Kayemet Le-Yisrael – Hebrew for the Jewish National Fund (JNF), founded in 1901.

Kibbutz (pl. Kibbutzim) – Communal, egalitarian agricultural settlements, with land and property in communal ownership. The first kibbutz was Degania, established in 1909. There are now 250 kibbutzim. The kibbutz and its members have been central to Israel's culture and ideology. Each kibbutz is a member of a larger movement, each with a distinct ideological point of view.

Kikar – Hebrew for public square or plaza.

Kilometer – A unit of length equal to .621 miles.

Kinneret – The Sea of Galilee. It is only twenty-one kilometers long and eight to twelve kilometers wide and 197 meters below sea level. It is the primary source of fresh water for the country and a prime recreational location.

Kumsitz – Traditional campfires that are lit during the holiday of Lag-ba-Omer.

Knesset – The Israeli Parliament.

Kurkar – A limestone found on the coastal plain and used as a building material.

Lag-ba-Omer – A Jewish holiday that falls in the spring between Passover and Shavuot.

Lulav – A bundle of palm branches carried during the service during Sukkot.

Ma'abarot – Temporary tent encampments for new immigrants.

Maatz – Mahleket Avdot Ziburiot, the Public Works Department, Israel's road builders.

Machtesh Ramon – An immense geological crater in the northern Negev.

Makom – Hebrew for place, but it can also refer to scared places and a divine presence.

Mandate – After the demise of the Ottoman Empire, under the League of Nations Palestine was under a British Mandate from the end of WWI until 1948.

Mangal – Grilling out-of-doors, especially meat: a barbeque. The practice is associated especially with the Sephardic and Israeli-Arab community.

Meter – A unit of length equal to 39.37 inches.

Midrachov – Hebrew for a pedestrian street.

Mirpeset (pl. mirpasot) – Hebrew for balcony.

Mishnah – The Oral Law. Along with the Gemara it forms the Talmud.

Misrad ha-shikkun – Hebrew for the Housing Ministry which historically has been responsible for much of the building in the country.

Mitzpor – Hebrew for observation point or lookout.

Mitzpe (pl. mitzpim) – Often used synonymously with *mitzpor*, in recent years it also refers to hilltop settlements in the Galilee.

Moledet – Hebrew for homeland, it refers to the broader area of study of the nation.

Moshav (pl. moshavot) – Cooperative agricultural settlements. In *moshav shitufi* family life is private, but the economy follows the communal pattern of collective production of the kibbutz.

Nabateans – A people who inhabited the area of the Negev between third century B.C and A.D. 500. Their cities included Avdat, Shivta, and Mamshit, with the capital in Petra, now in Jordan.

Nahal – Hebrew for stream. See *wadi*.

Negev – The southern desert region of Israel, occupying almost 60% of its area.

Nof – Hebrew for landscape or view.

Oleh Chadash – Hebrew for a new immigrant.

Oleh (pl. olim) – Hebrew for immigrant.

Pardes (pl. pardesim) – Hebrew for orchard, particularly citrus.

Passover (*Pesach* in Hebrew) – One of the major Jewish festivals commemorating the exodus from Egypt.

Purim – The Festival of Lots, celebrating the deliverance of Persian Jewry. During the holiday it is customary, especially for children, to dress up in costume.

Sabra – A native-born Israeli, after the eponymous cactus.

Sde Boker – A kibbutz in the northern Negev where David Ben-Gurion made his home after his retirement. Nearby is the site of a desert research station.

Sephardic – Originally referring to Jews from Spain (*Sepharad* in Hebrew), but extended to Jews from the Mediterranean, North Africa, and the Middle East.

Shabbat – Hebrew for the Sabbath.

Sharon – The central plain region of Israel between Haifa and Tel Aviv. It has been a major agricultural region, especially citrus orchards. It is now under great pressure for development.

Shekhuna (pl. shekhunot) – The residential quarters of a community.

Shikkun (pl. shikkunim) – Housing projects.

Shoah – The Hebrew term for the Holocaust.

Shoresh – Hebrew for the three-letter root of words.

Souk – Arabic for market.

Sukkah – A temporary structure where people eat and sometimes sleep during Sukkot.

Sukkot – The fall Feast of the Tabernacles. One of three ancient pilgrimage festivals, along with Passover and Shavuot.

Talmud – The basic codification and compilation of Jewish Law, combining the Mishnah (the Oral law) and the Gemara, commentaries on the Mishnah. The study of the Talmud is the fundamental source of Jewish learning.

Tayelet (pl. tayalot) – Hebrew for a promenade.

Tel – Artificial mounds or hills which cover ruins, often of cities.

Templar – Refers to the Crusader order of the Templars and to a German-Christian sect that settled in Palestine in the nineteenth century.

Tiulim – Hebrew for trips.

Tichnun – Hebrew for design.

Tu' bi-shevat – Described in the Talmud as the "New Year for Trees," it is much like Arbor Day in the United States of America, but with songs and festivity.

T'zofim – A youth scouting movement.

Ulpan – Intensive language classes oriented toward new immigrants.

Wadi – Arabic for a dry river bed. See *nahal*.

Yad Lebanim – A memorial for fallen soldiers.

Yad Vashem – Israel's national memorial to the Shoah (holocaust), located in Jerusalem.

Yediat ha-aretz – The study of the land, encompassing natural and cultural history.

Yishuv – The term applies to the Jewish community in Palestine before 1948.

Yizkor book – The compilation of the deceased and the histories of communities destroyed in the Holocaust.

Yom Ha Atzmaut – Israel Independence Day.

Yom Hazikaron – Israel's Memorial Day, it falls the day before Yom Hatzmaut.

Yom Kippur – The Day of Atonement, which follows Rosh Hashanah (the New Year). Together they are known as the High Holidays. Yom Kippur is the most solemn day in the Jewish calendar.

Zionism – Modern Zionism is the political, social, and religious movement to establish a Jewish state in its ancient homeland. The first Zionist Congress was held in Basel in 1897, convened by Theodor Herzl.

Alon Mozes, Tal, and Amir, Shaul. "Landscape and Ideology: The Emergence of Vernacular Gardening Culture in Pre-State Israel." *Landscape Journal 21*(2) (2002): forthcoming.

Alter, Robert. *Modern Hebrew Literature.* New York: Behrman, 1975.

Altman, Elisabeth A., and Betsey R. Rosenbaum. "Principles of Planning and Zionist Ideology: The Israeli Development Town." *American Institute of Planning Journal 9*(10) (1973): 316–325.

Aronson, Shlomo. "From Yatir to the Negev: Greening the Israeli Landscape." *Landscape Architecture.* 67(5) (1977): 394–398.

Ben Arav, Josef. *Gardens and Landscape of Israel.* Tel Aviv: Hakibbutz ha'Meuhad, 1981.

Ben-Ari, Eyal, and Yoram Bilu, eds. *Grasping Land: Space and Place in Contemporary Israeli Discourse and Experience.* Albany: State University of New York Press, 1997.

Benvenisti, Meron. *Conflicts and Contradictions.* New York: Villard, 1986.

Bernstein, Ellen. *Ecology & the Jewish Spirit.* Woodstock, VT: Jewish Lights, 1998.

Bigelman, Shimon. *Ganei Yerushalaim (The Gardens of Jerusalem).* Jerusalem: Bet ha-hotsa'ah ha-Yerushalami, 1988.

Blocker, Joel, ed. *Israeli Stories: A Selection of the Best Writing in Israel Today.* New York: Schocken, 1962.

Braudo, Alisa. "The Bustan: A Garden of the Past in Today's Landscapes." Master's thesis, University of Oregon, 1983.

Burmil, Shmuel. "Protected Areas and Management Agencies in Arid Landscapes." Ph.D. dissertation, University of Arizona, 1994.

Further Reading

"… they shall know the land…"
—Numbers 14:31

Carta's Historical Atlas of Israel. Jerusalem: Carta, 1977.

Cohen, Shaul Ephriam. *The Politics of Planting: Israeli-Palestinian Competition for Control of Land in the Jerusalem Periphery.* Chicago: University of Chicago Press, 1993.

Danziger, Yitzhak. *The Rehabilitation of the Nesher Quarry.* Jerusalem: Central, 1971.

Debel, Ruth. "What Does It Mean To Be An Israeli Artist?" *ARTNews* 77(5) (1978): 52–56.

Devir, Ori. *Off the Beaten Track in Israel: A Guide to Beautiful Places.* New York: Adama, 1985.

Efrat, Elisha. *Urbanization in Israel.* London: Croom Helm, 1984.

Enis, Ruth. "On the Pioneering Work of Landscape Architects in Israel: A Historical Review." *Landscape Journal* 11(1) (1992): 22–34.

——— "Kibbutz Ideology and Lifestyle as Reflected in the Kubbutz Gardens." *Landscape Research* 18(3) (1993):110–119.

——— "The Impact of the 'Israelitische Gartenbauschule Ahlem' on Landscape Architecture in Israel." *Die Gartenkunst. 10*(2) (1998): 311–330.

Enis, Ruth, and Joseph Ben-Arav. *Ganim vanof bakibbutz (Sixty Years of Kibbutz Gardens and Landscape [1910-1970]).* Ministry of Defense: Israel, 1994.

Evenari, Michael, Leslie Shanan and Naphtali Tadmor. *The Negev: The Challenge of the Desert.* Cambridge: Harvard University Press, 1982.

Eyal Ben-Ari, and Yoram Bilu, eds. *Space and Place in Contemporary Israeli Discourse and Experience.* Albany: State University of New York Press, 1997.

Fischer, Yona. *25 Years of Art in Israel: From Landscape to Abstraction—From Abstraction to Nature.* Jerusalem: Israel Museum, 1972.

Friedländer, Saul. "Memory of the Shoah in Israel." In *The Art of Memory: Holocaust Memorials,* edited by James E. Young. Munich: Prestel-Verlag, 1994.

Gilbert, Martin. *Jerusalem History Atlas.* New York: Macmillan, 1977.

Glikson, Artur. "Urban Design in New Towns and Neighborhoods." *Landscape Architecture* 52(3) (1962):169–172.

Glueck, Nelson. *Rivers in the Desert: A History of the Negev.* New York: Grove, 1959.

Goodman, Susan Tumarkin. *Artists of Israel: 1920-1980,* New York: Jewish Museum, 1981.

Gradus, Yehuda, and Gabriel Lipshitz. *The Mosaic of Israeli Geography.* Beer Sheva: Ben-Gurion University of the Negev, 1996.

Halprin, Lawrence. "New Life in an Old Land." *Landscape Architecture.* 52(3) (1962): 155–157.

———— *Lawrence Halprin: Changing Places.* San Francisco: San Francisco Museum of Modern Art, 1986.

Har-gil, Gil. "An Historical Analysis of the Landscape of the Kibbutz Garden." Ph.D. dissertation, Technion, Israel Institute of Technology, 1992.

Hareuveni, Nogah. *Nature in Our Biblical Heritage.* Translated by Helen Frenkley. Kiryat Ono: Neot Kedumin, 1980.

———— *Tree and Shrub in Our Biblical Heritage.* Translated by Helen Frenkley. Kiryat Ono: Neot Kedumin, 1984.

Harlap, Amiram. *New Israeli Architecture.* Rutherford, NJ: Fairleigh Dickinson University Press, 1992.

Helphand, Kenneth. "Constants and Variables: Basic Themes in Landscape Architecture." In *Point of View: Four Approaches to Landscape Architecture in Israel,* by Mordechai Omer *et al.* Tel Aviv: Genia Schreiber University Art Center, 1996.

Herbert, Gilbert, and Silvina Sosnovsky. *Bauhaus on the Carmel and the Crossroads of the Empire: Architecture and Planning in Haifa during the British Mandate.* Jerusalem: Yad Izhak Ben-Zvi, 1993.

Herzl, Theodor. *Altneuland:.* Haifa: Haifa, 1960 [1902].

Heschel, Abraham Joshua. *The Sabbath: It's Meaning for Modern Man.* New York: Noonday, 1951.

Hirshfeld, Ariel. *Reshimot al Makom (Local Notes),* Tel Aviv: Am Oved, 2000.

Howe, Kathleen Stewart. *Revealing the Holy Land: Photographic Exploration of Palestine.* Berkeley: University of California Press, 1997.

Jacobs, Peter, and Kenneth Helphand. *Shlomo Aronson: Making Peace with the Land.* Washington, D. C.: Spacemaker Press, 1998.

Kauffmann, Richard, "Planning of Jewish Settlements in Palestine." *The Town Planning Review 12*(2) (1926): 93–116.

Kendall, Henry. *Jerusalem: The City Plan.* London: H.M. Stationery Office and The Admiralty Chart Establishment, 1948.

Kiriaty, Josef. "Contemporary Israeli Architecture." *Process: Architecture 44* (1984).

Kolodny, Joseph. *Two Millenia in Kfar Saba.* Kfar Saba: Hatsa'at Iriyot Kfar Saba, 1988.

Kroyanker, David. *Jerusalem Architecture.* New York: Vendome, 1994.

Kutcher, Arthur. *The New Jerusalem: Planning and Politics.* Cambridge: MIT Press, 1973.

Meljon, Zeev, ed. *Towns and Villages in Israel.* Tel Aviv: Japheth, 1966.

Melville, Herman. Edited by Raymond Weaver. *Journal up the Straits, October 11, 1856–May 5, 1857.* New York: Copper Square, 1971.

Mishal, Nissim. *Those Were The Years…Israel's Jubilee.* Tel Aviv: Miskal, 1997.

Nahon, S.U., ed. *Mount Herzl.* Jerusalem: Jerusalem Post, 1968.

Newberry, Paul. "Collective Agriculture: The Kibbutzim of Israel." In *A Geography of Agriculture*, edited by MacDonald and Evans, Plymouth: Estover, 1980.

Omer, Mordechai. *Hiriya in the Museum.* Jerusalem: Beracha Foundation, Tel Aviv Museum of Art, 1999.

Omer, Mordechai *et al. Point of View: Four Approaches to Landscape Architecture in Israel.* Tel Aviv: Genia Schreiber University Art Center, 1996.

Onne, Eyal. *Photographic Heritage of the Holy Land, 1839–1914.* Manchester: Institute of Advanced Studies, Manchester Polytechnic, 1980.

Oren, Ruth. "Zionist Photography, 1910–41: Constructing and Landscape." *History of Photography 19*(3) (1995): 201–209.

Orgel, Anna, and Alexander Tzonis, eds. "Architecture in Israel, 1948–1998." *Le Carré Bleu* (Mar/April), 1999.

Rabinowitz, Louis I. *Torah and Flora.* New York: Sanhedrin, 1977.

Schlör, Joachim. *Tel Aviv: From Dream to City.* Translated by Helen Atkins. London: Reaktion, 1999.

Sharon, Arieh. *Planning Jerusalem: The Master Plan for the Old City of Jerusalem and Its Environs.* New York: McGraw-Hill, 1973.

——— *Kibbutz + Bauhaus: An Architect's Way in a New Land.* Tel Aviv: Massada, 1976.

Sprin, Anne Whiston. *The Language of Landscape.* New Haven: Yale University Press, 1998.

Sosnovsky, Silvina, ed. *Yohanan Ratner: The Man the Architect and His Work.* Haifa: Architectural Heritage Research Centre, Technion, 1992.

Stanley, Arthur Penrhyn. *Sinai and Palestine: In Connection with Their History.* New York: Armstrong. 1890.

Stein, Achva Benzinberg. "Landscape Elements of the Makam: Sacred Places in Israel." *Landscape Journal 6*(2) (1987):123–131.

Tammuz, Benjamin and Max Wykes-Joyce. *Art in Israel.* Philadelphia: Chilton, 1967.

Tartakover, David. *A Trip Across the Country: Games from Mr. Barlevy's Store.* Tel Aviv: Eretz Israel Museum, 1999.

Tsorfati, Ruth. *A Chapter in the Life of My Father—The Garden.* Tel Aviv: Massada, 1982.

Twain, Mark. *The Innocents Abroad: Roughing It.* New York: Literary Classics of the U.S., 1984 [1869]

Vilnay, Zev. *The New Israel Atlas: Bible to Present Day.* Translated by Moshe Aumann. New York: McGraw-Hill, 1969.

Waterman, S. "Ideology and Events in Israeli Human Landscapes." *Geography* 65(3) (1979):171–181.

Weitz, Joseph. *Forests and Afforestation in Israel.* Translated by Shlomo Levenson. Jerusalem: Massada, 1974.

Yalan, E. *The Design of Agricultural Settlements: Technological Aspects of Rural Community Developments.* Haifa: Michlol, 1975.

Young, James E. *The Texture of Memory: Holocaust Memorials and Meaning.* New Haven: Yale University Press, 1993.

———*The Art of Memory: Holocaust Memorials in History.* Munich: Prestel-Verlag, 1994.

Zararoni, Irit, ed. *Israel Roots and Routes: A Nation Living in its Landscape.* Tel Aviv: Peli, 1990.

Zerubavel, Yael. *Recovered Roots: Collective Memory and the Making of Israeli National Tradition.* Chicago: University of Chicago Press, 1995.

——— "The Forest as National Icon: Literature, Politics, and the Archeology of Memory," *Israel Studies* 1(1) (1996): 60–99.

About the Author

Kenneth Helphand is a professor of landscape architecture at the University of Oregon. He has been a frequent visiting professor at Technion—Israel Institute of Technology, and is familiar with the Israeli landscape and the practice of the profession in Israel. Helphand is the author of the award-winning books *Colorado: Visions of an American Landscape* (Roberts Rinehart, 1992) and, with Cynthia Girling, *Yard, Street, Park: The Design of Suburban Open Space* (John Wiley, 1994). He is editor of *Landscape Journal* and former book reviews editor of *Landscape Architecture* magazine. He is also the recipient of the University of Oregon's Distinguished Teaching Award (1993), the Council of Educators in Landscape Architecture Award of Distinction (1997), the Bradford Williams Medal (2001), a Fellow of the American Society of Landscape Architects, and an Honorary Member of the Israel Association of Landscape Architects.

The Center for American Places is a tax-exempt 501(c)(3) nonprofit organization, founded in 1990, whose educational mission is to enhance the public's understanding of, and appreciation for, the natural and built environment. It is guided by the belief that books provide an indispensible foundation for comprehending—and caring for—the places where we live, work, and explore. Books live. Books endure. Books make a difference. Books are gifts to civilization.

With offices in New Mexico and Virginia, Center editors bring to publication 20–25 books per year under the Center's own imprint or in association with its publishing partners. The Center is also engaged in numerous other programs that emphasize the interpretation of place through art, literature, scholarship, exhibitions, and field research. The Center's Cotton Mather Library in Arthur, Nebraska, its Martha A. Strawn Photographic Library in Davidson, North Carolina, and a 10-acre reserve along the Santa Fe River in Florida are available as retreats upon request.

The Center strives every day to make a difference through books, research, and education. For more information, please send inquiries to P. O. Box 23225, Santa Fe, NM 87502, U.S.A. or visit the Center's Web site (*www.americanplaces.org*).

ABOUT THE BOOK:
The text for *Dreaming Gardens: Landscape Architecture and the Making of Modern Israel* was set in Bembo and Serif Gothic. The paper is 200m Supreme gloss Four-color separations, printing, and binding were professionally rendered through Global Ink Inc. Harrisonburg, VA 22802.

FOR THE CENTER FOR AMERICAN PLACES:

George F. Thompson, president and publisher

Randall B. Jones, editor and publishing liaison

Denis Wood, manuscript editor

David Skolkin, designer and typesetter

Dave Keck, of Global Ink, Inc., production coordinator

FOR THE UNIVERSITY OF VIRGINIA PRESS

Penelope Kaiserlian, director

Martha A. Farlow, design and production

Mark Saunders, marketing